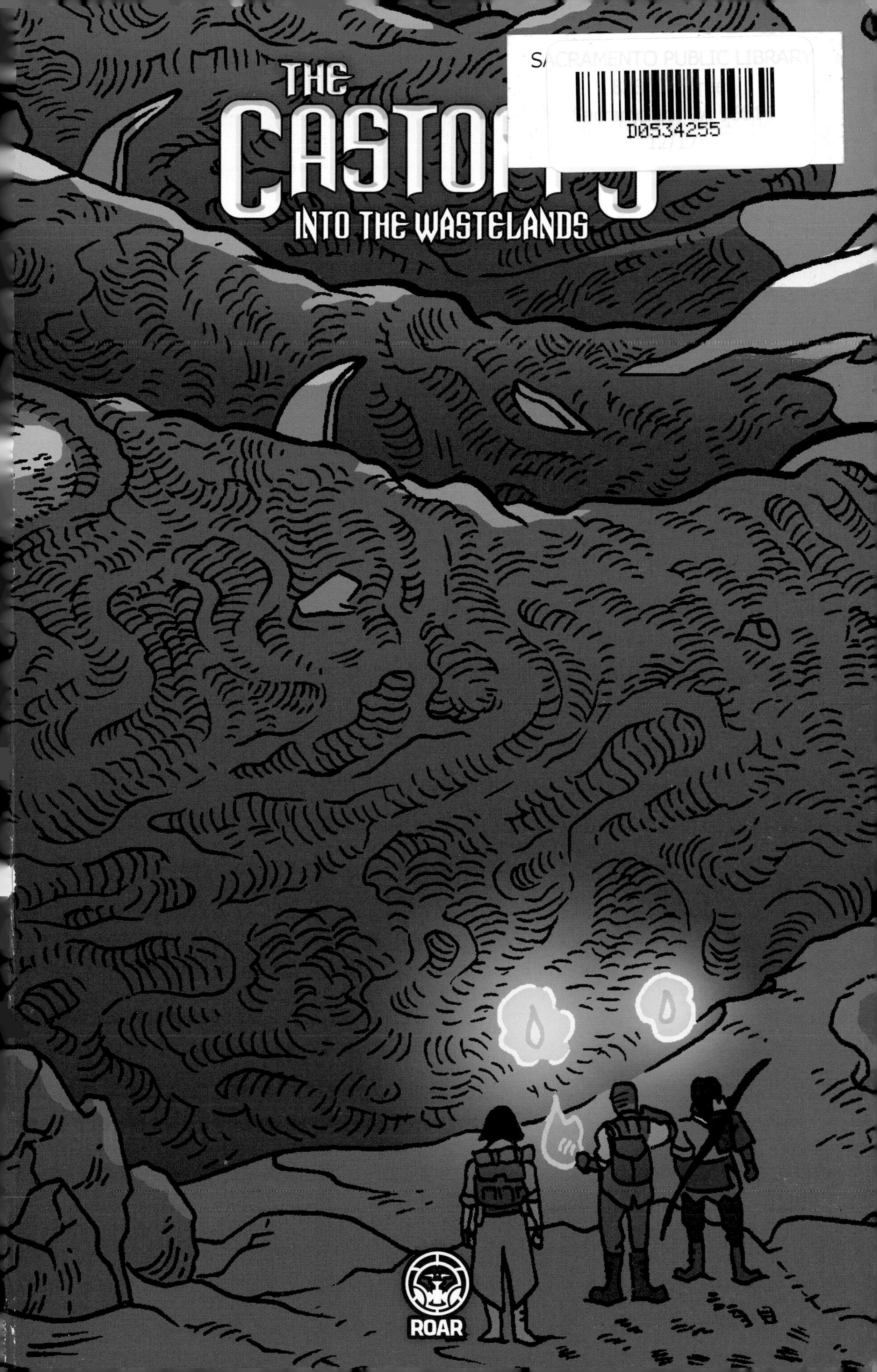
THE
INTO THE WASTELANDS
ROAR

MK REED
BRIAN "SMITTY" SMITH
WYETH YATES
KENDRA WELLS

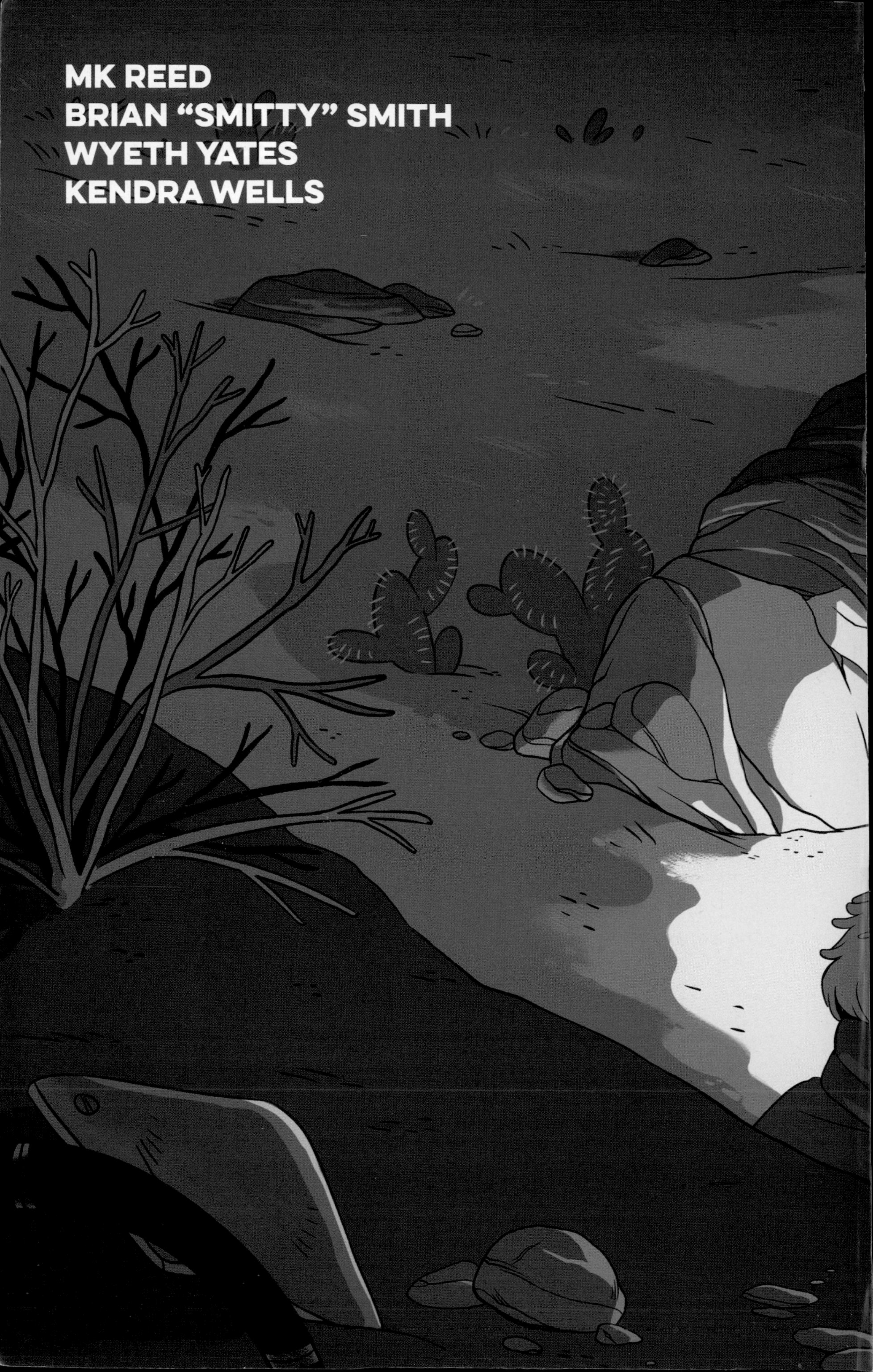

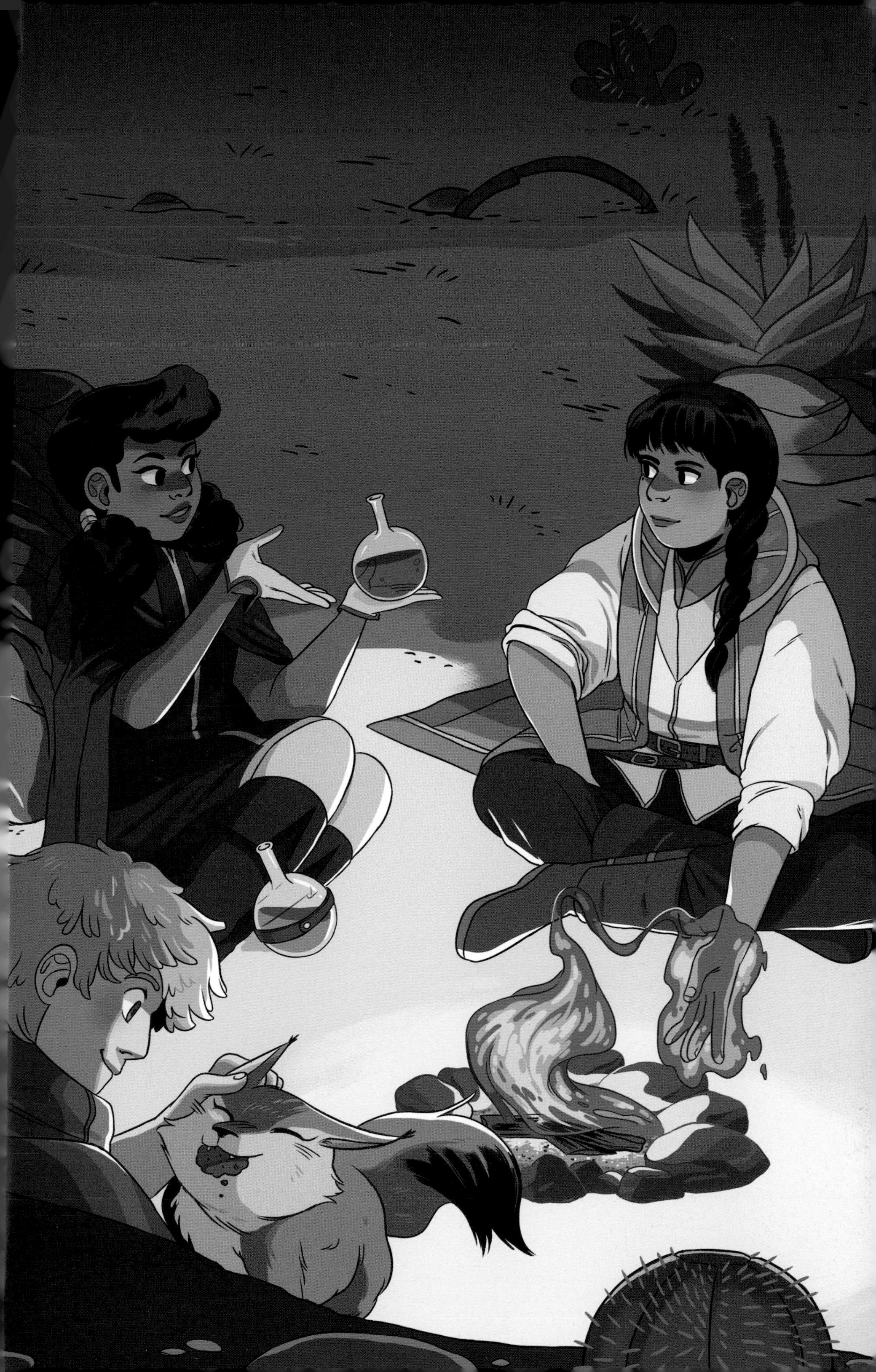

THE CASTOFFS

VOLUME 2

INTO THE WASTELANDS

MK REED & BRIAN "SMITTY" SMITH *WRITERS*

WYETH YATES *ARTIST*

BRIAN "SMITTY" SMITH
COLORIST, Issues 5-6, Covers

KENDRA WELLS
COLORIST, Issues 7-9

WYETH YATES
COLORIST, Collection Cover

AW'S D.C. HOPKINS
LETTERER

CHAN CHAU
TITLE SPREAD ILLUSTRATION

ANDREA COLVIN
EDITOR

HAZEL NEWLEVANT
ASSISTANT EDITOR

ANDWORLD DESIGN
DESIGNER

Publisher's Cataloging-In-Publication Data

(Prepared by The Donohue Group, Inc.)

Names: Reed, M. K. | Smith, Brian (Comic book writer), author, colorist. | Yates, Wyeth, illustrator. | Wells, Kendra, colorist. | Hopkins, D. C., letterer. | Chou, Chan, illustrator. | Colvin, Andrea, editor. | Newlevant, Hazel, editor. | AndWorld Design (Firm), designer.

Title: The Castoffs. Volume 2, Into the wastelands / MK Reed & Brian "Smitty" Smith, writers ; Wyeth Yates, artist ; Brian "Smitty" Smith, colorist, issues 5-6, covers ; Kendra Wells, colorist, issues 7-9 ; Wyeth Yates, colorist, collection cover ; AW's D.C. Hopkins, letterer ; Chan Chou, title spread illustration ; Andrea Colvin, editor ; Hazel Newlevant, assistant editor ; Andworld Design, designer.

Other Titles: Into the wastelands

Description: [St. Louis, Missouri] : The Lion Forge, LLC, 2017. | Interest age level: 12 and up. | "Roar." | "Portions of this book were previously published in The Castoffs, Vol. 2, Issues 5-9." | Summary: "Charris, Trinh, and Ursa have managed to work together long enough to defeat the evil Priestess and her hive-mind robot army, the Surrogate. They journey back to the village of Clifton to reunite with their guild, but once there, they discover that the Priestess may not be defeated after all, and a much larger threat may be looming. A secret from Ursa's past threatens to break the fragile trust between the three mages, but they must overcome their differences and work together if they stand a chance of surviving the coming darkness."-- Provided by publisher.

Identifiers: ISBN 978-1-941302-32-3

Subjects: LCSH: Teenagers--Comic books, strips, etc. | Magic--Comic books, strips, etc. | Women priests--Comic books, strips, etc. | Good and evil--Comic books, strips, etc. | LCGFT: Graphic novels. | Science fiction.

Classification: LCC PN6728 .C372 2017 | DDC 741.5973 [Fic]--dc23

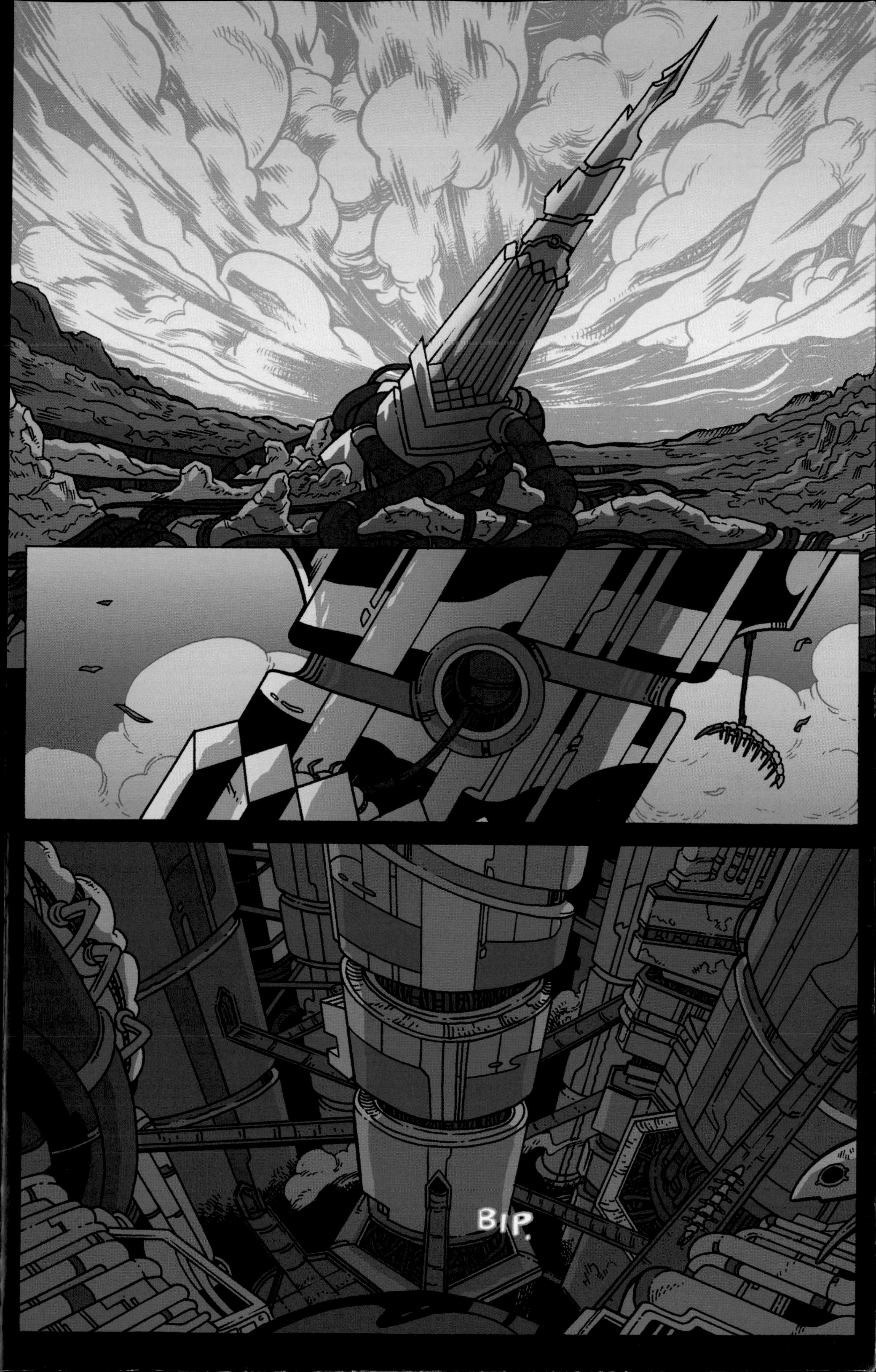
BIP.

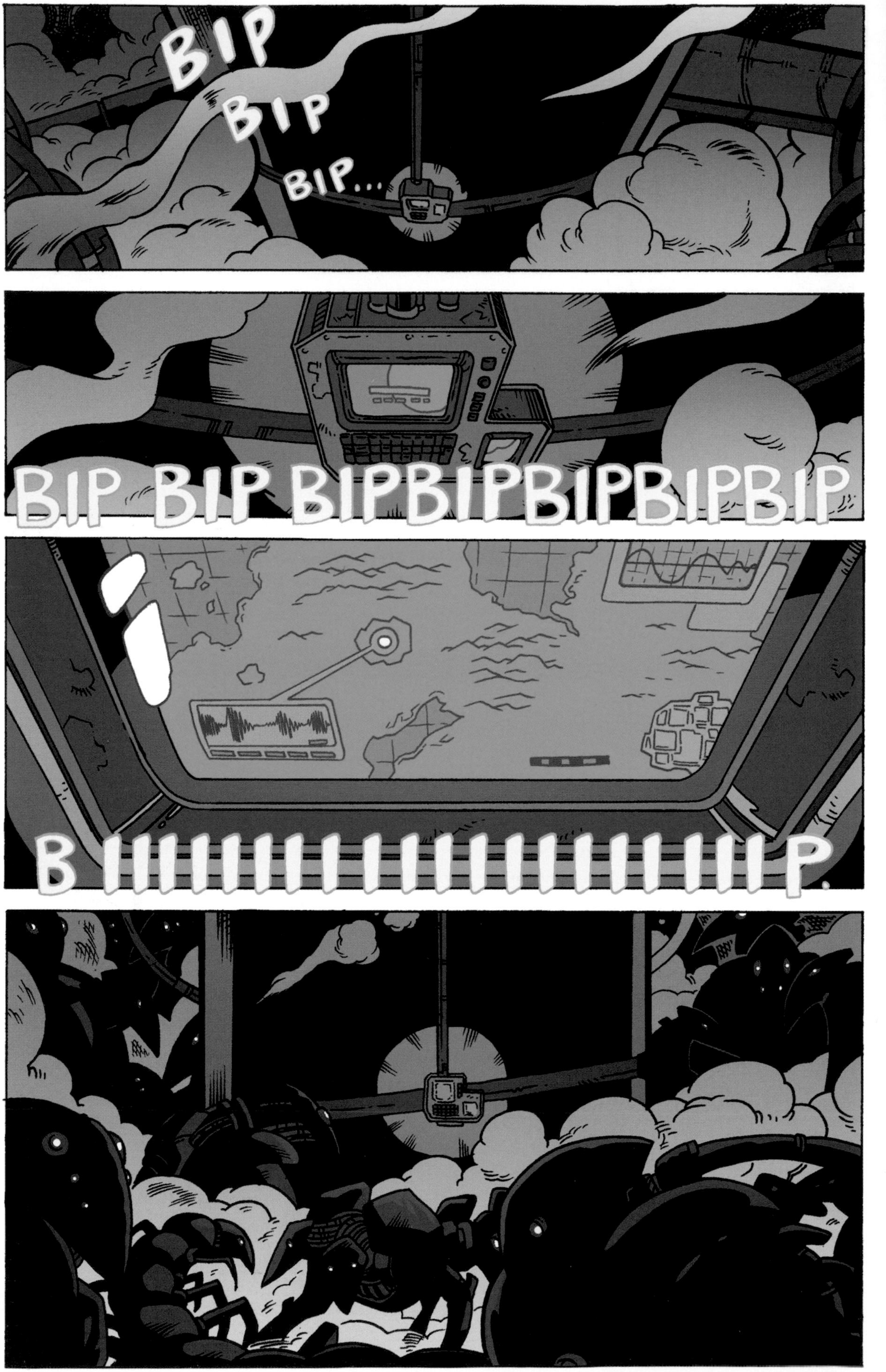
BIP
BIP
BIP...
BIP BIP BIPBIPBIPBIPBIP
B IIIIIIIIIIIIIIIIIIIIIIP.

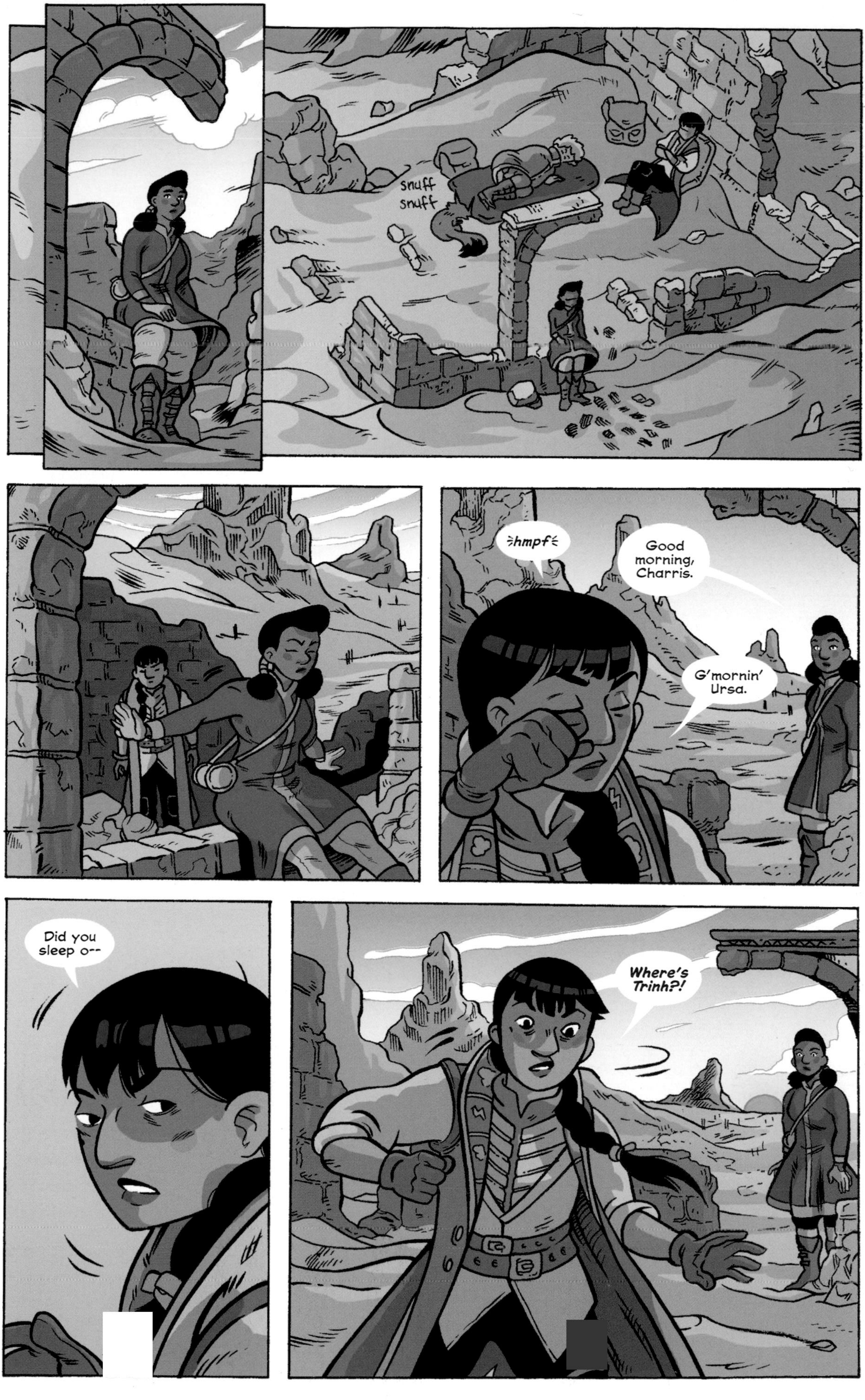
snuff
snuff
hmpf
Good morning, Charris.
G'mornin' Ursa.
Did you sleep o--
Where's Trinh?!

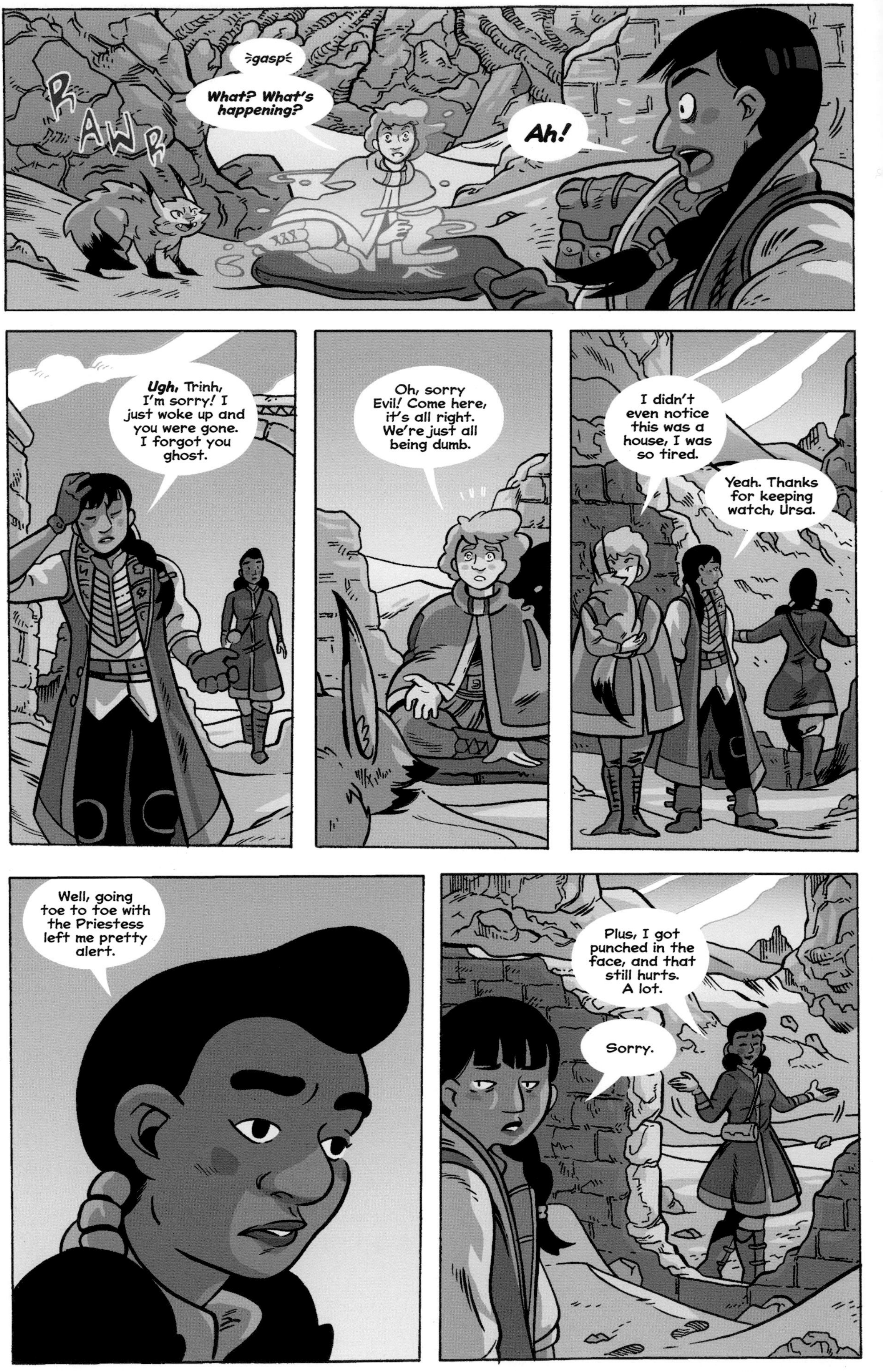
RAWR
gasp
What? What's happening?
Ah!
Ugh, Trinh, I'm sorry! I just woke up and you were gone. I forgot you ghost.
Oh, sorry Evil! Come here, it's all right. We're just all being dumb.
I didn't even notice this was a house, I was so tired.
Yeah. Thanks for keeping watch, Ursa.
Well, going toe to toe with the Priestess left me pretty alert.
Plus, I got punched in the face, and that still hurts. A lot.
Sorry.

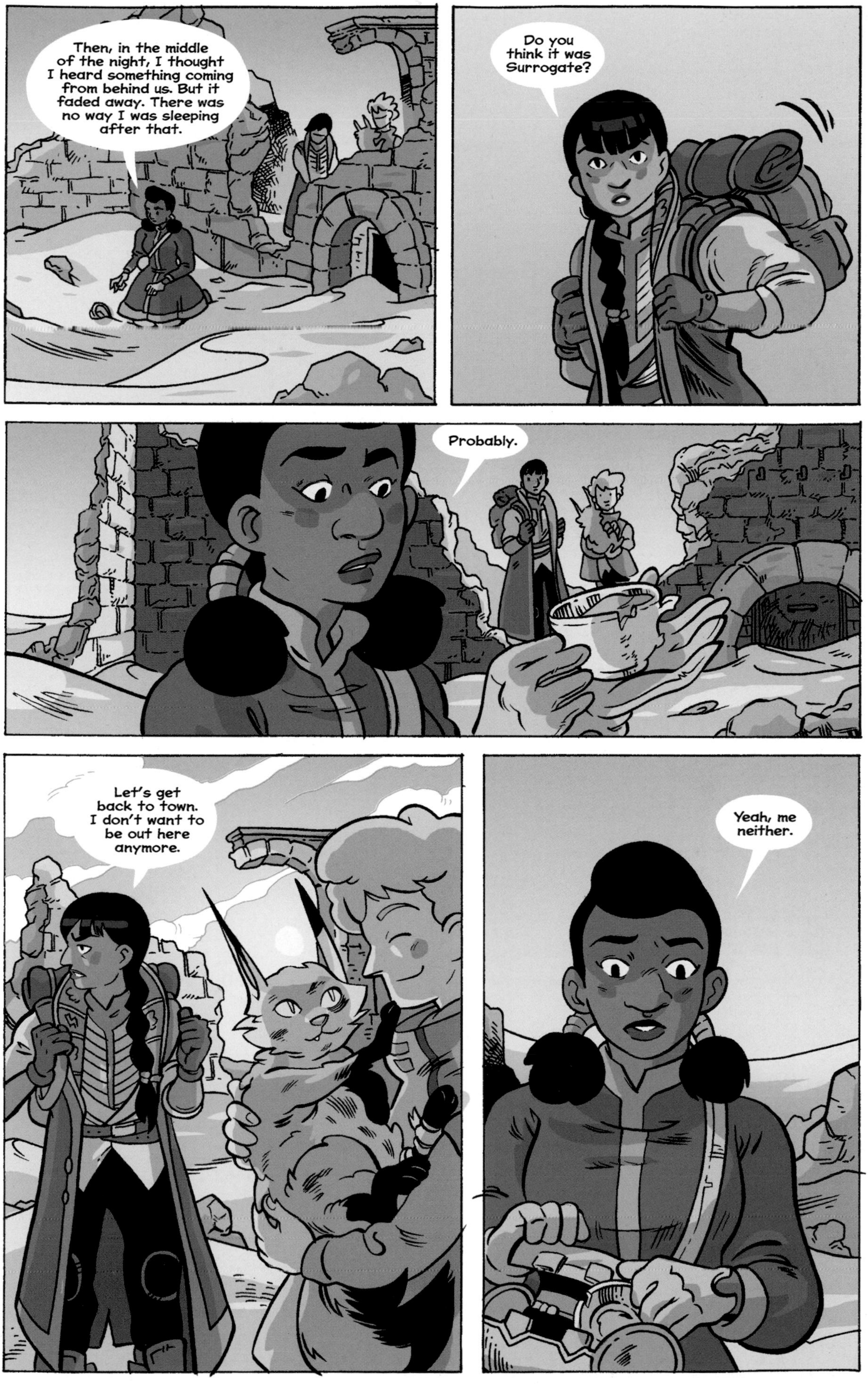
Then, in the middle of the night, I thought I heard something coming from behind us. But it faded away. There was no way I was sleeping after that.
Do you think it was Surrogate?
Probably.
Let's get back to town. I don't want to be out here anymore.
Yeah, me neither.

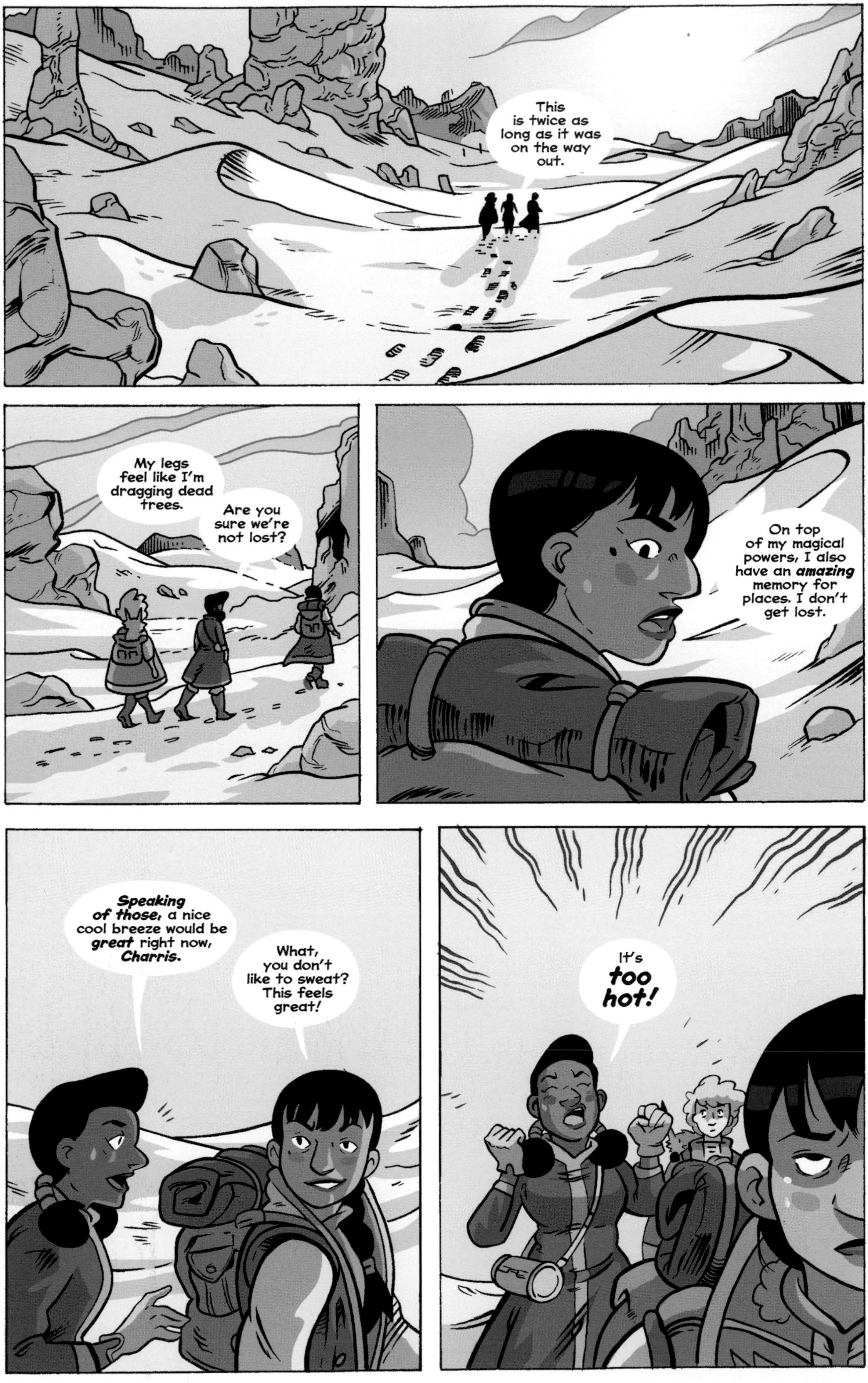
This is twice as long as it was on the way out.
My legs feel like I'm dragging dead trees.
Are you sure we're not lost?
On top of my magical powers, I also have an ***amazing*** memory for places. I don't get lost.
Speaking of those, a nice cool breeze would be ***great*** right now, ***Charris.***
What, you don't like to sweat? This feels great!
It's ***too hot!***

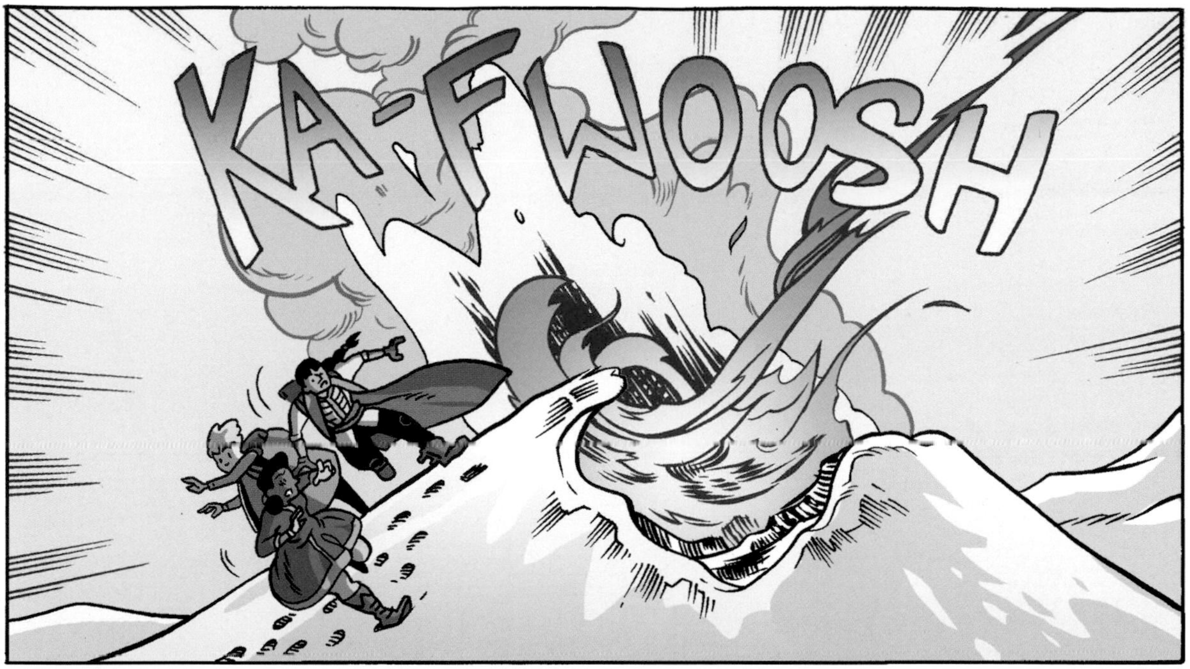
KA-FWOOSH

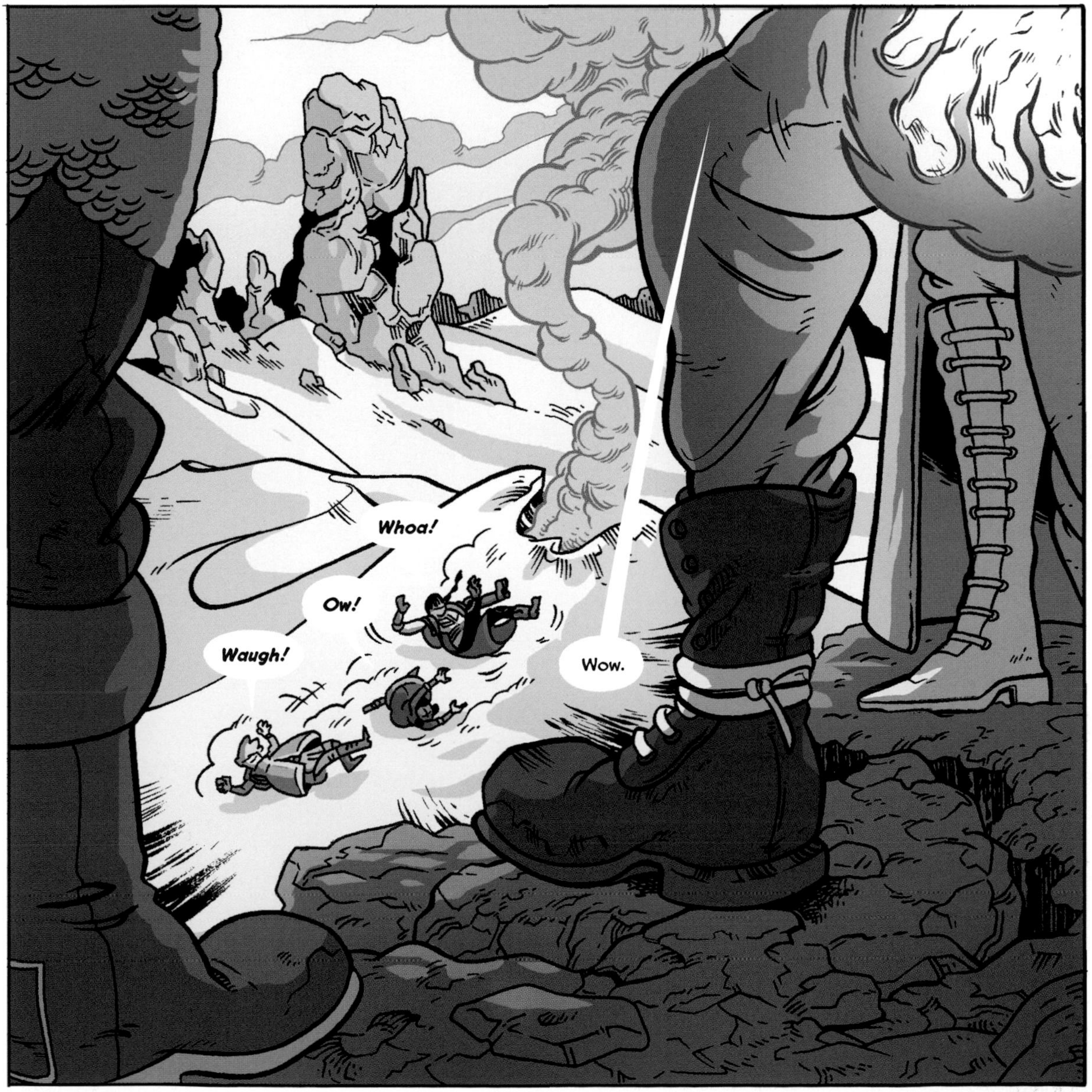
Whoa!
Ow!
Waugh!
Wow.

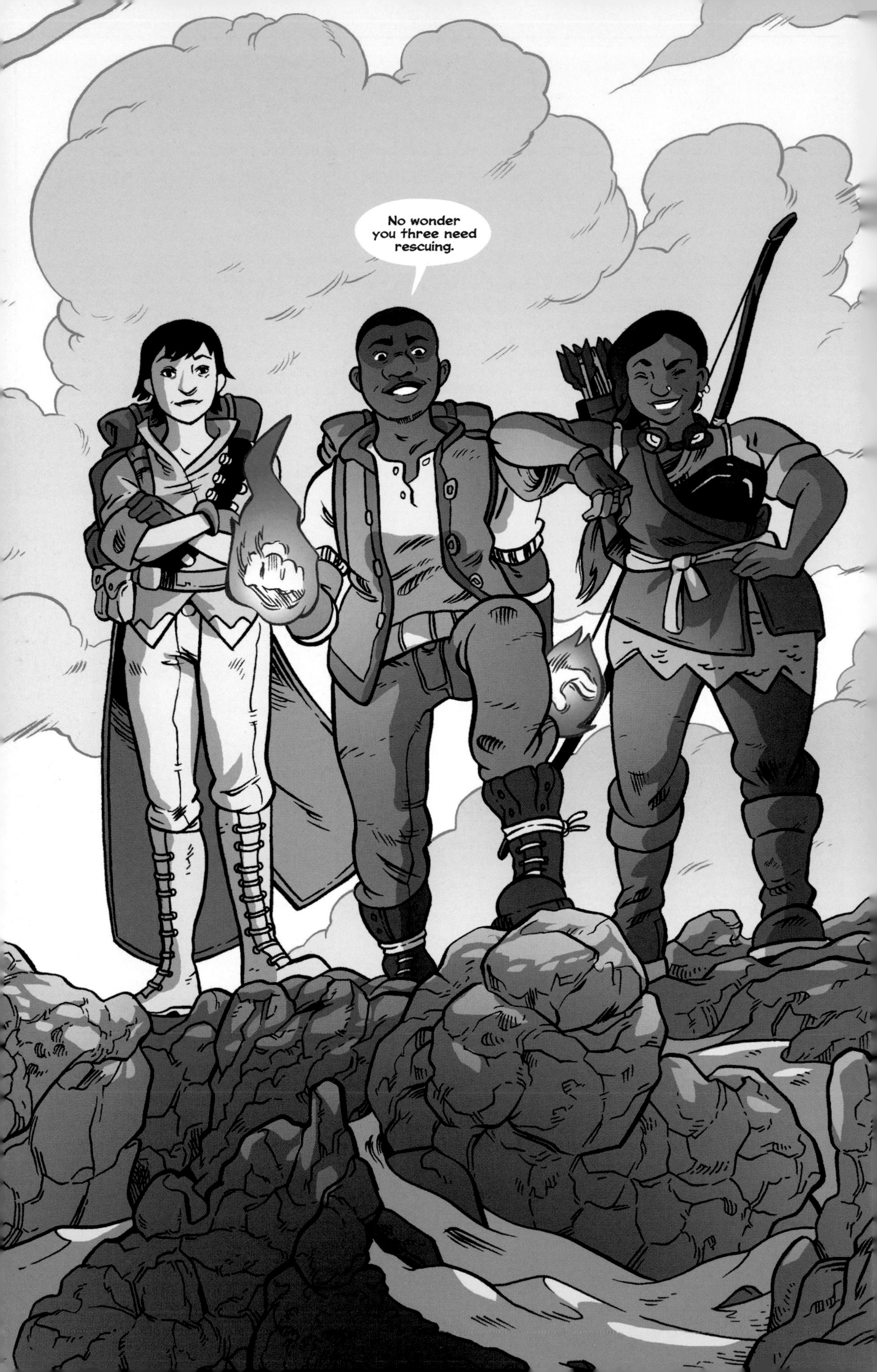
No wonder you three need rescuing.

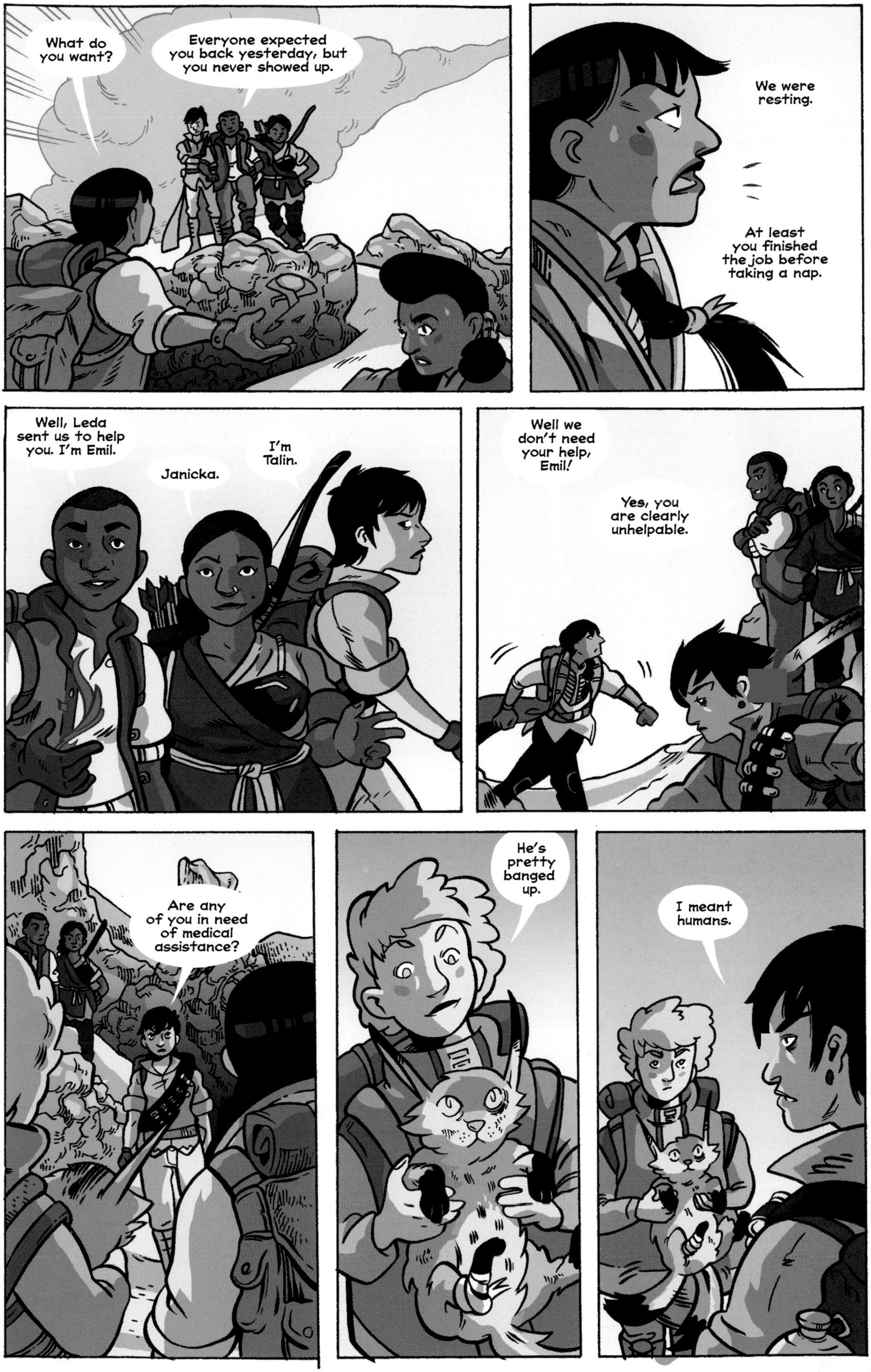
What do you want?
Everyone expected you back yesterday, but you never showed up.
We were resting.
At least you finished the job before taking a nap.
Well, Leda sent us to help you. I'm Emil.
Janicka.
I'm Talin.
Well we don't need your help, Emil!
Yes, you are clearly unhelpable.
Are any of you in need of medical assistance?
He's pretty banged up.
I meant humans.

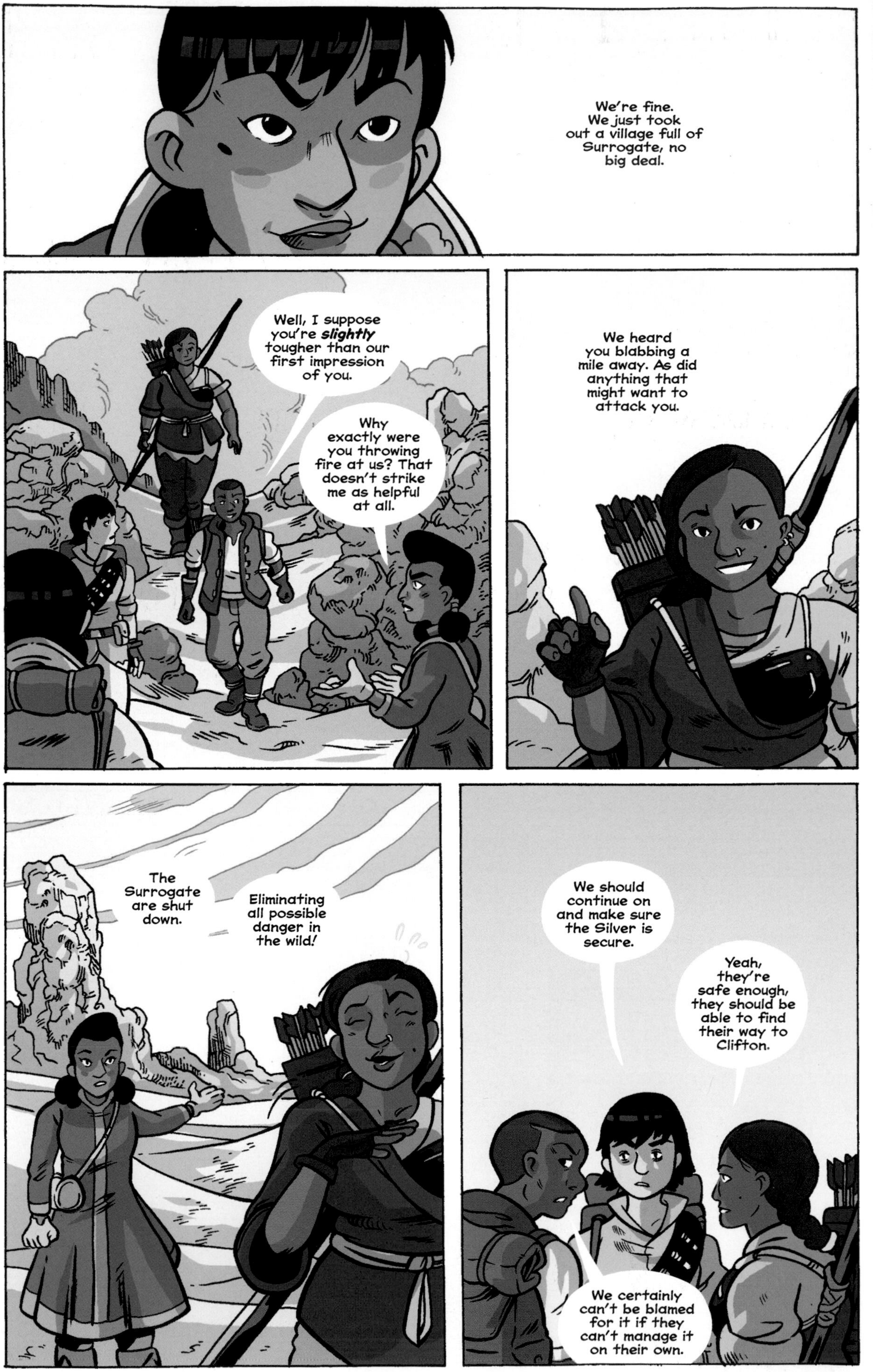
We're fine. We just took out a village full of Surrogate, no big deal.
Well, I suppose you're *slightly* tougher than our first impression of you.
Why exactly were you throwing fire at us? That doesn't strike me as helpful at all.
We heard you blabbing a mile away. As did anything that might want to attack you.
The Surrogate are shut down.
Eliminating all possible danger in the wild!
We should continue on and make sure the Silver is secure.
Yeah, they're safe enough, they should be able to find their way to Clifton.
We certainly can't be blamed for it if they can't manage it on their own.

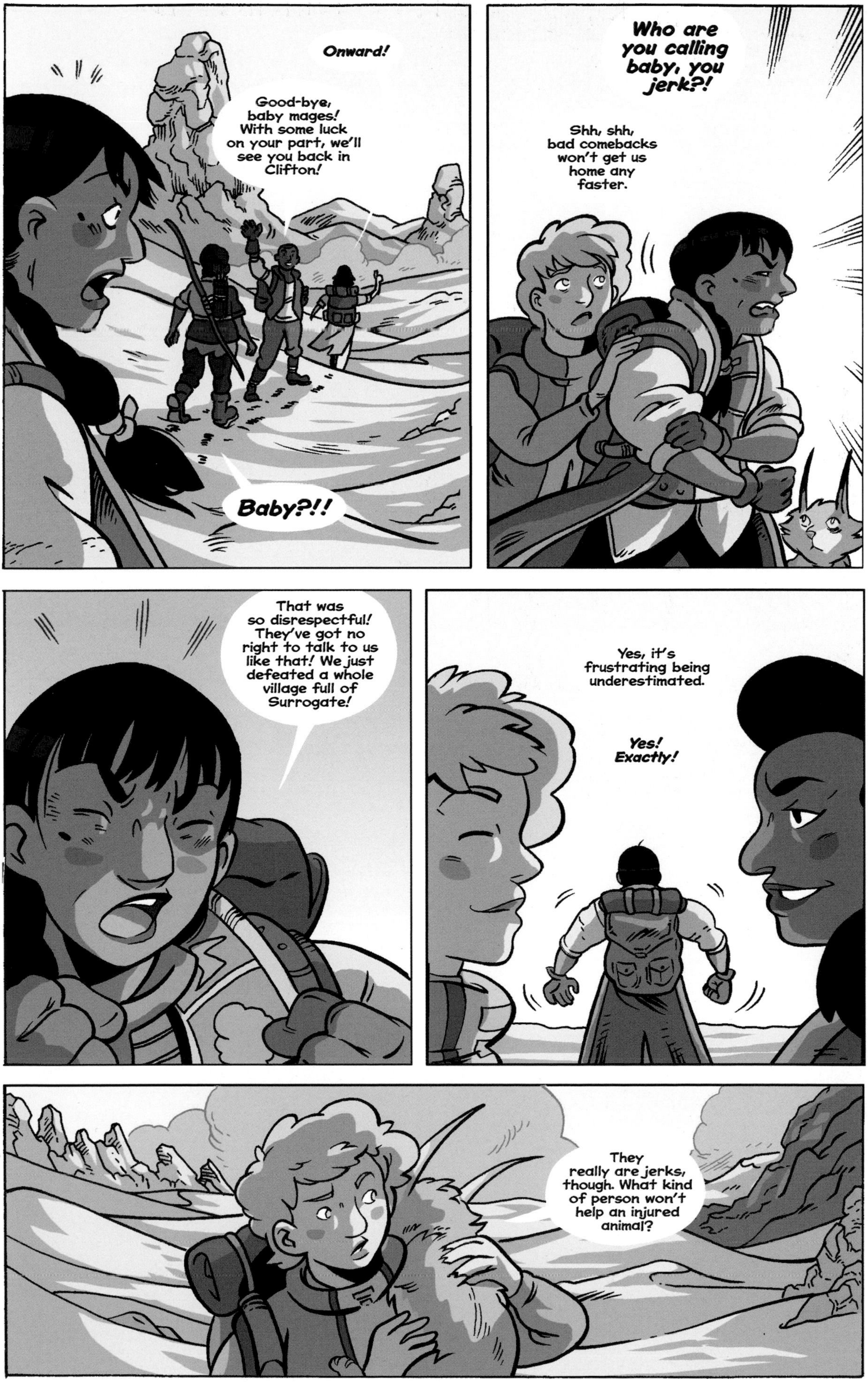
Onward!
Good-bye, baby mages! With some luck on your part, we'll see you back in Clifton!
Baby?!!
Who are you calling baby, you jerk?!
Shh, shh, bad comebacks won't get us home any faster.
That was so disrespectful! They've got no right to talk to us like that! We just defeated a whole village full of Surrogate!
Yes, it's frustrating being underestimated.
Yes! Exactly!
They really are jerks, though. What kind of person won't help an injured animal?

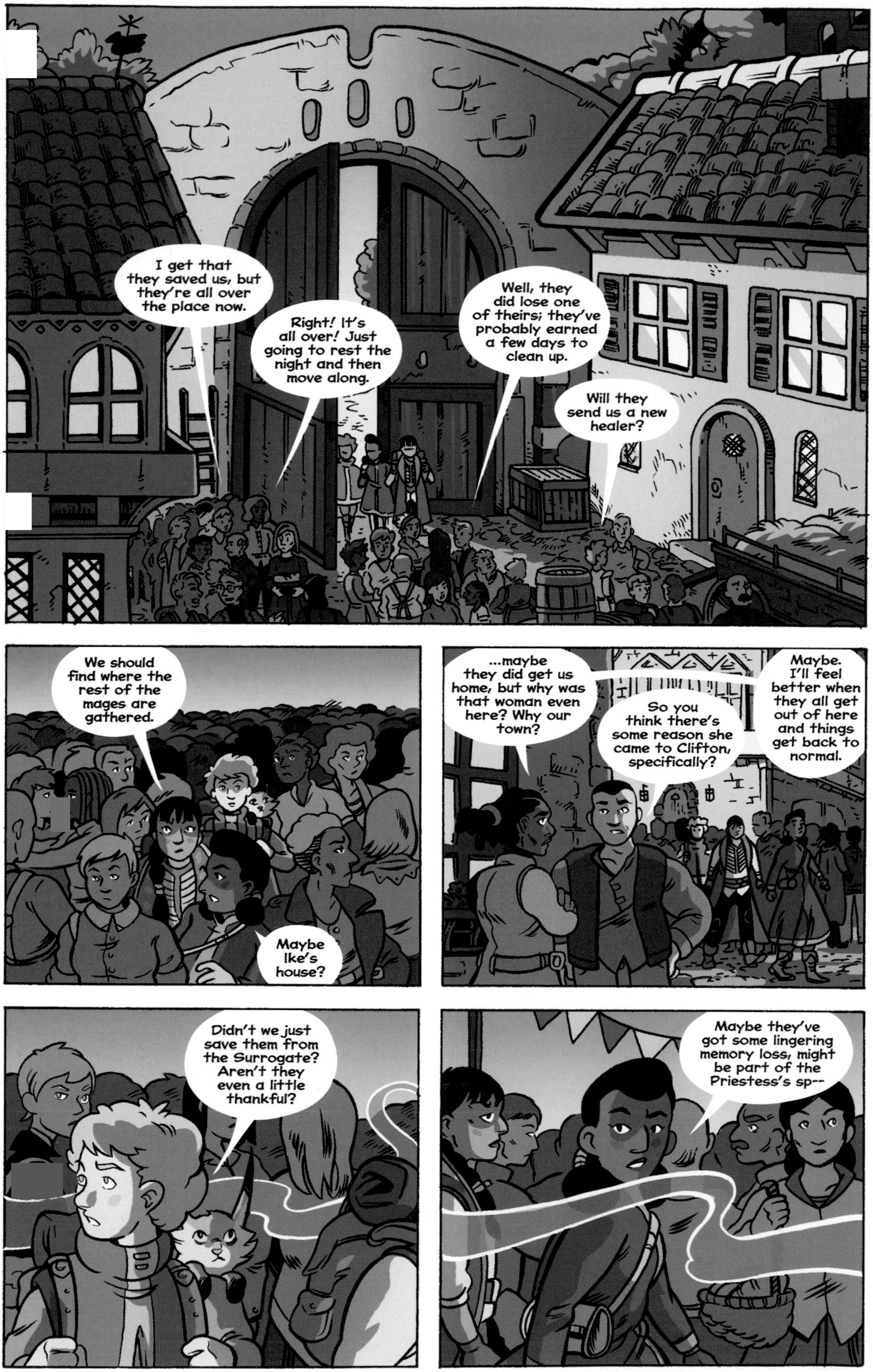
I get that they saved us, but they're all over the place now.
Right! It's all over! Just going to rest the night and then move along.
Well, they did lose one of theirs; they've probably earned a few days to clean up.
Will they send us a new healer?
We should find where the rest of the mages are gathered.
Maybe Ike's house?
...maybe they did get us home, but why was that woman even here? Why our town?
So you think there's some reason she came to Clifton, specifically?
Maybe. I'll feel better when they all get out of here and things get back to normal.
Didn't we just save them from the Surrogate? Aren't they even a little thankful?
Maybe they've got some lingering memory loss, might be part of the Priestess's sp--

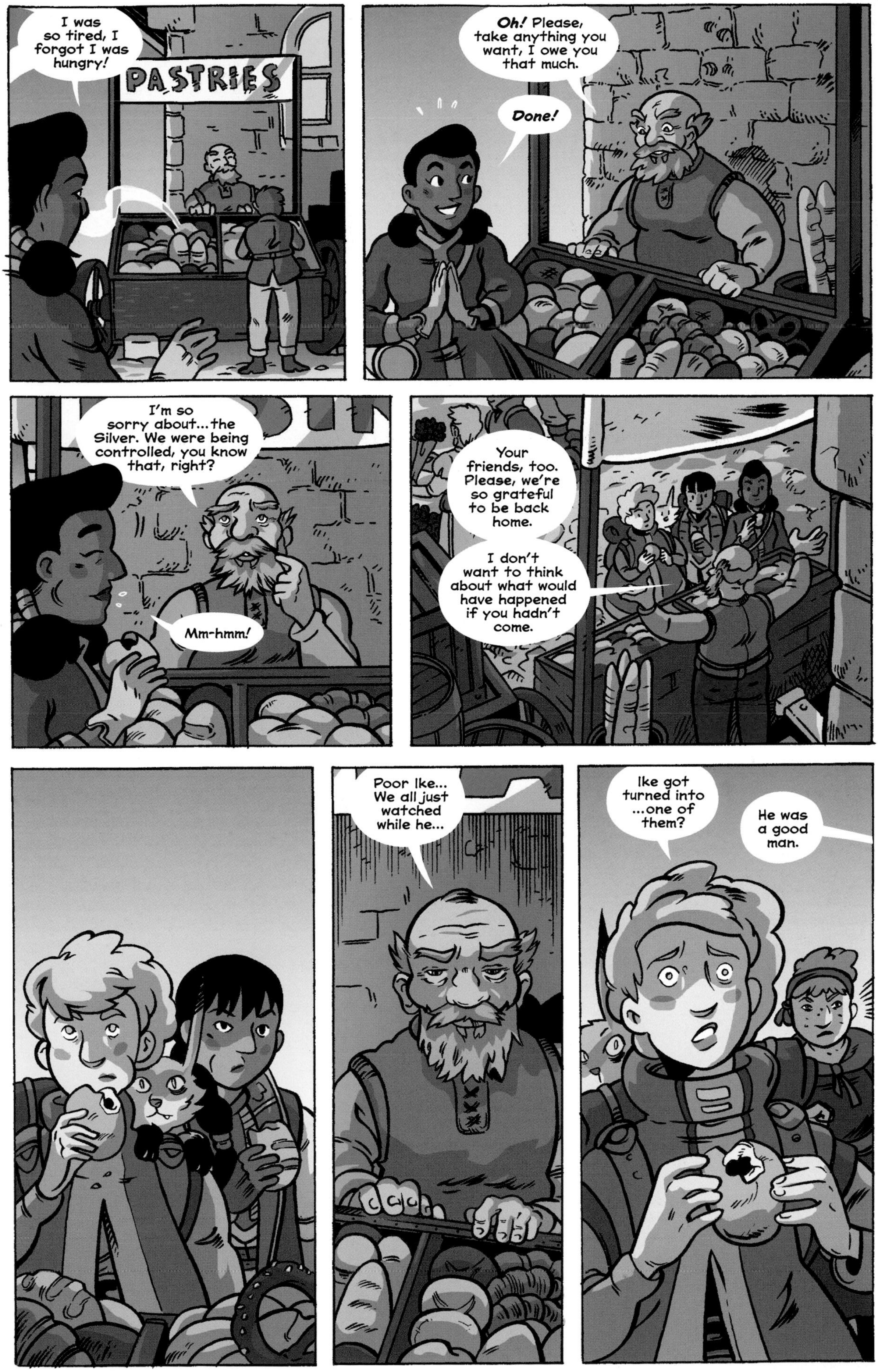
I was so tired, I forgot I was hungry!
PASTRIES
Oh! Please, take anything you want, I owe you that much.
Done!
I'm so sorry about...the Silver. We were being controlled, you know that, right?
Mm-hmm!
Your friends, too. Please, we're so grateful to be back home.
I don't want to think about what would have happened if you hadn't come.
Poor Ike... We all just watched while he...
Ike got turned into ...one of them?
He was a good man.

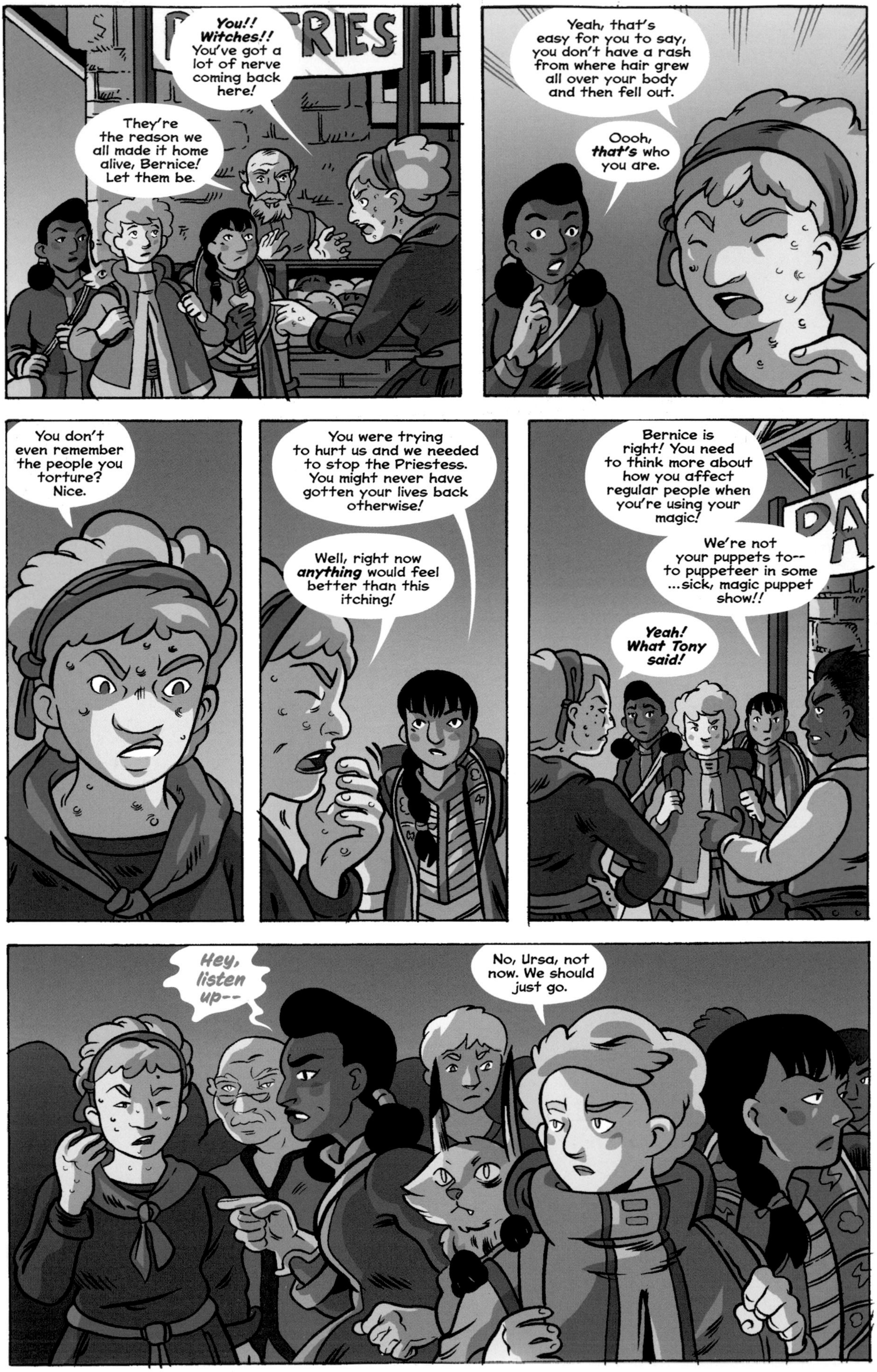

RIES
You!! Witches!! You've got a lot of nerve coming back here!
They're the reason we all made it home alive, Bernice! Let them be.
Yeah, that's easy for you to say, you don't have a rash from where hair grew all over your body and then fell out.
Oooh, that's who you are.
You don't even remember the people you torture? Nice.
You were trying to hurt us and we needed to stop the Priestess. You might never have gotten your lives back otherwise!
Well, right now anything would feel better than this itching!
Bernice is right! You need to think more about how you affect regular people when you're using your magic!
We're not your puppets to-- to puppeteer in some ...sick, magic puppet show!!
Yeah! What Tony said!
Hey, listen up--
No, Ursa, not now. We should just go.

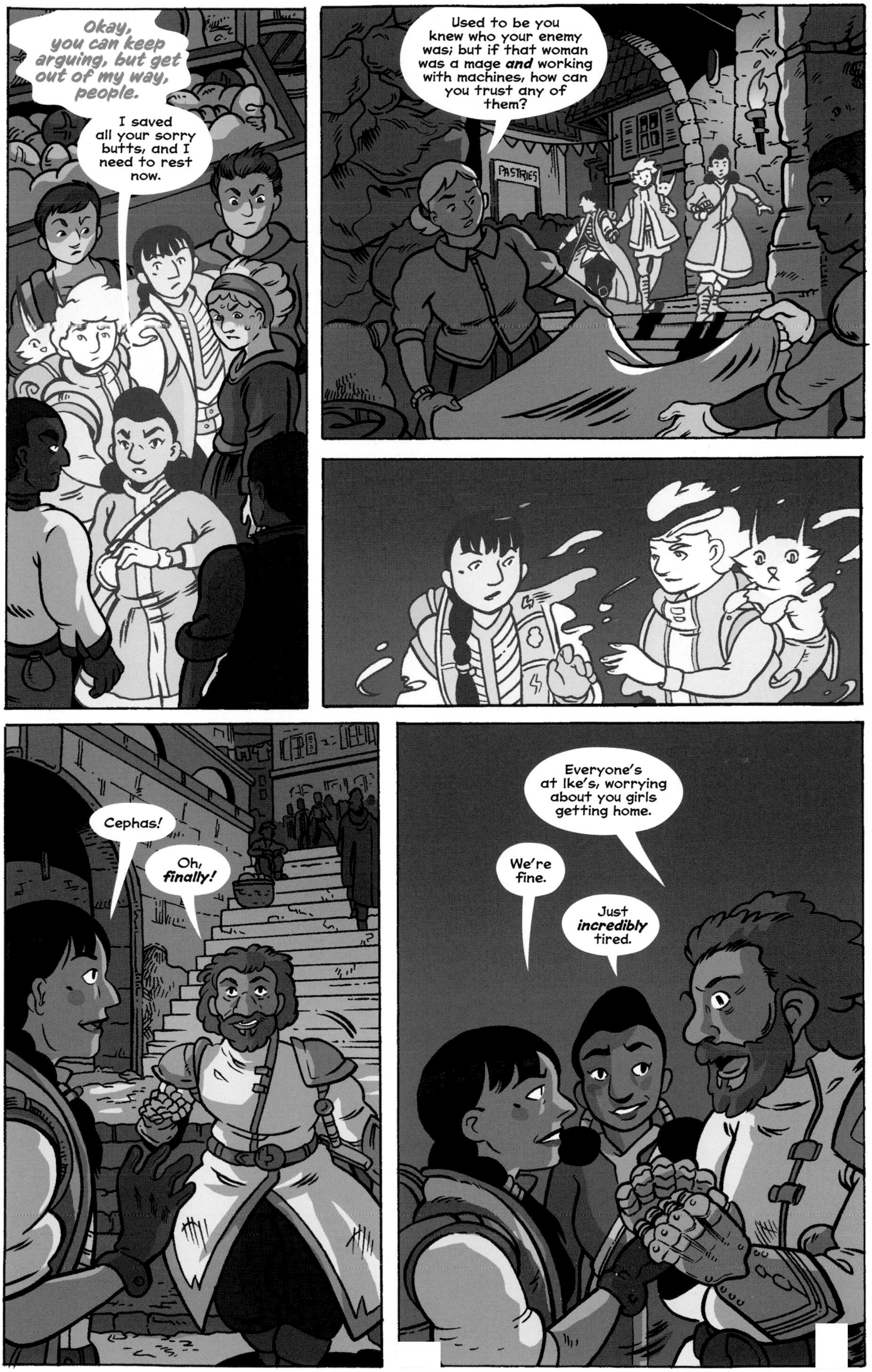
Okay, you can keep arguing, but get out of my way, people.
I saved all your sorry butts, and I need to rest now.
Used to be you knew who your enemy was; but if that woman was a mage *and* working with machines, how can you trust any of them?
PASTRIES
Cephas!
Oh, *finally!*
Everyone's at Ike's, worrying about you girls getting home.
We're fine.
Just *incredibly* tired.

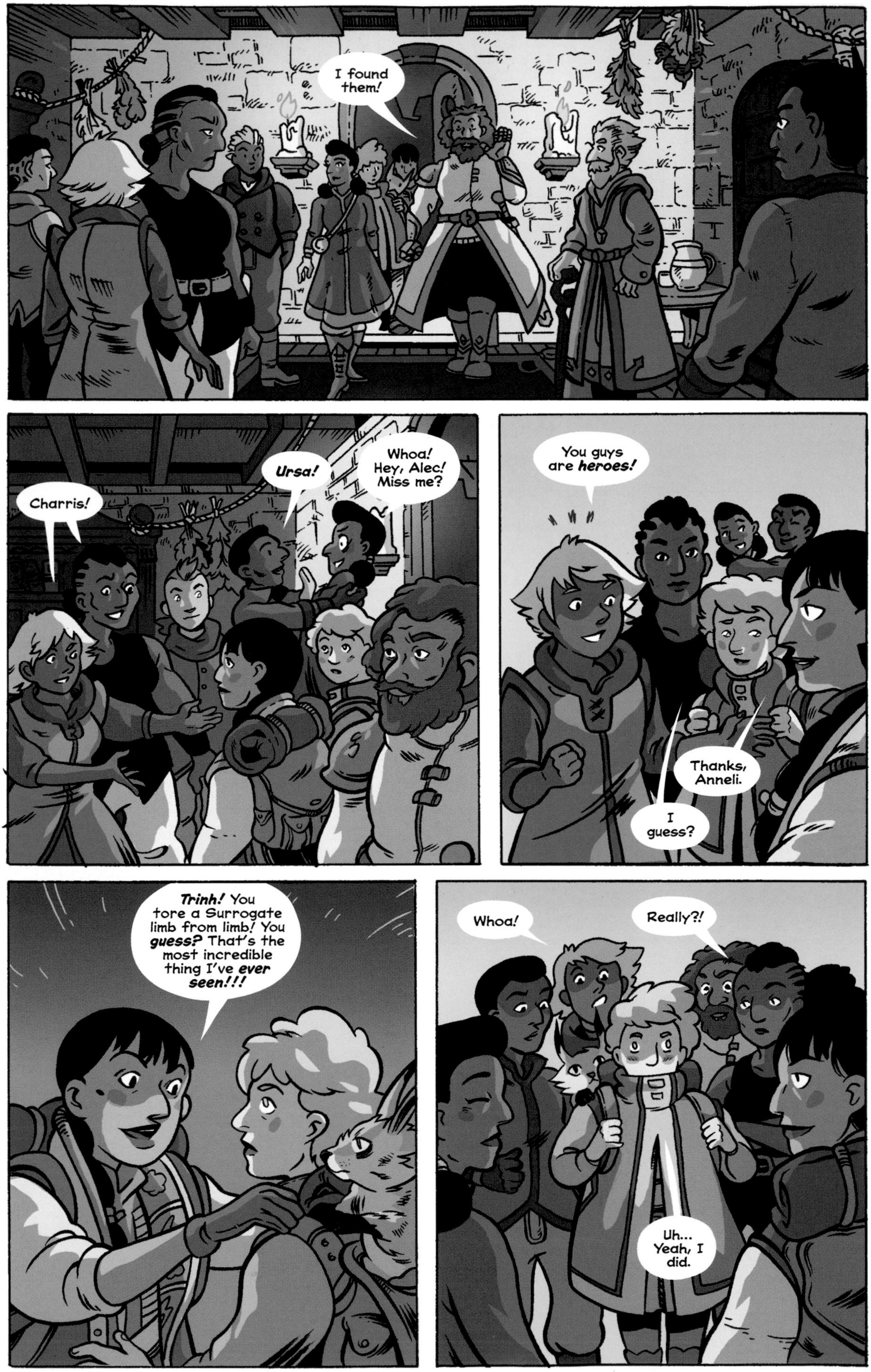
I found them!
Charris!
Ursa!
Whoa! Hey, Alec! Miss me?
You guys are **heroes!**
Thanks, Anneli.
I guess?
Trinh! You tore a Surrogate limb from limb! You **guess?** That's the most incredible thing I've **ever seen!!!**
Whoa!
Really?!
Uh... Yeah, I did.

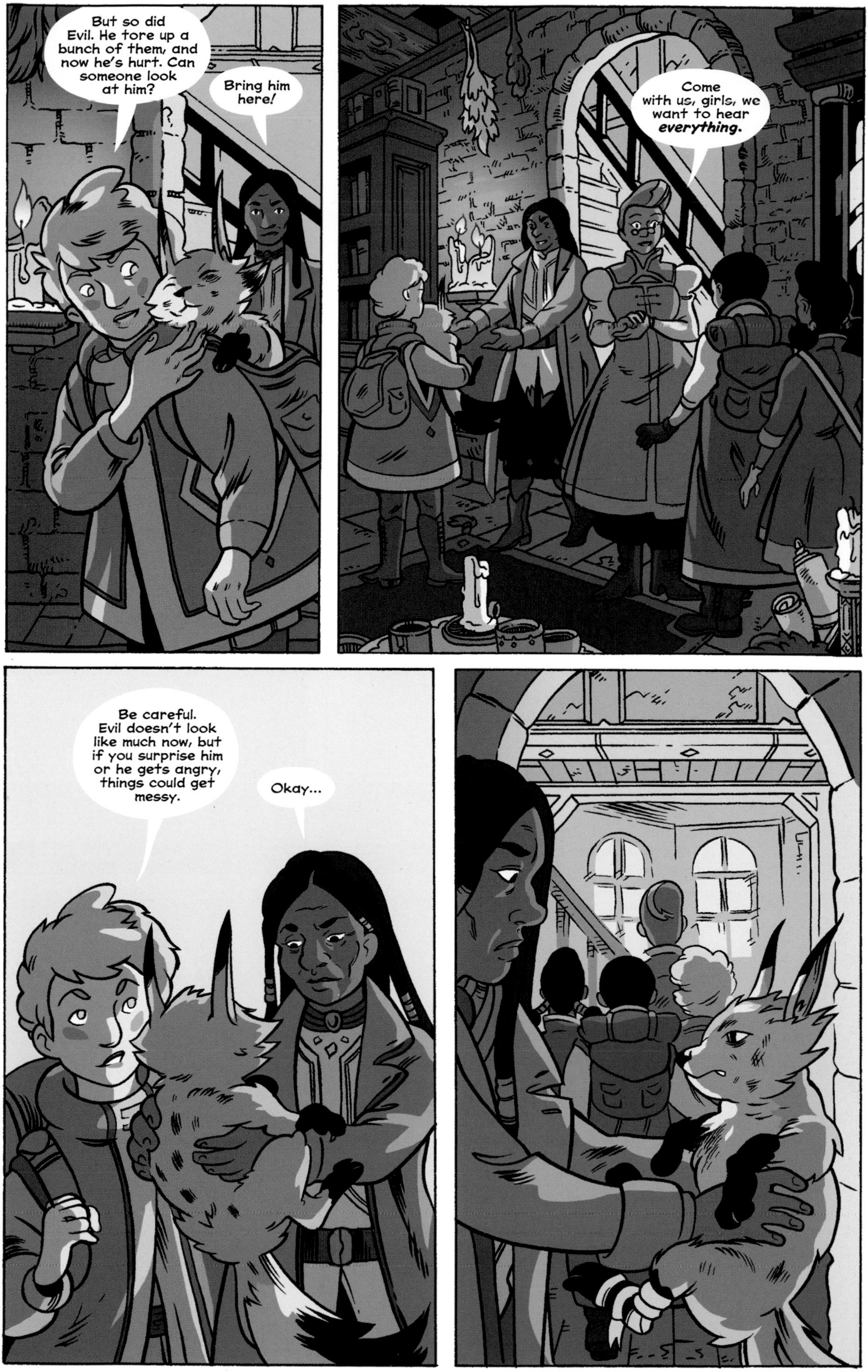

But so did Evil. He tore up a bunch of them, and now he's hurt. Can someone look at him?
Bring him here!
Come with us, girls, we want to hear *everything.*
Be careful. Evil doesn't look like much now, but if you surprise him or he gets angry, things could get messy.
Okay...

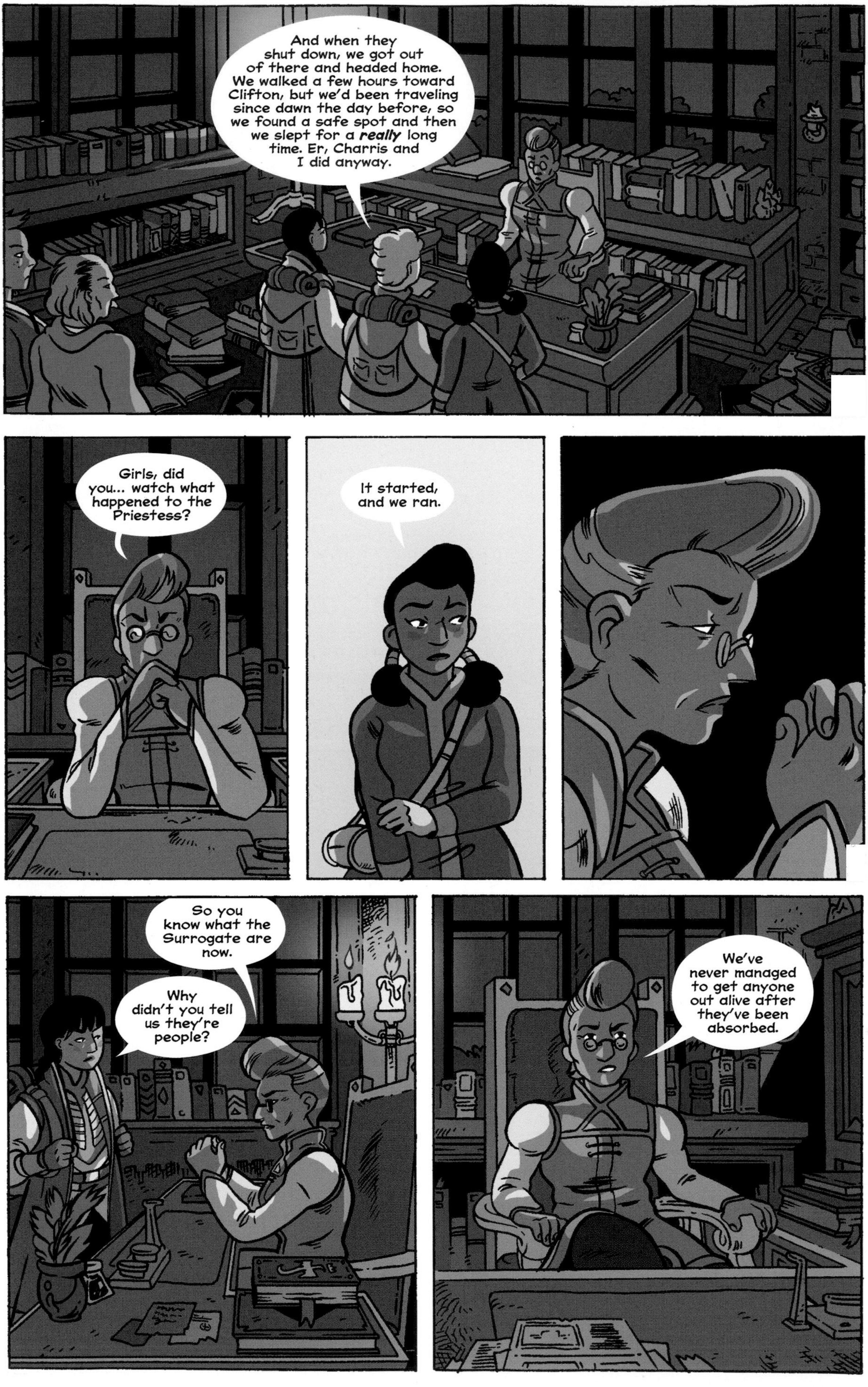
And when they shut down, we got out of there and headed home. We walked a few hours toward Clifton, but we'd been traveling since dawn the day before, so we found a safe spot and then we slept for a ***really*** long time. Er, Charris and I did anyway.
Girls, did you... watch what happened to the Priestess?
It started, and we ran.
So you know what the Surrogate are now.
Why didn't you tell us they're people?
We've never managed to get anyone out alive after they've been absorbed.

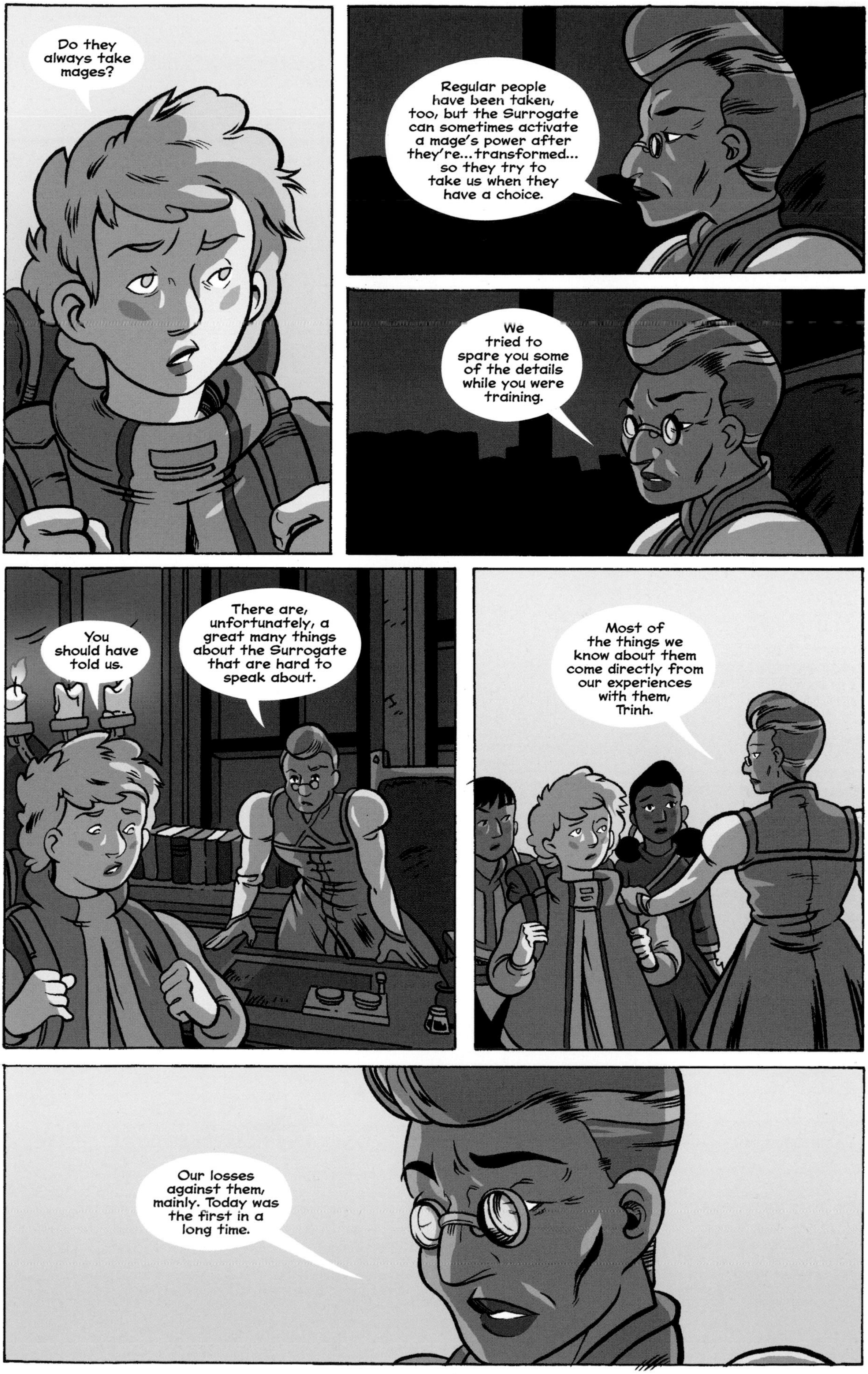
Do they always take mages?
Regular people have been taken, too, but the Surrogate can sometimes activate a mage's power after they're...transformed... so they try to take us when they have a choice.
We tried to spare you some of the details while you were training.
You should have told us.
There are, unfortunately, a great many things about the Surrogate that are hard to speak about.
Most of the things we know about them come directly from our experiences with them, Trinh.
Our losses against them, mainly. Today was the first in a long time.

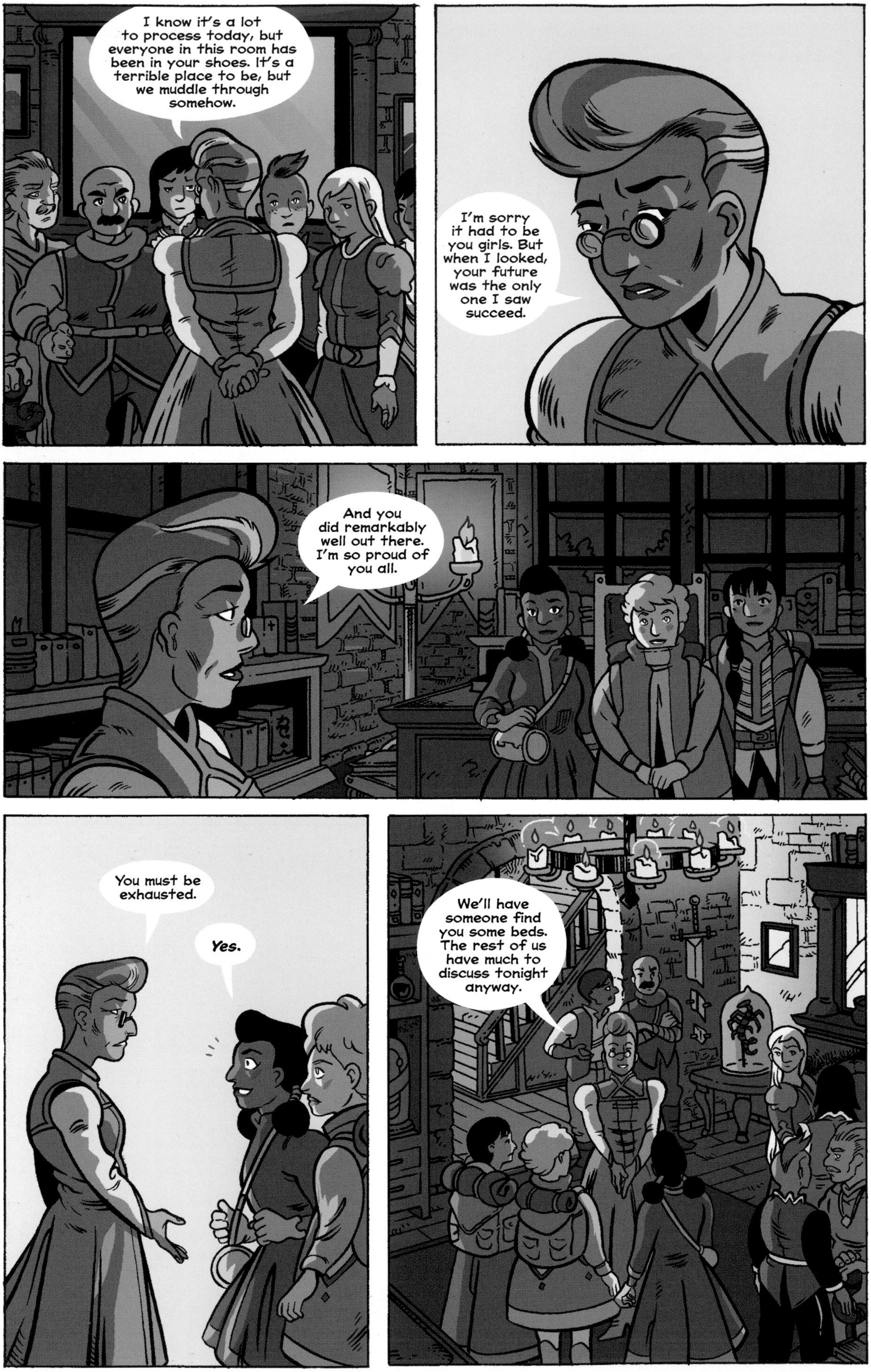
I know it's a lot to process today, but everyone in this room has been in your shoes. It's a terrible place to be, but we muddle through somehow.
I'm sorry it had to be you girls. But when I looked, your future was the only one I saw succeed.
And you did remarkably well out there. I'm so proud of you all.
You must be exhausted.
Yes.
We'll have someone find you some beds. The rest of us have much to discuss tonight anyway.

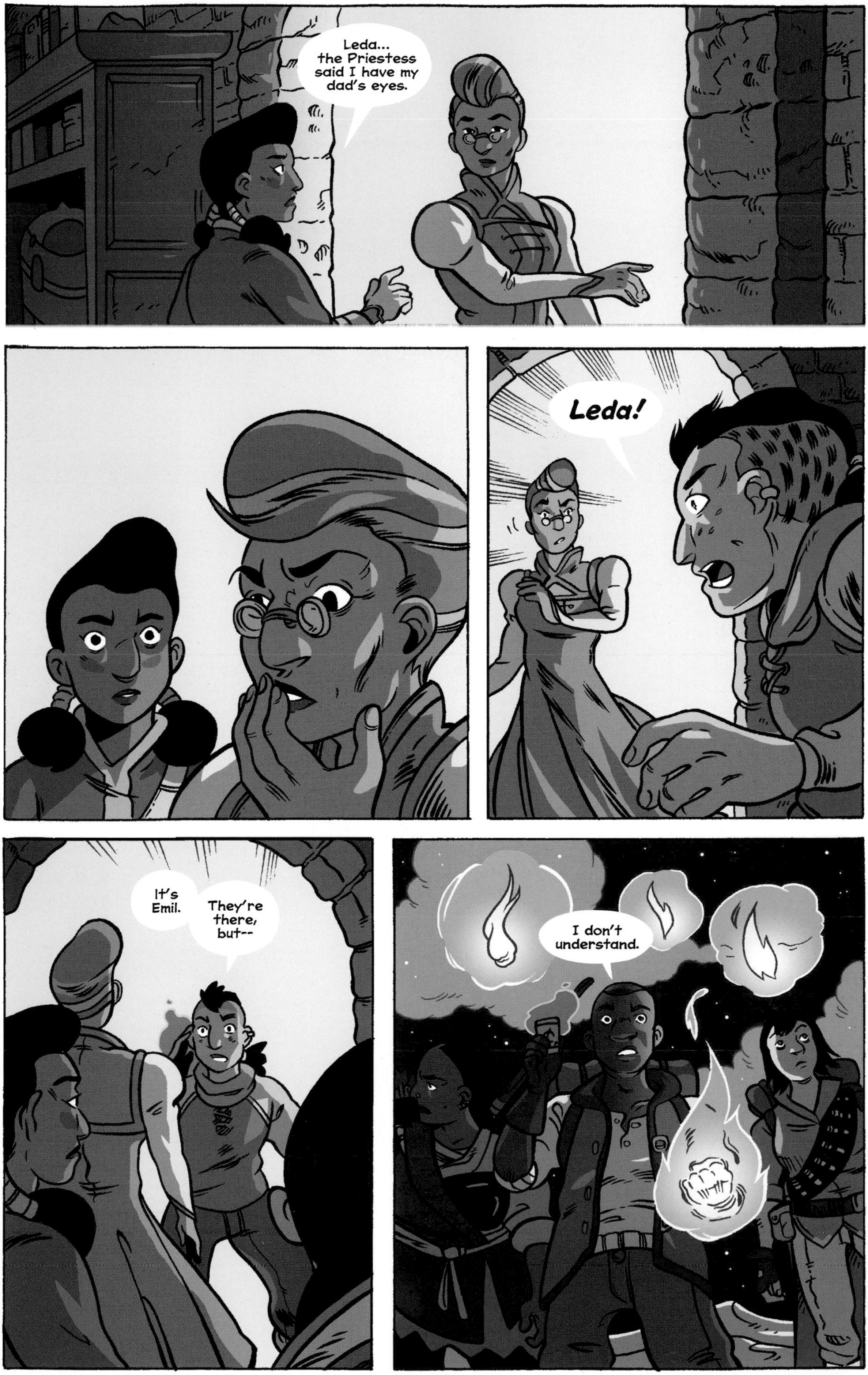
Leda... the Priestess said I have my dad's eyes.
Leda!
It's Emil.
They're there, but--
I don't understand.

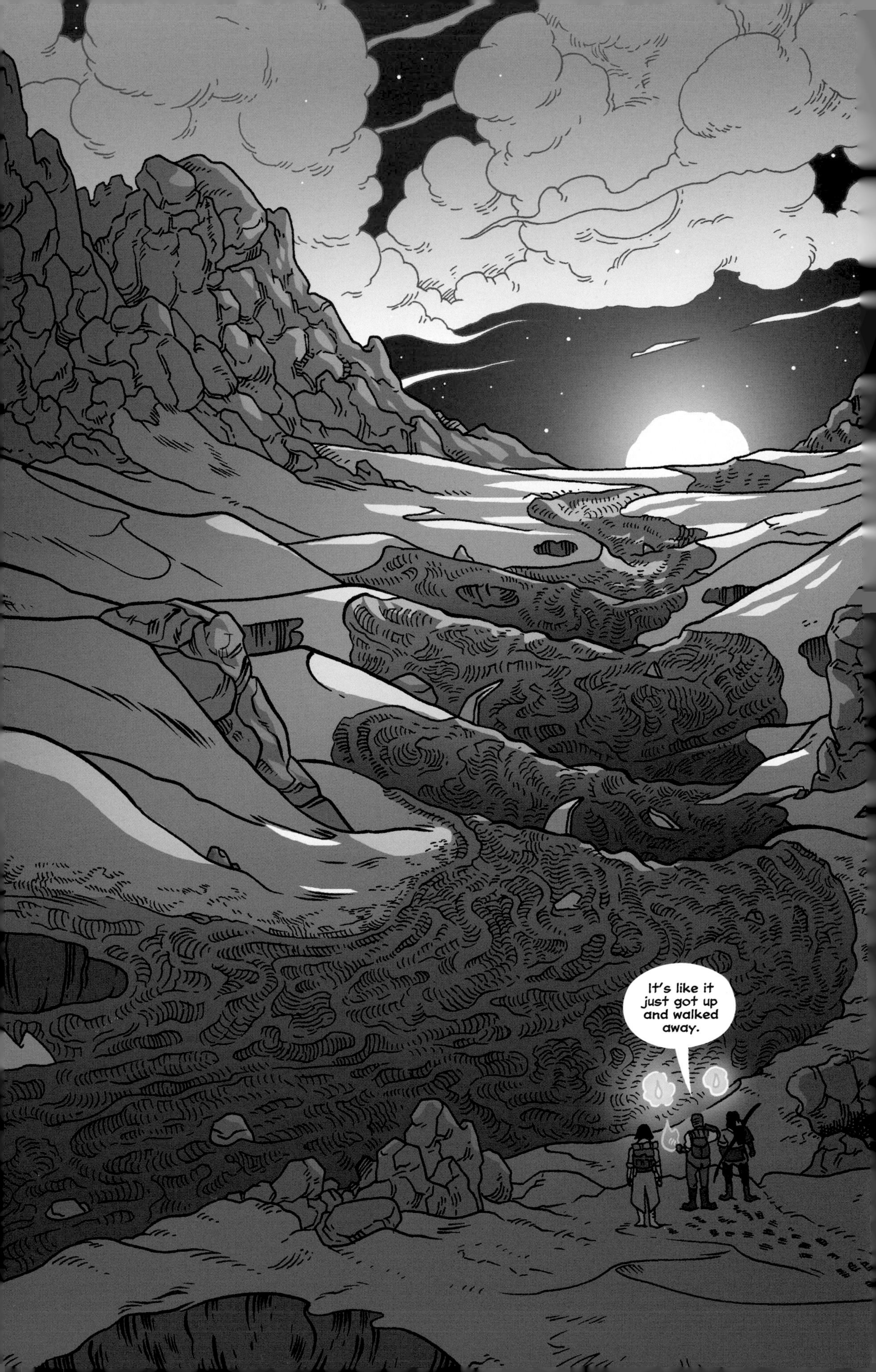
It's like it just got up and walked away.

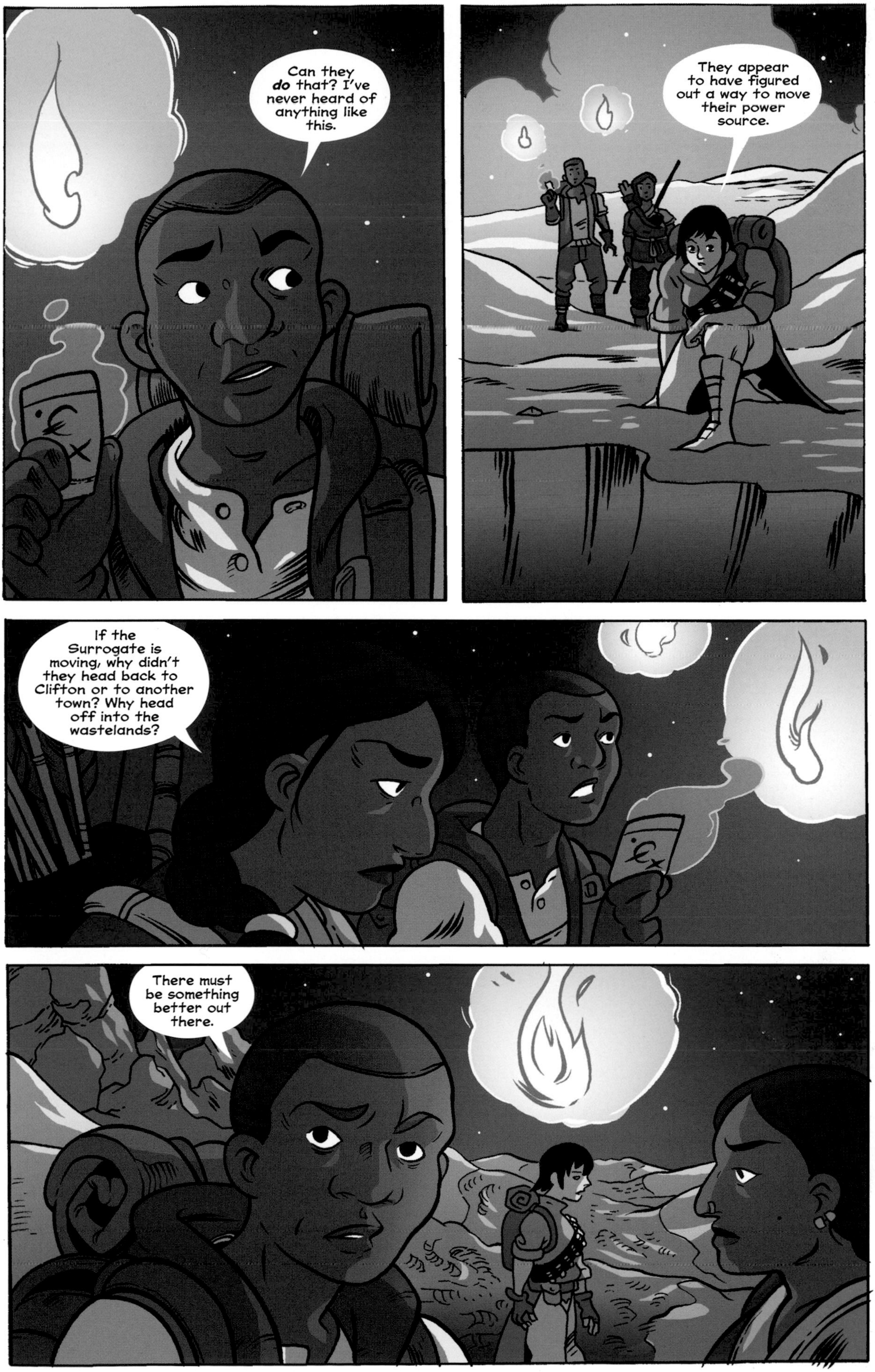

Can they *do* that? I've never heard of anything like this.
They appear to have figured out a way to move their power source.
If the Surrogate is moving, why didn't they head back to Clifton or to another town? Why head off into the wastelands?
There must be something better out there.

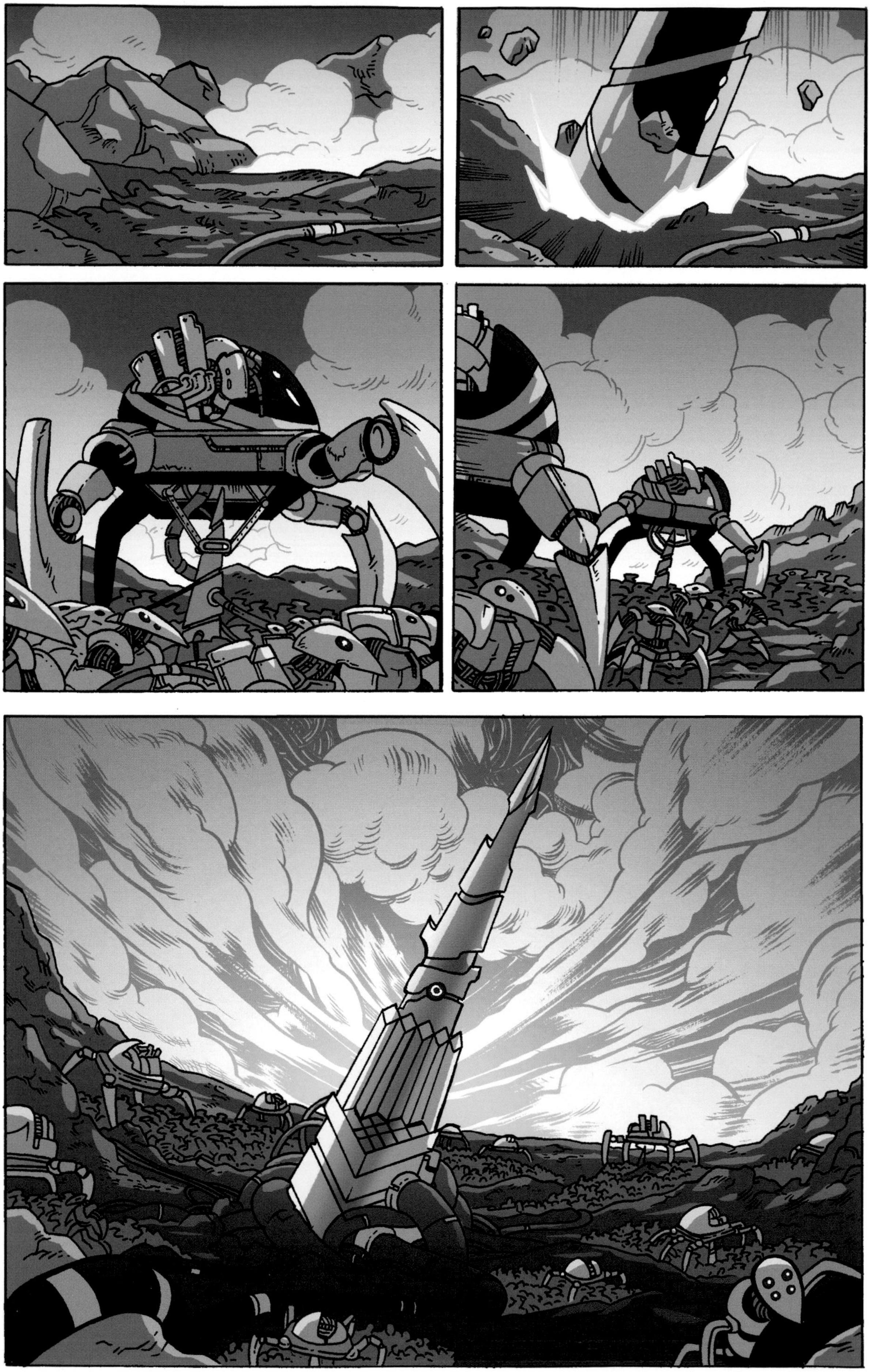

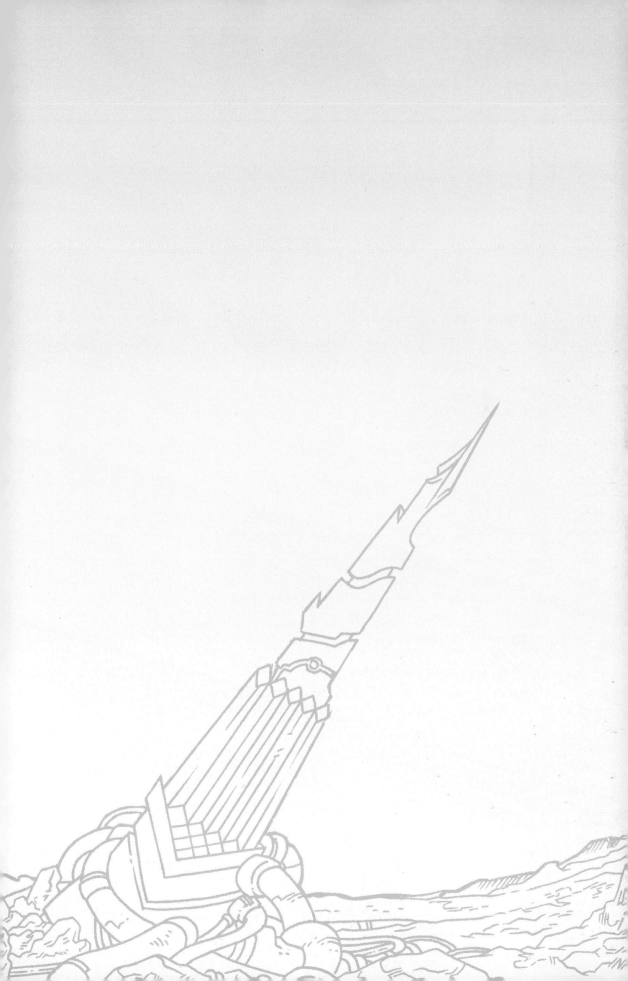

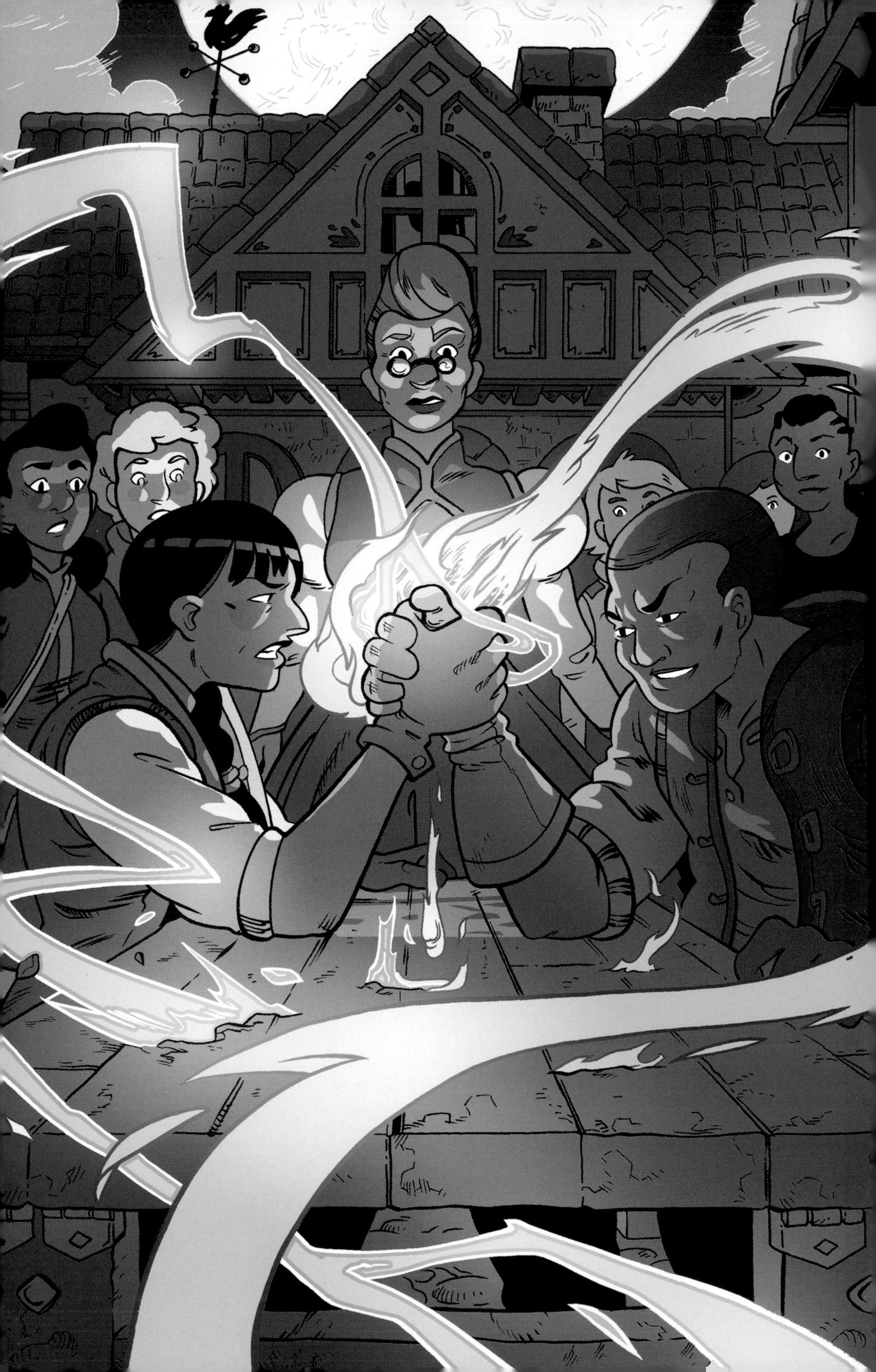

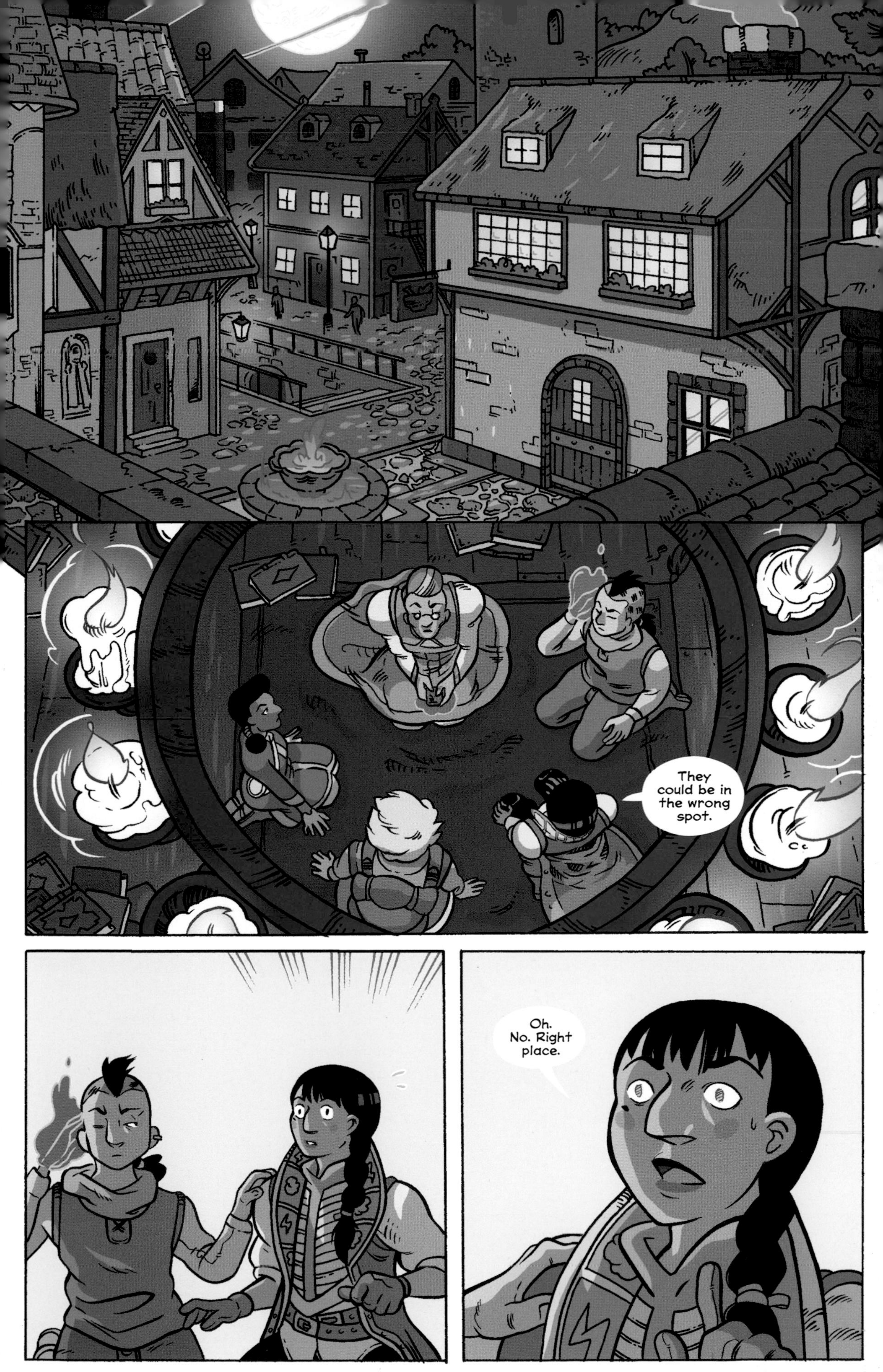
They could be in the wrong spot.
Oh. No. Right place.

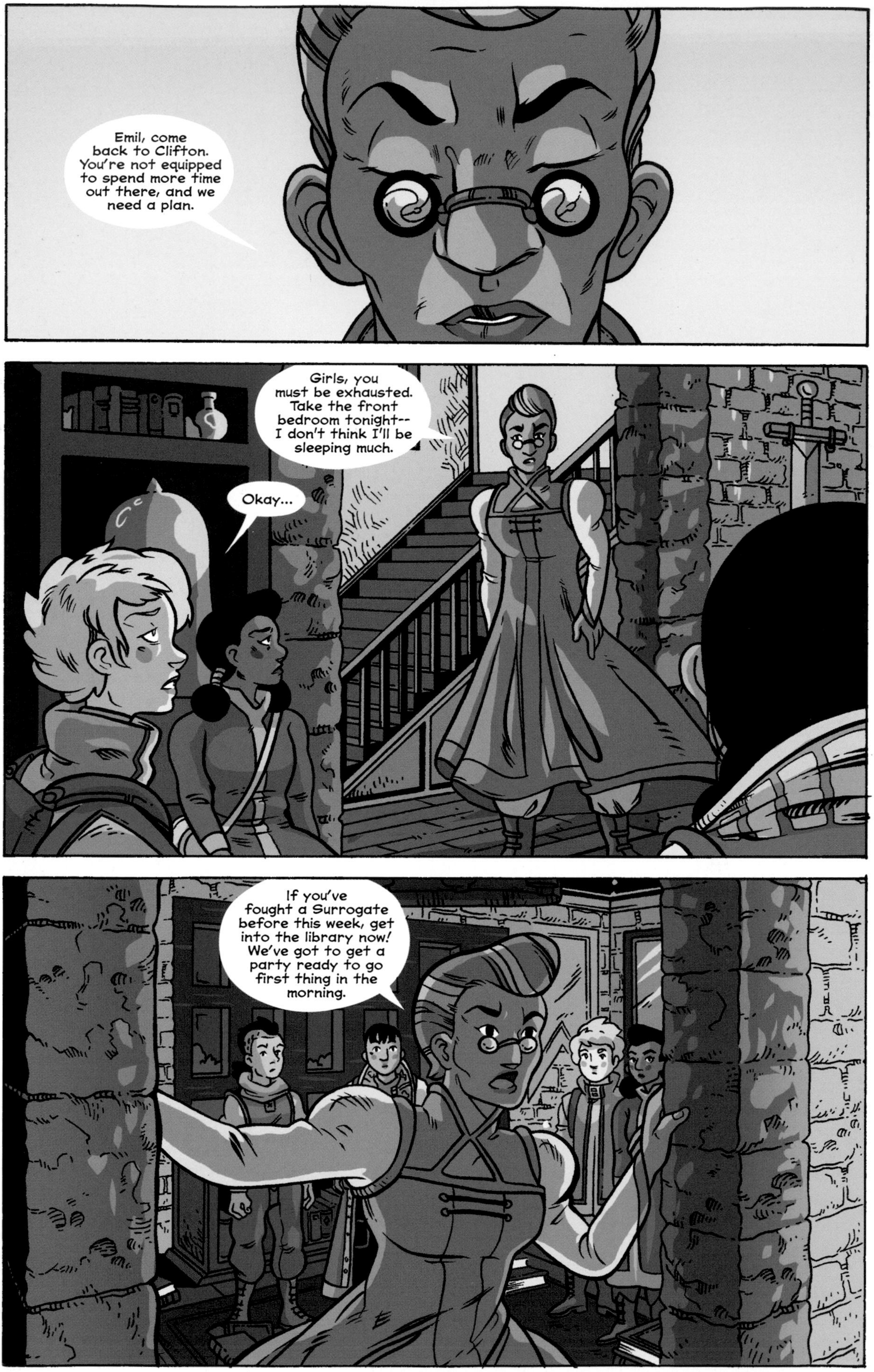
Emil, come back to Clifton. You're not equipped to spend more time out there, and we need a plan.
Girls, you must be exhausted. Take the front bedroom tonight-- I don't think I'll be sleeping much.
Okay...
If you've fought a Surrogate before this week, get into the library now! We've got to get a party ready to go first thing in the morning.

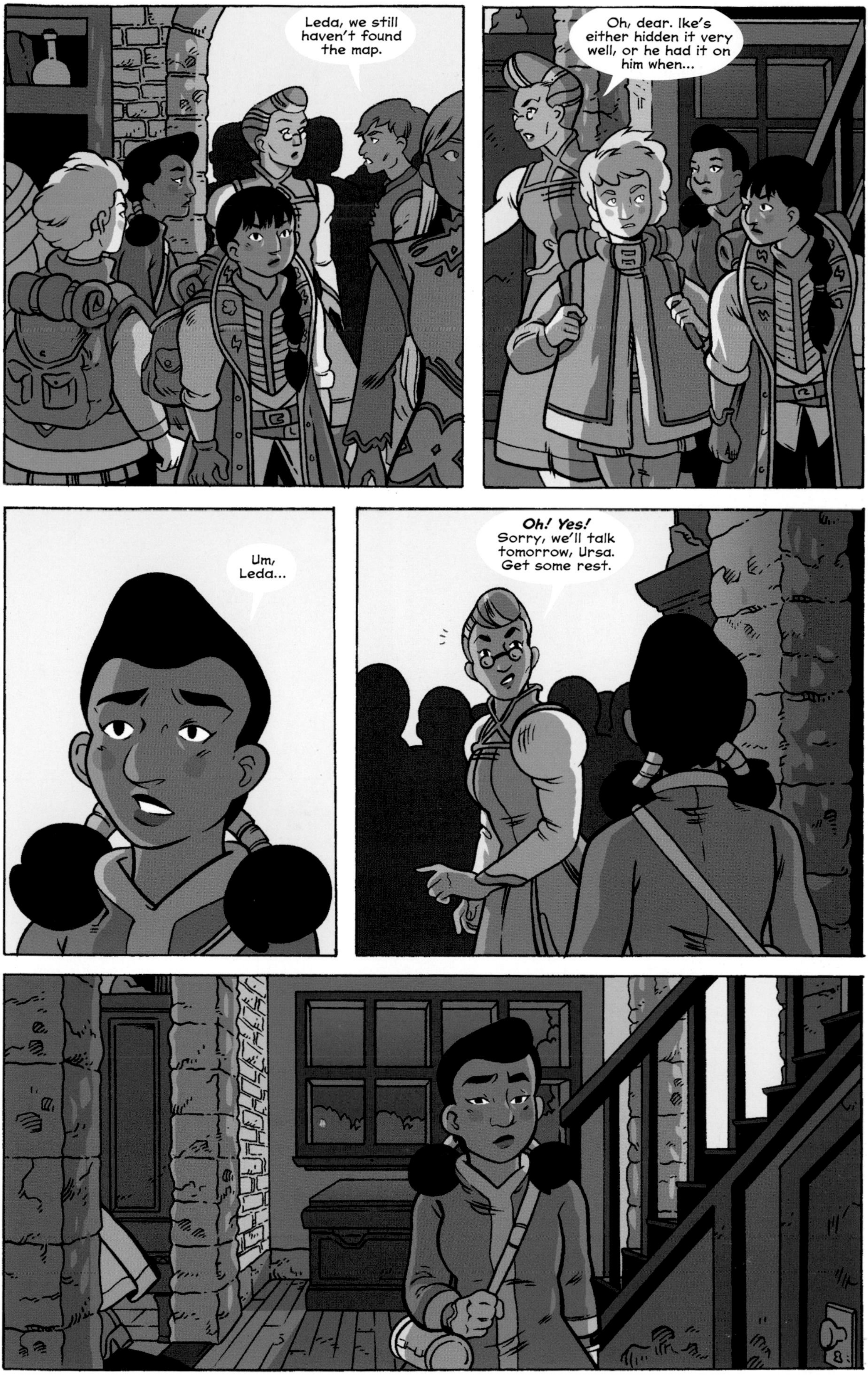
Leda, we still haven't found the map.
Oh, dear. Ike's either hidden it very well, or he had it on him when...
Um, Leda...
Oh! Yes! Sorry, we'll talk tomorrow, Ursa. Get some rest.

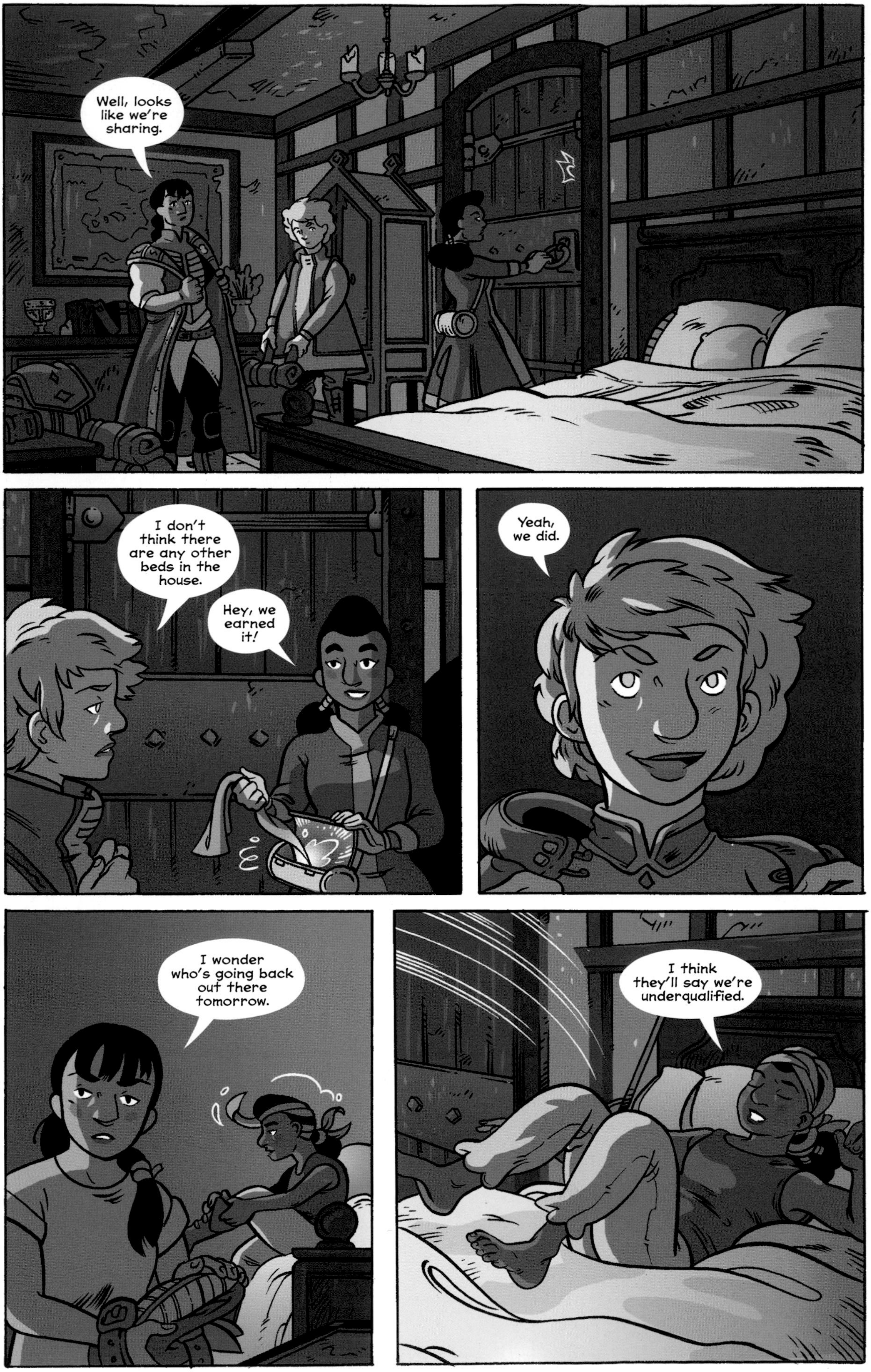
Well, looks like we're sharing.
I don't think there are any other beds in the house.
Hey, we earned it!
Yeah, we did.
I wonder who's going back out there tomorrow.
I think they'll say we're underqualified.

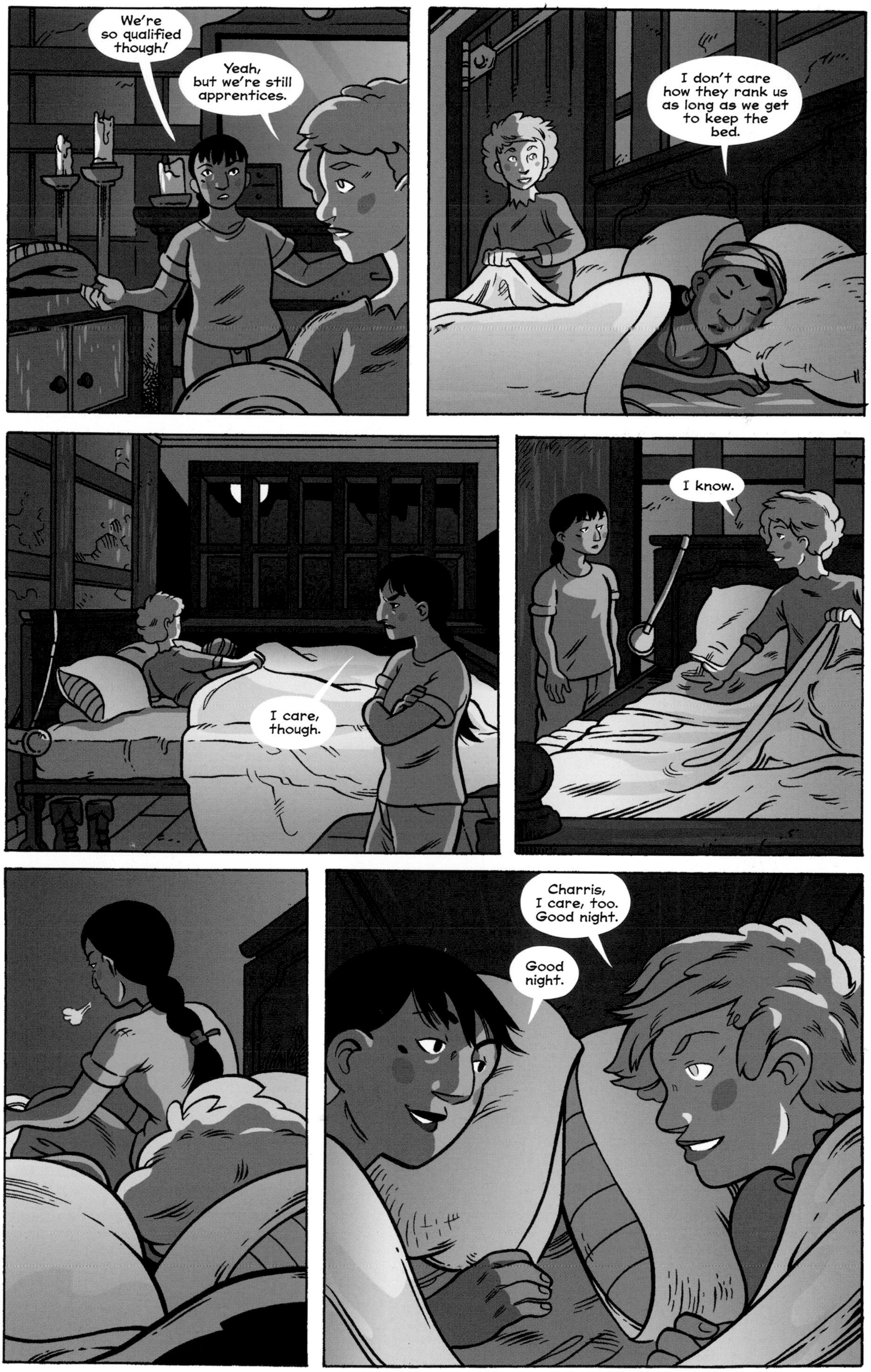
We're so qualified though!
Yeah, but we're still apprentices.
I don't care how they rank us as long as we get to keep the bed.
I care, though.
I know.
Charris, I care, too. Good night.
Good night.

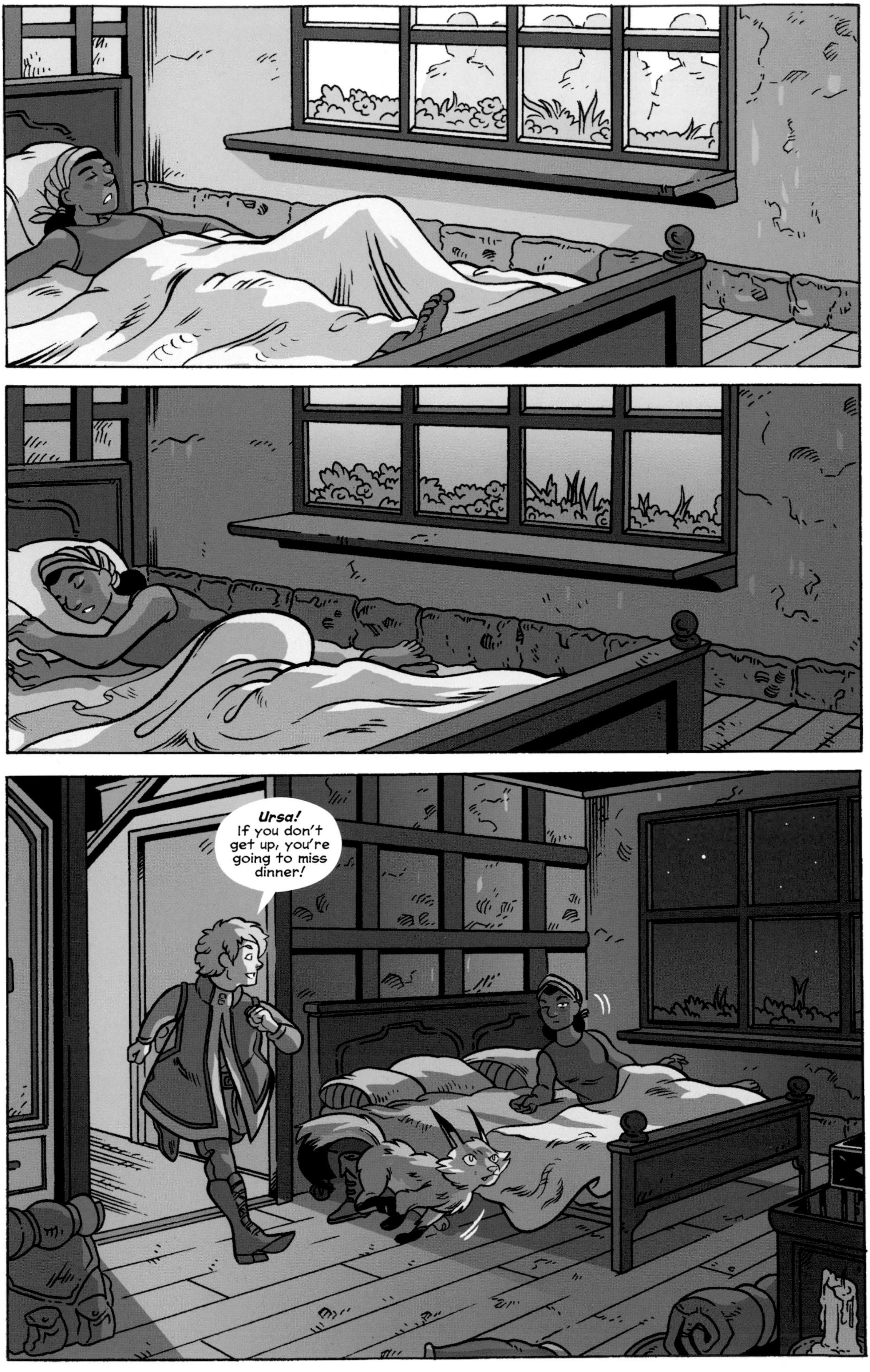
Ursa!
If you don't get up, you're going to miss dinner!

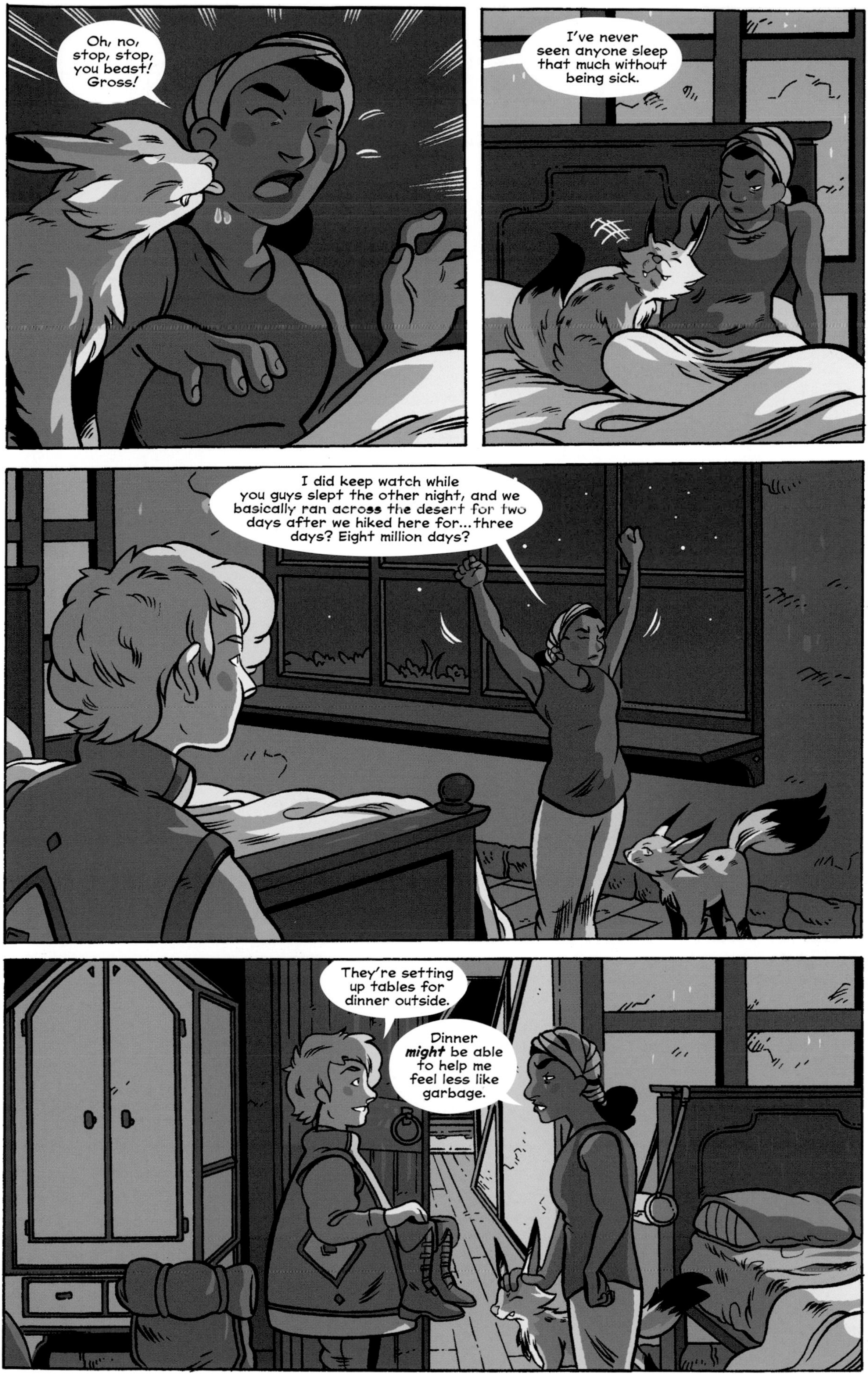
Oh, no, stop, stop, you beast! Gross!
I've never seen anyone sleep that much without being sick.
I did keep watch while you guys slept the other night, and we basically ran across the desert for two days after we hiked here for...three days? Eight million days?
They're setting up tables for dinner outside.
Dinner *might* be able to help me feel less like garbage.

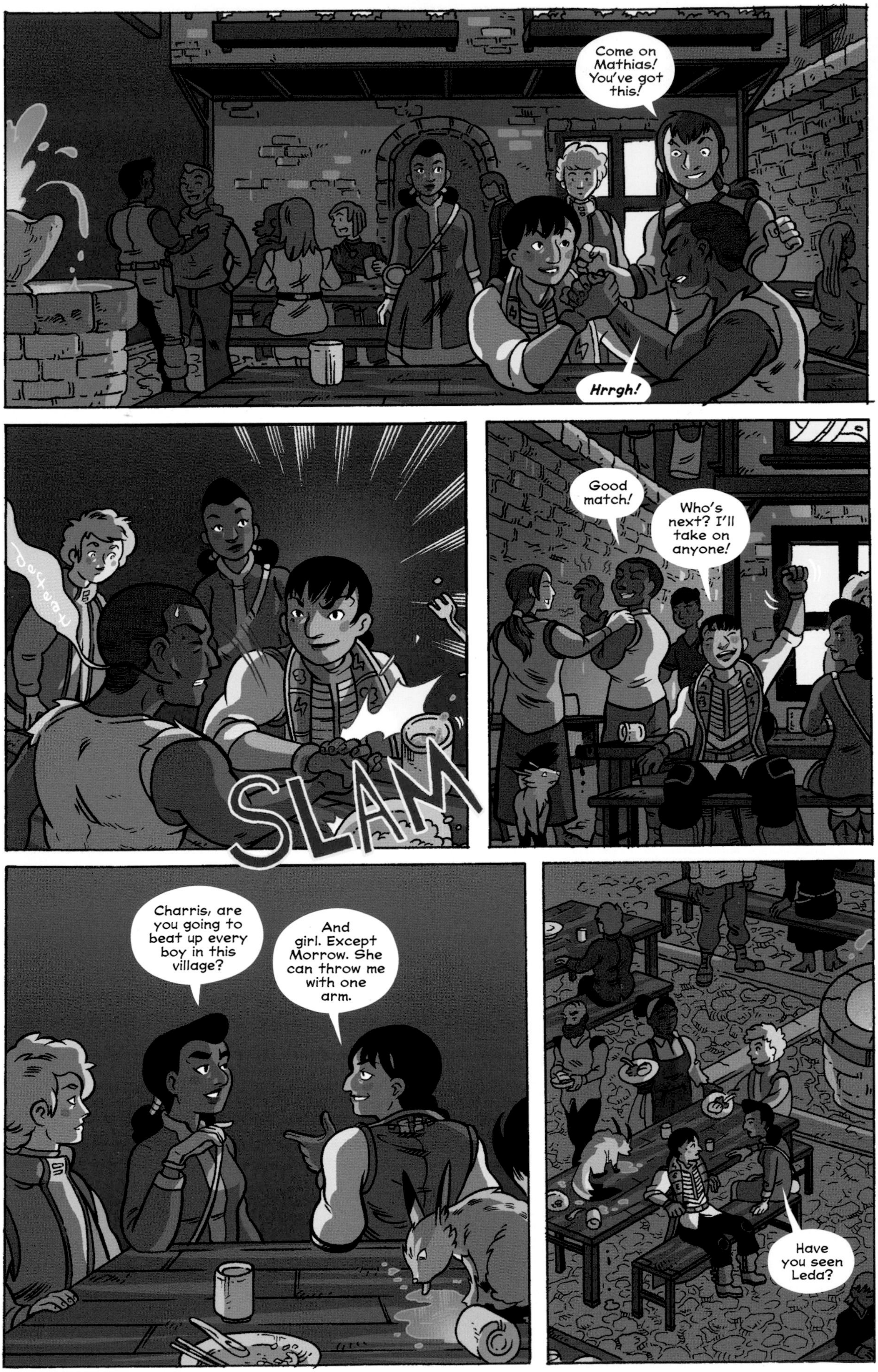

Come on Mathias! You've got this!
Hrrgh!
SLAM
Good match!
Who's next? I'll take on anyone!
Charris, are you going to beat up every boy in this village?
And girl. Except Morrow. She can throw me with one arm.
Have you seen Leda?

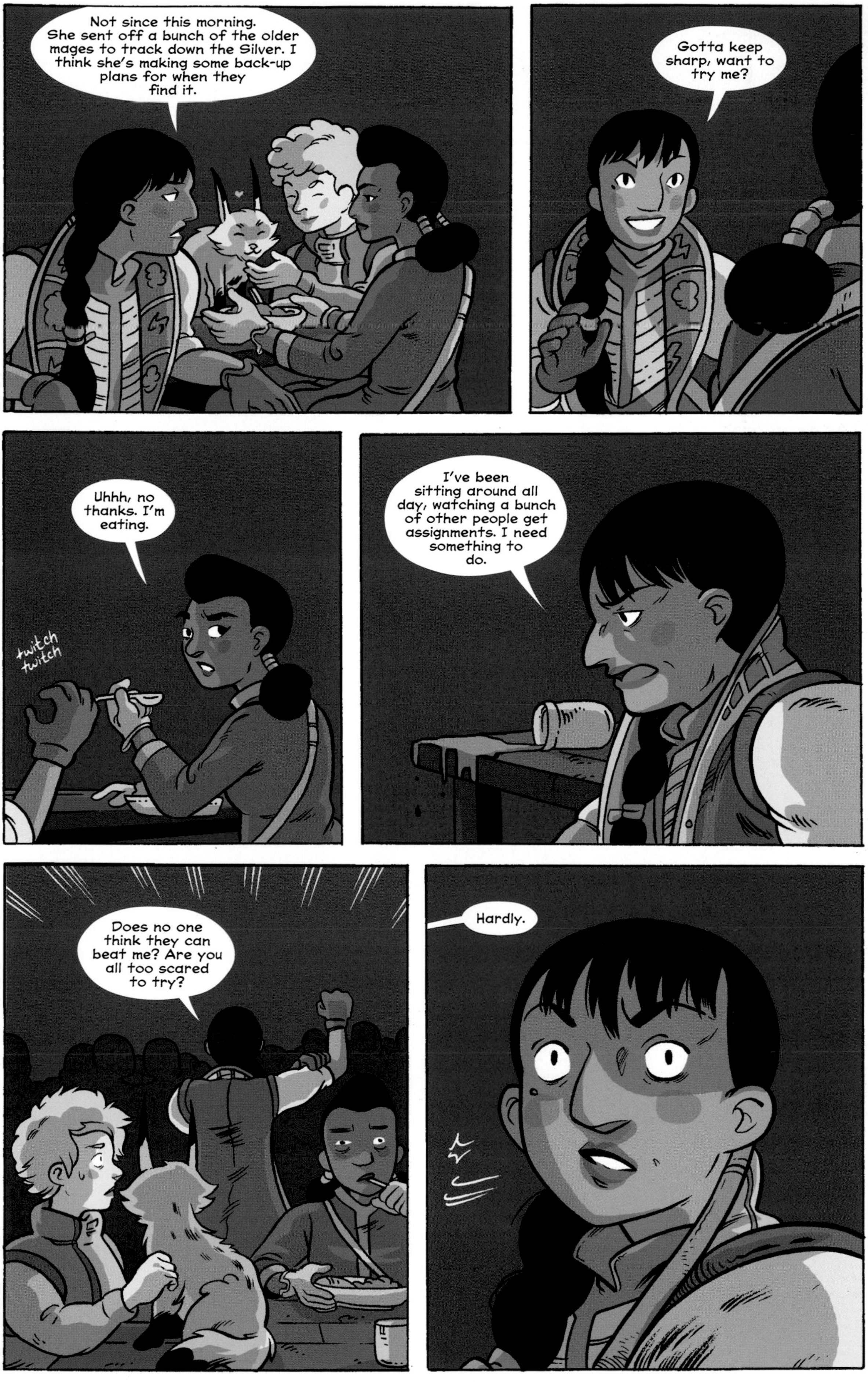
Not since this morning. She sent off a bunch of the older mages to track down the Silver. I think she's making some back-up plans for when they find it.
Gotta keep sharp, want to try me?
Uhhh, no thanks. I'm eating.
twitch twitch
I've been sitting around all day, watching a bunch of other people get assignments. I need something to do.
Does no one think they can beat me? Are you all too scared to try?
Hardly.

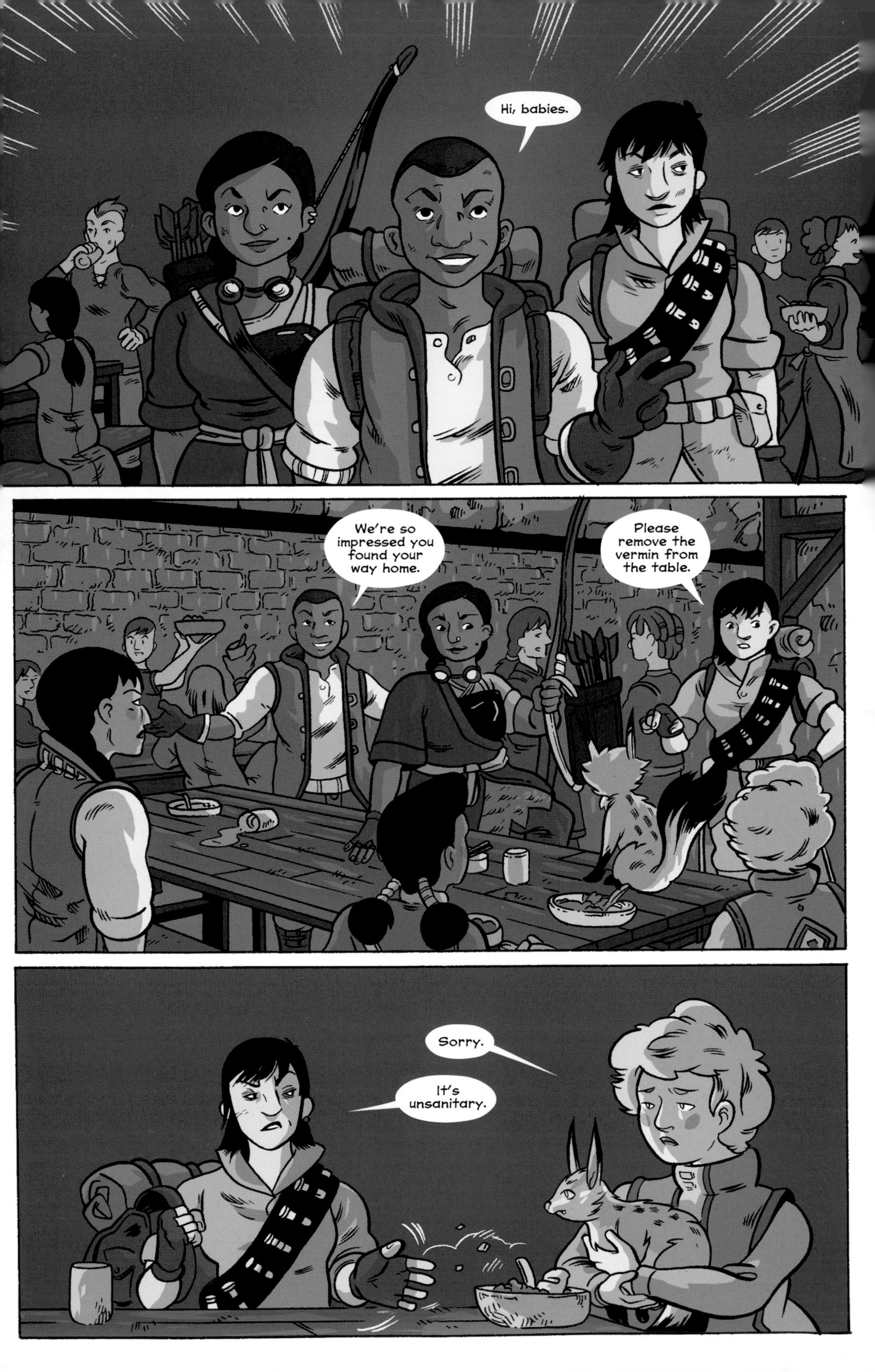
Hi, babies.
We're so impressed you found your way home.
Please remove the vermin from the table.
Sorry.
It's unsanitary.

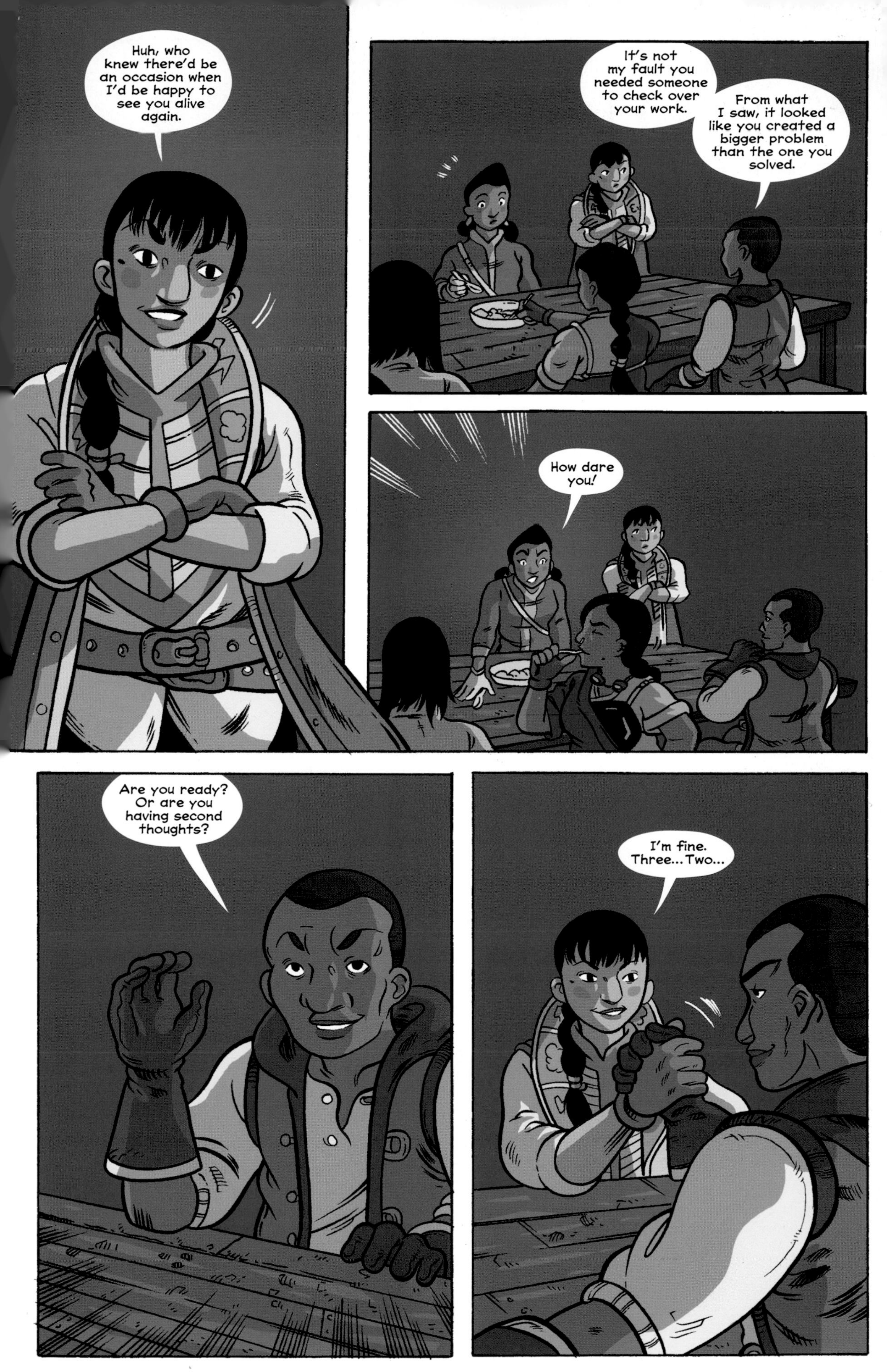
Huh, who knew there'd be an occasion when I'd be happy to see you alive again.
It's not my fault you needed someone to check over your work.
From what I saw, it looked like you created a bigger problem than the one you solved.
How dare you!
Are you ready? Or are you having second thoughts?
I'm fine. Three... Two...

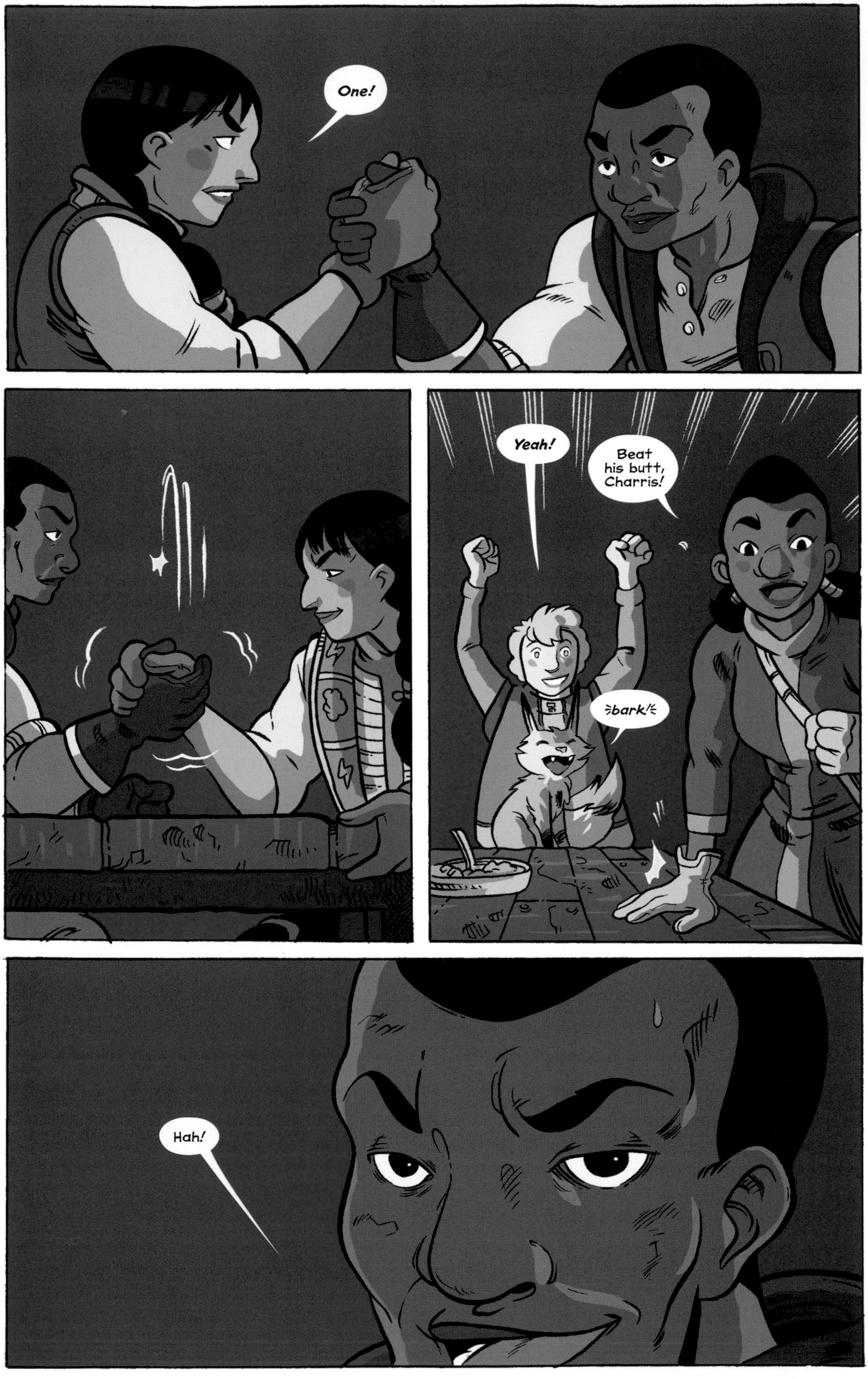
One!
Yeah!
Beat his butt, Charris!
bark!
Hah!

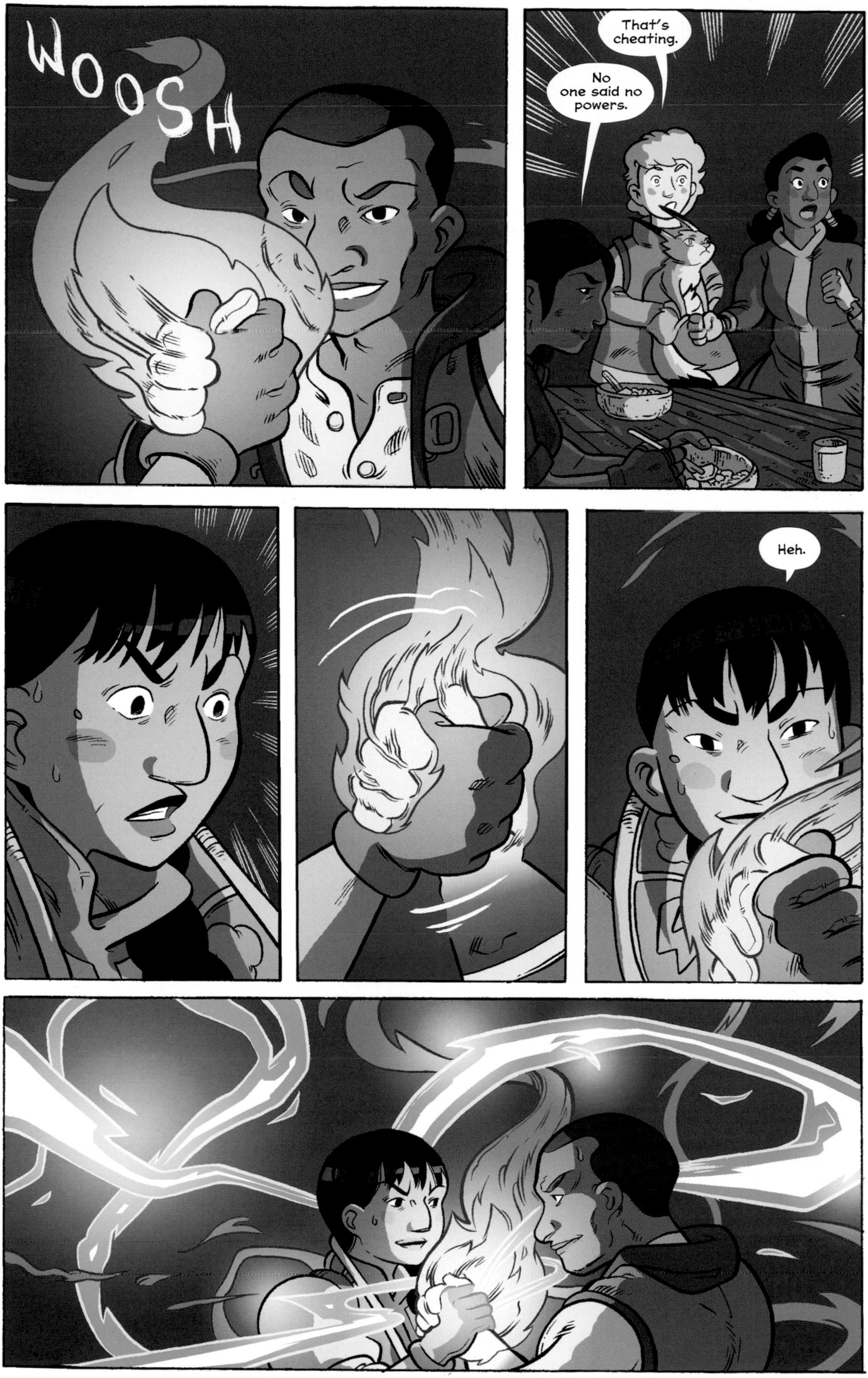
WOOSH
That's cheating.
No one said no powers.
Heh.

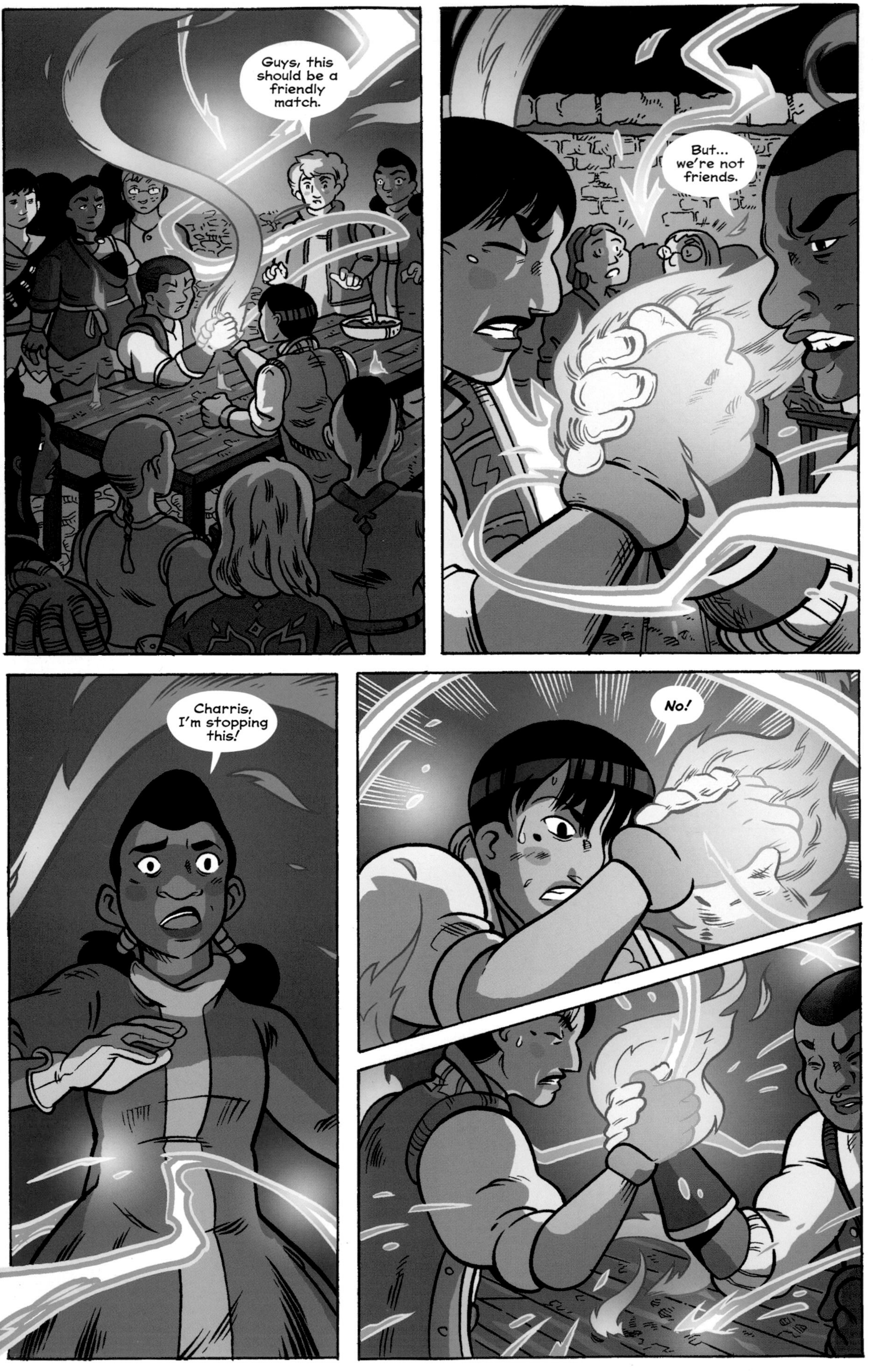
Guys, this should be a friendly match.
But... we're not friends.
Charris, I'm stopping this!
No!

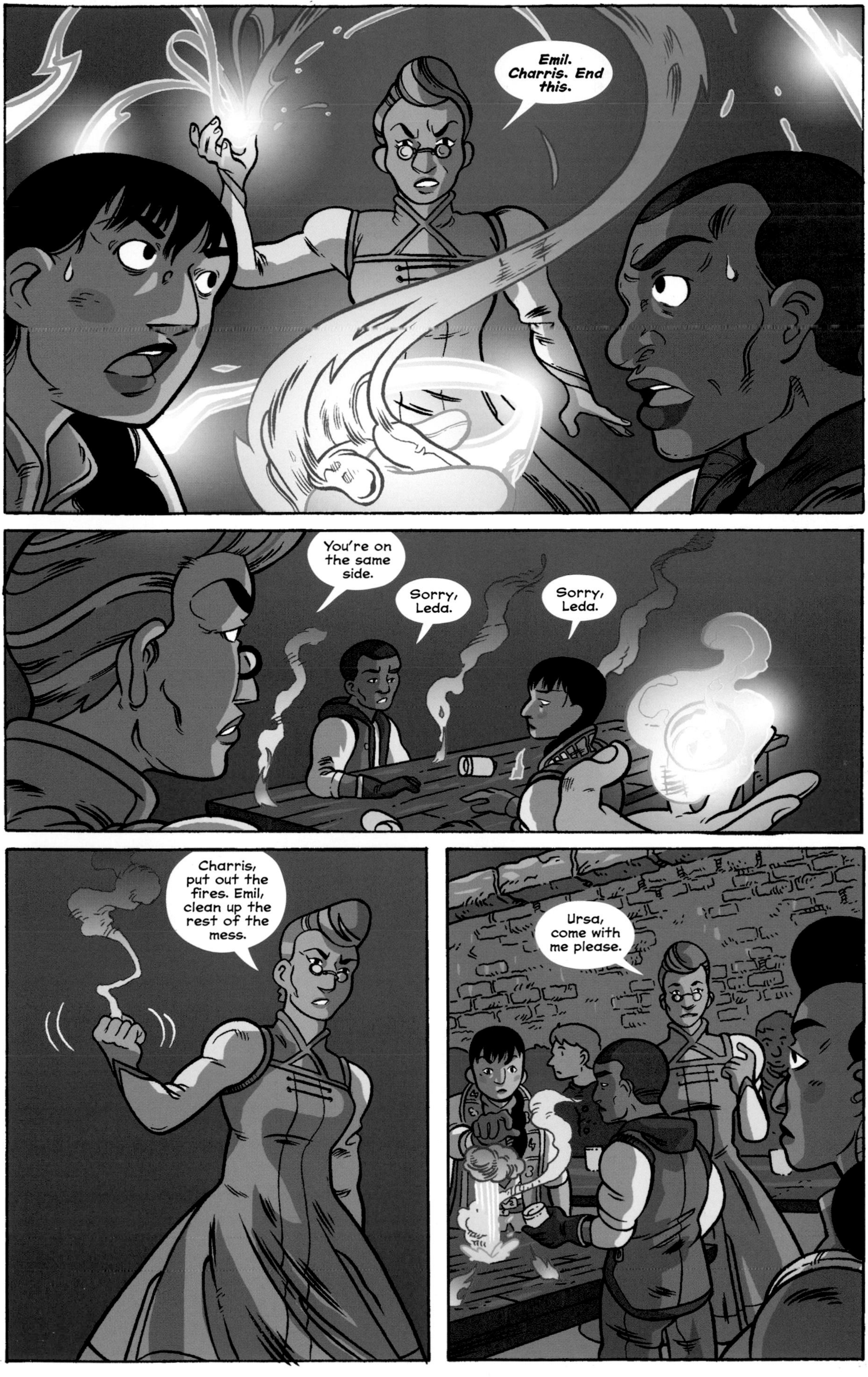
Emil. Charris. End this.
You're on the same side.
Sorry, Leda.
Sorry, Leda.
Charris, put out the fires. Emil, clean up the rest of the mess.
Ursa, come with me please.

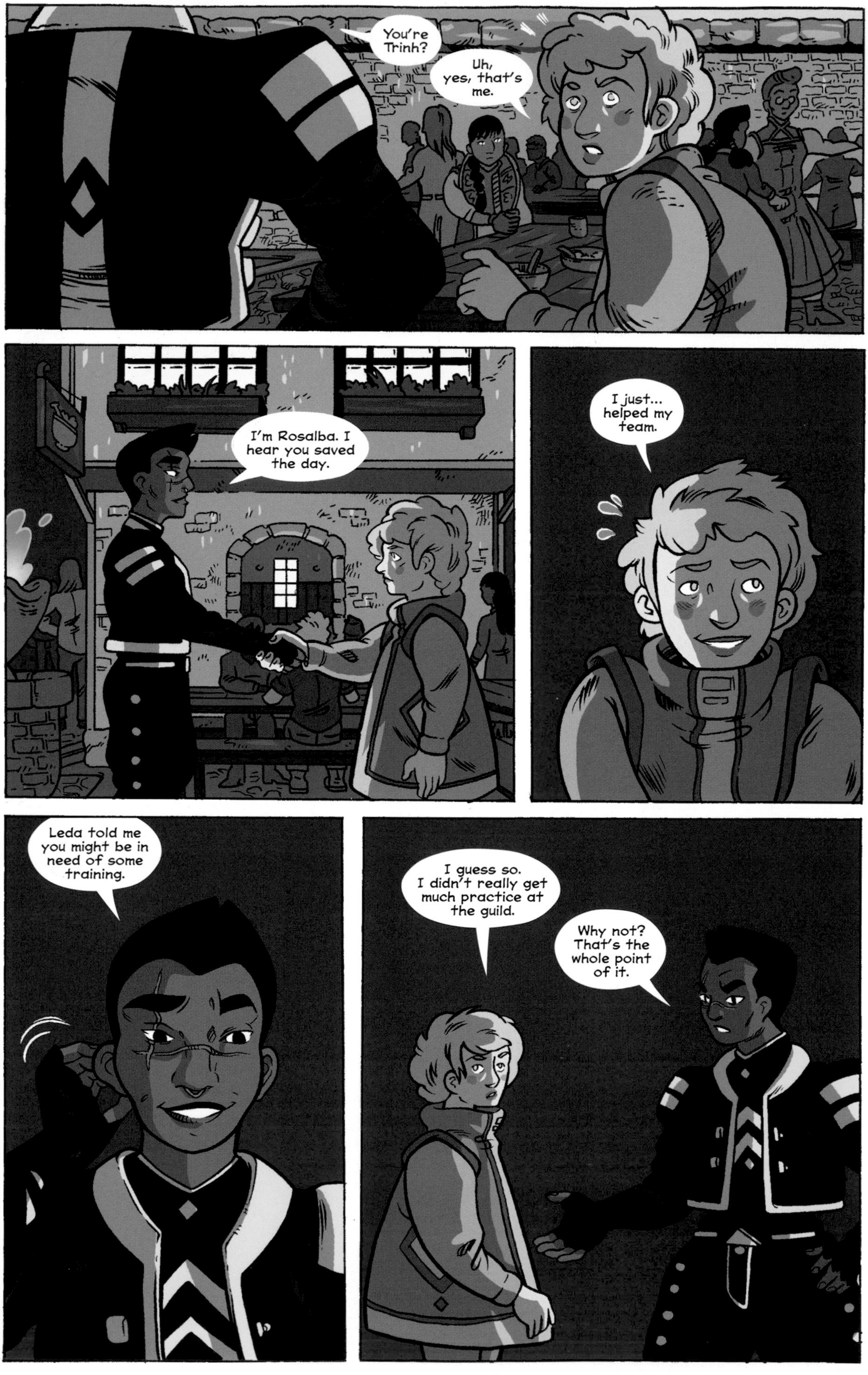
You're Trinh?
Uh, yes, that's me.
I'm Rosalba. I hear you saved the day.
I just... helped my team.
Leda told me you might be in need of some training.
I guess so. I didn't really get much practice at the guild.
Why not? That's the whole point of it.

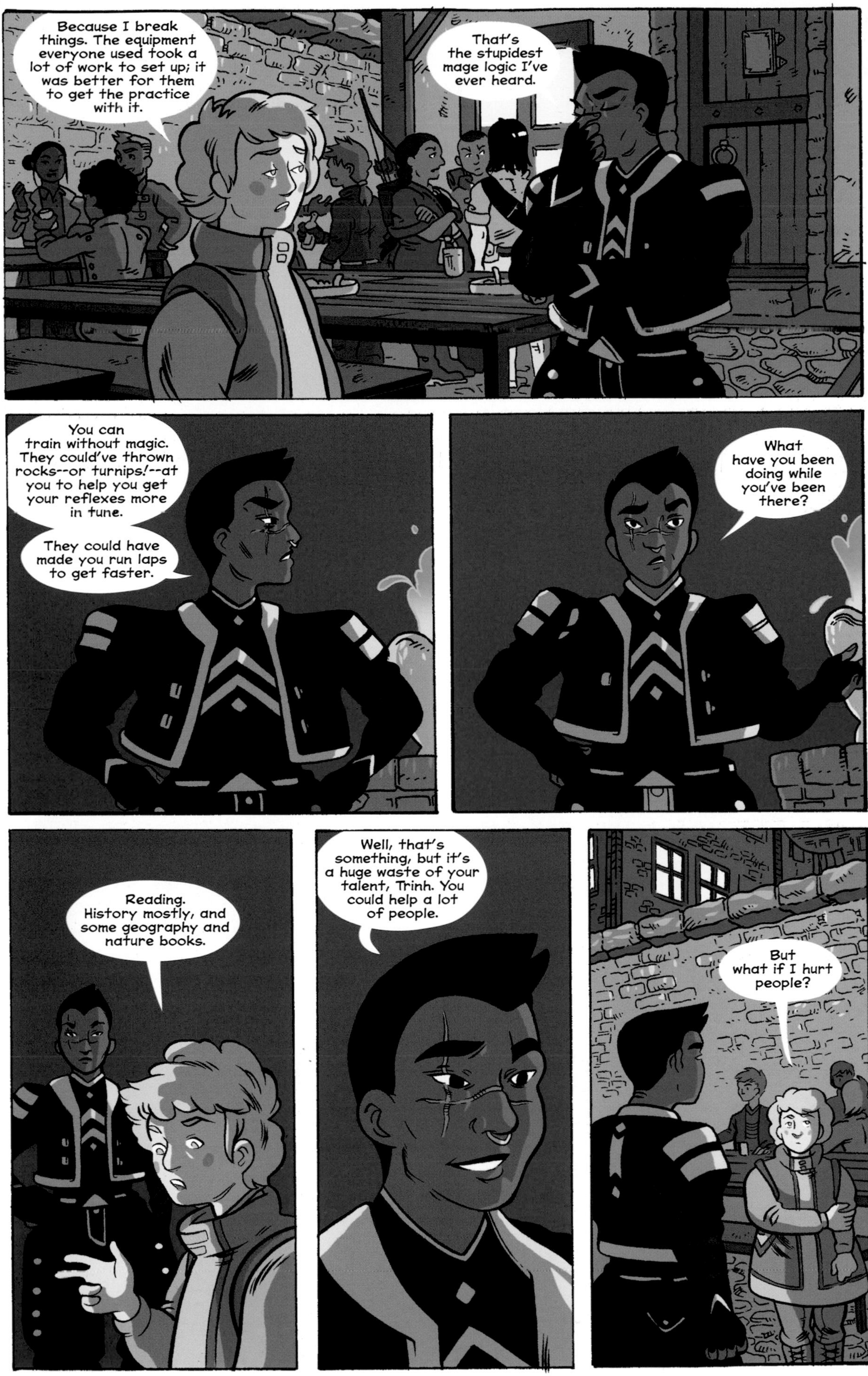

Because I break things. The equipment everyone used took a lot of work to set up; it was better for them to get the practice with it.
That's the stupidest mage logic I've ever heard.
You can train without magic. They could've thrown rocks--or turnips!--at you to help you get your reflexes more in tune.
They could have made you run laps to get faster.
What have you been doing while you've been there?
Reading. History mostly, and some geography and nature books.
Well, that's something, but it's a huge waste of your talent, Trinh. You could help a lot of people.
But what if I hurt people?

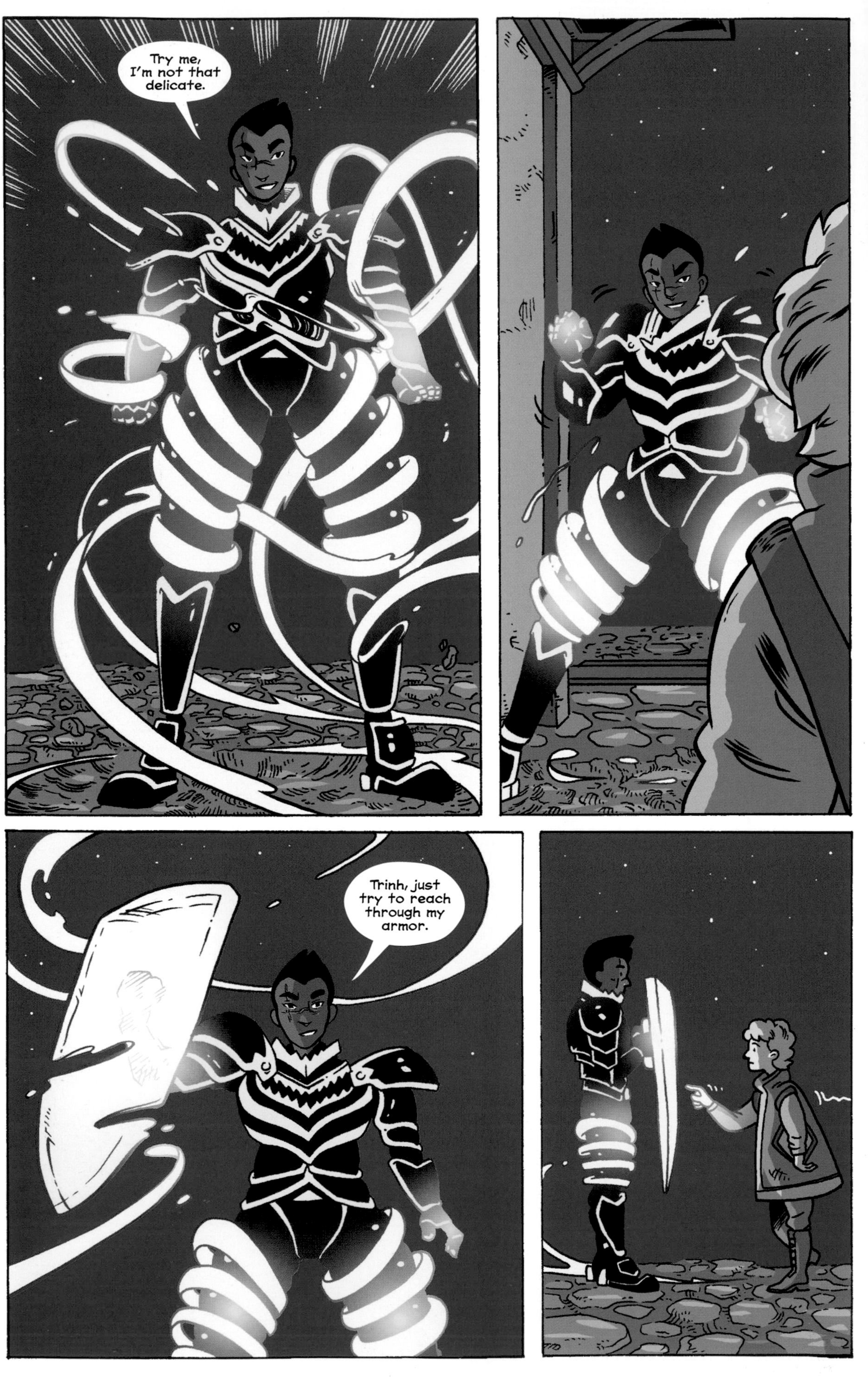
Try me, I'm not that delicate.
Trinh, just try to reach through my armor.

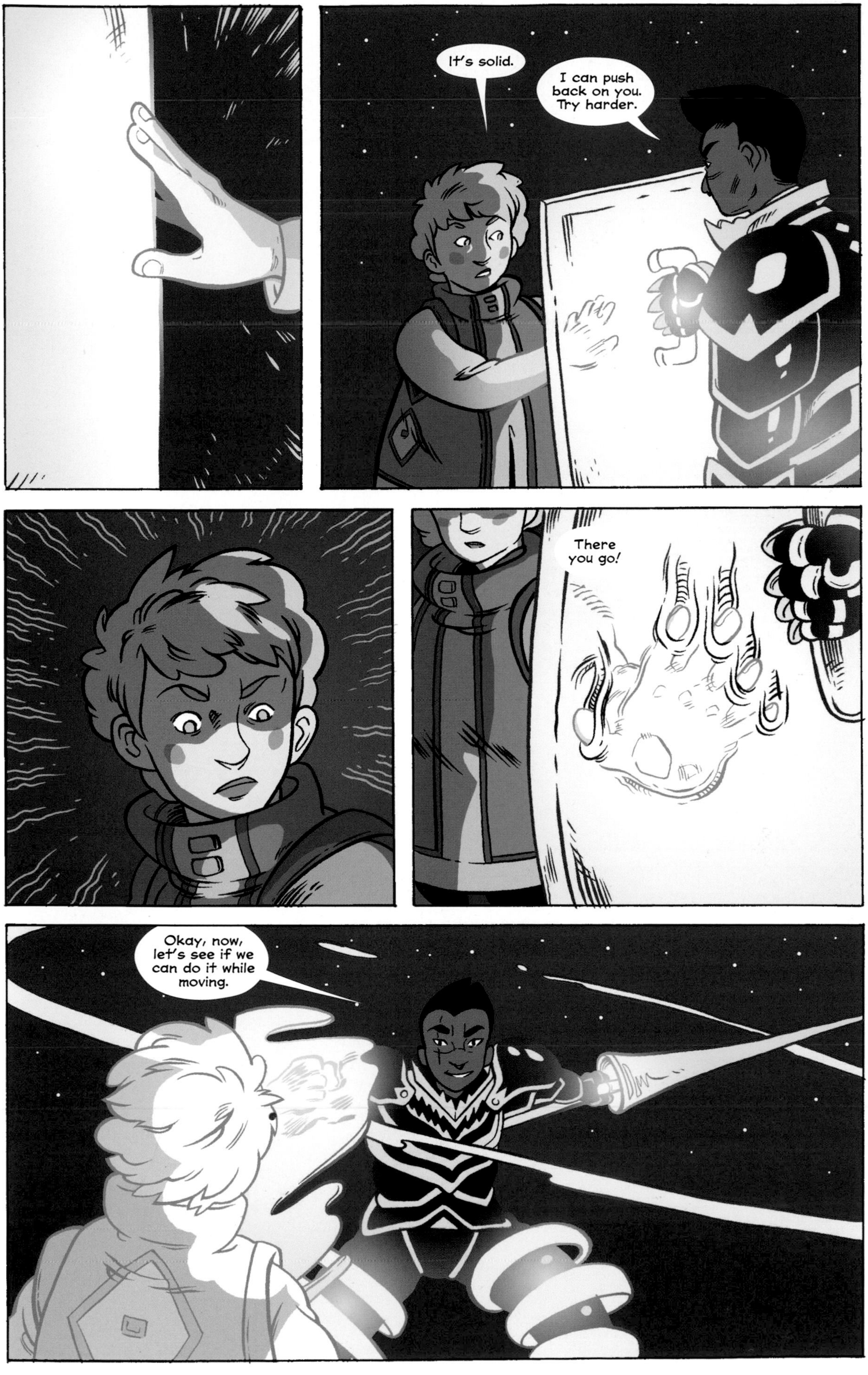
It's solid.
I can push back on you. Try harder.
There you go!
Okay, now, let's see if we can do it while moving.

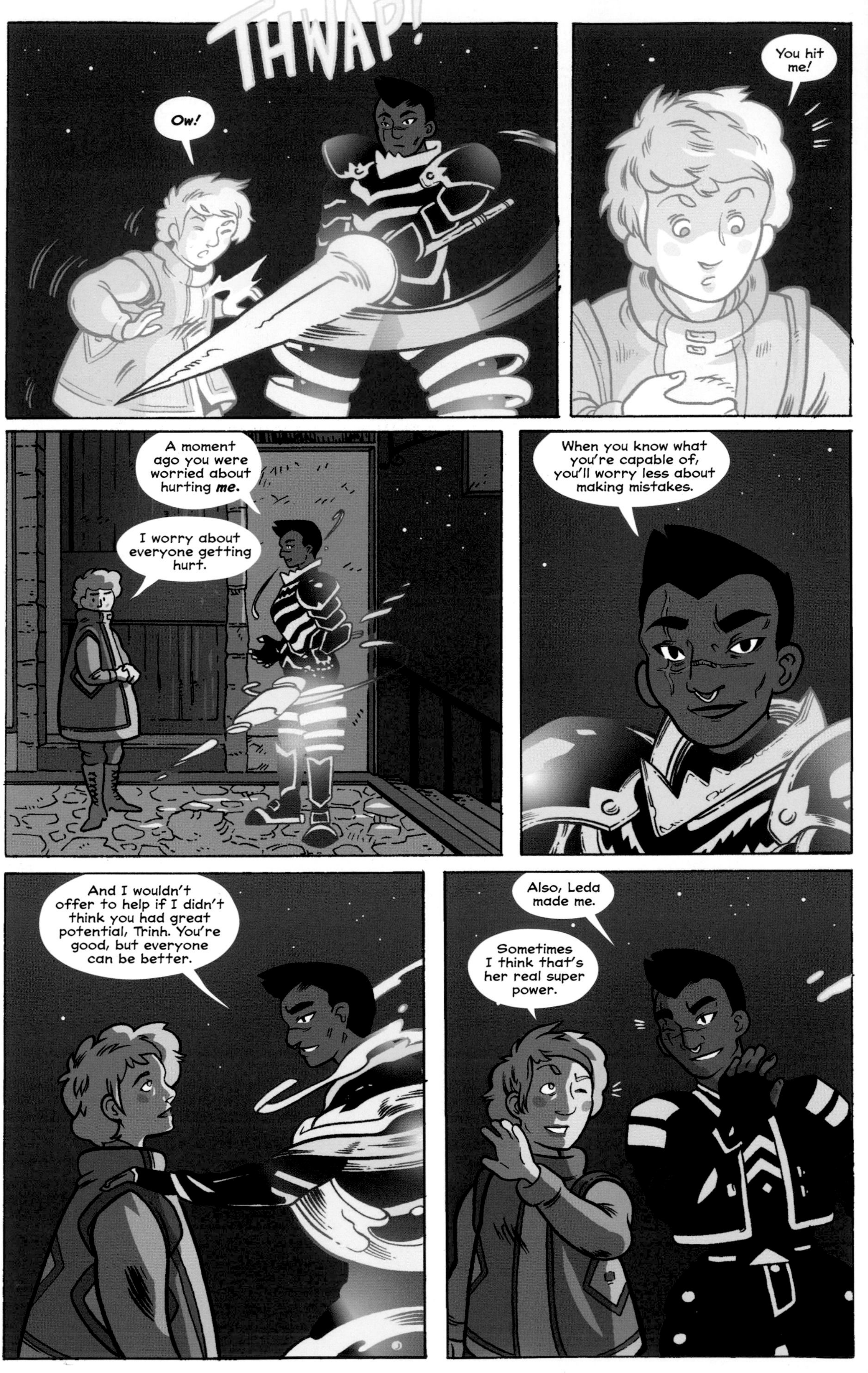
THWAP!
Ow!
You hit me!
A moment ago you were worried about hurting *me*.
I worry about everyone getting hurt.
When you know what you're capable of, you'll worry less about making mistakes.
And I wouldn't offer to help if I didn't think you had great potential, Trinh. You're good, but everyone can be better.
Also, Leda made me.
Sometimes I think that's her real super power.

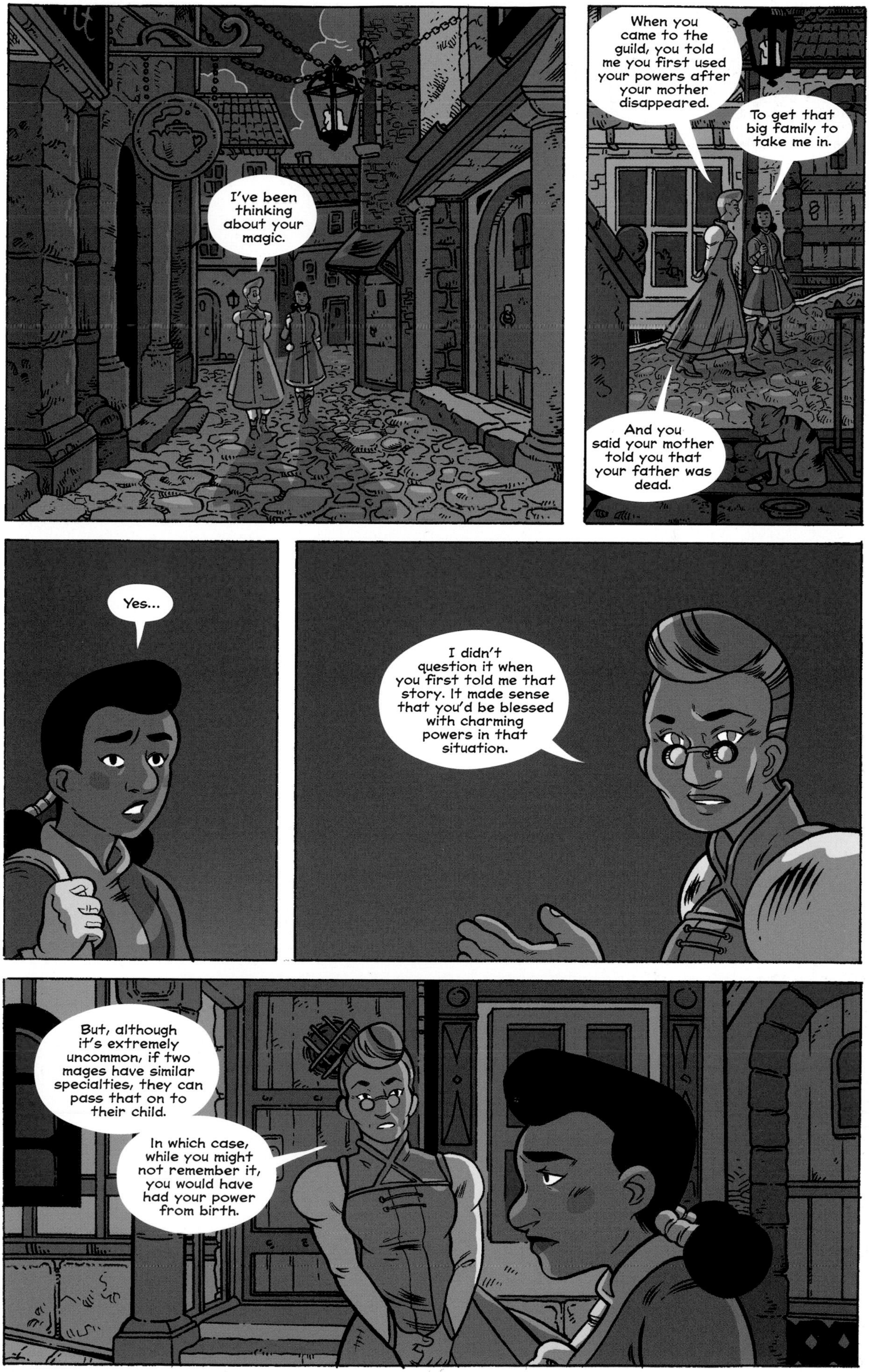
I've been thinking about your magic.
When you came to the guild, you told me you first used your powers after your mother disappeared.
To get that big family to take me in.
And you said your mother told you that your father was dead.
Yes...
I didn't question it when you first told me that story. It made sense that you'd be blessed with charming powers in that situation.
But, although it's extremely uncommon, if two mages have similar specialties, they can pass that on to their child.
In which case, while you might not remember it, you would have had your power from birth.

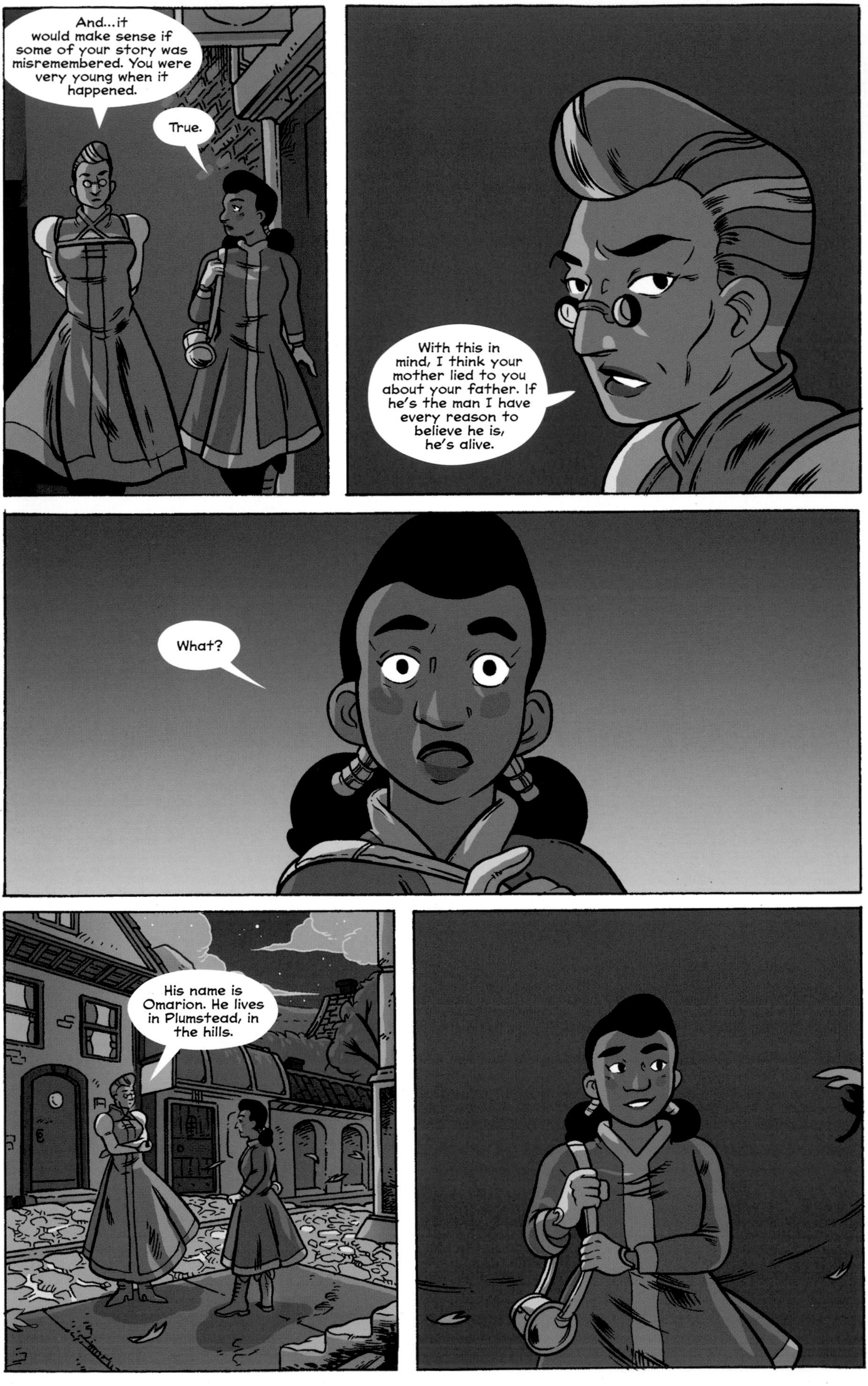
And...it would make sense if some of your story was misremembered. You were very young when it happened.
True.
With this in mind, I think your mother lied to you about your father. If he's the man I have every reason to believe he is, he's alive.
What?
His name is Omarion. He lives in Plumstead, in the hills.

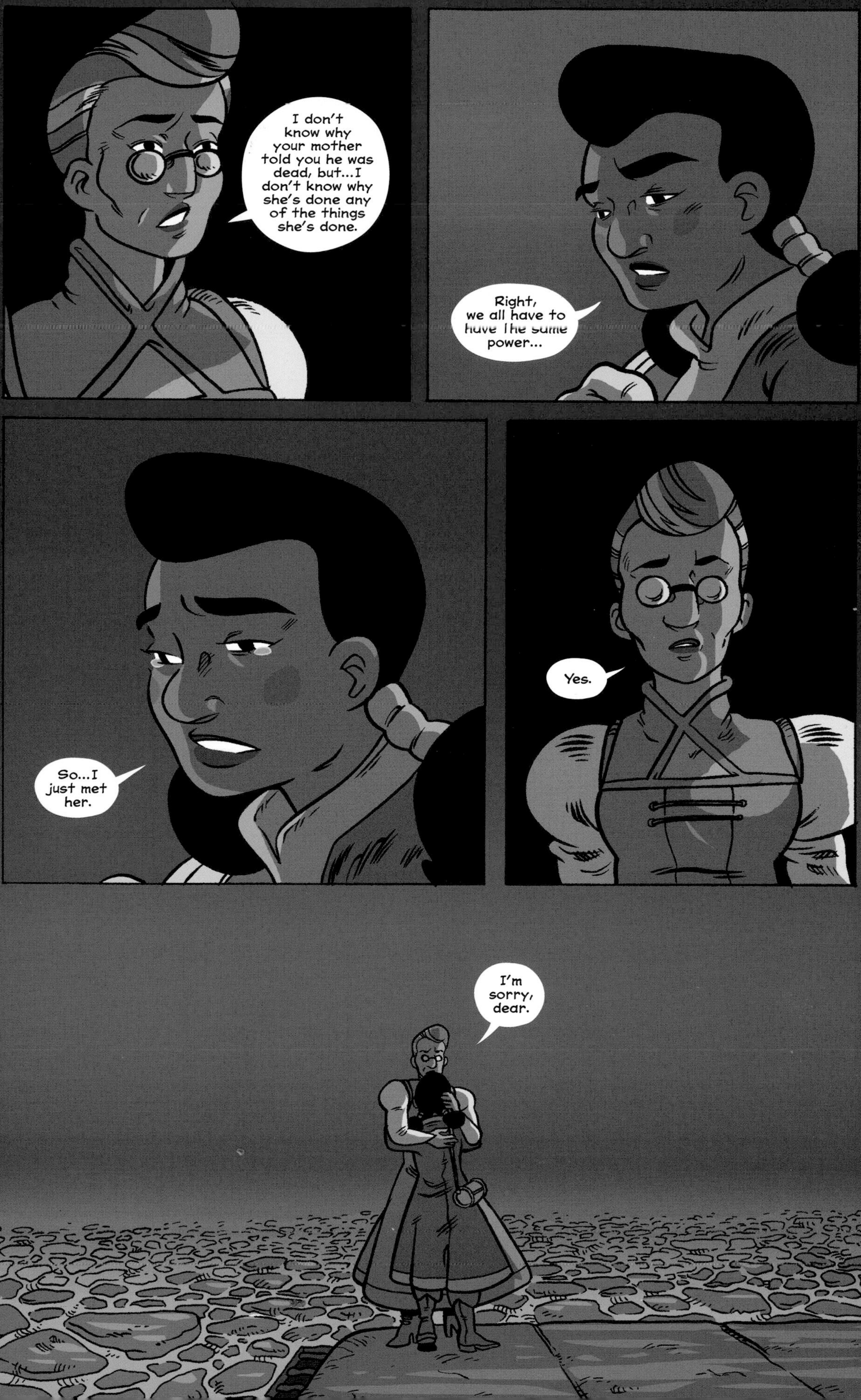
I don't know why your mother told you he was dead, but...I don't know why she's done any of the things she's done.
Right, we all have to have the same power...
So...I just met her.
Yes.
I'm sorry, dear.

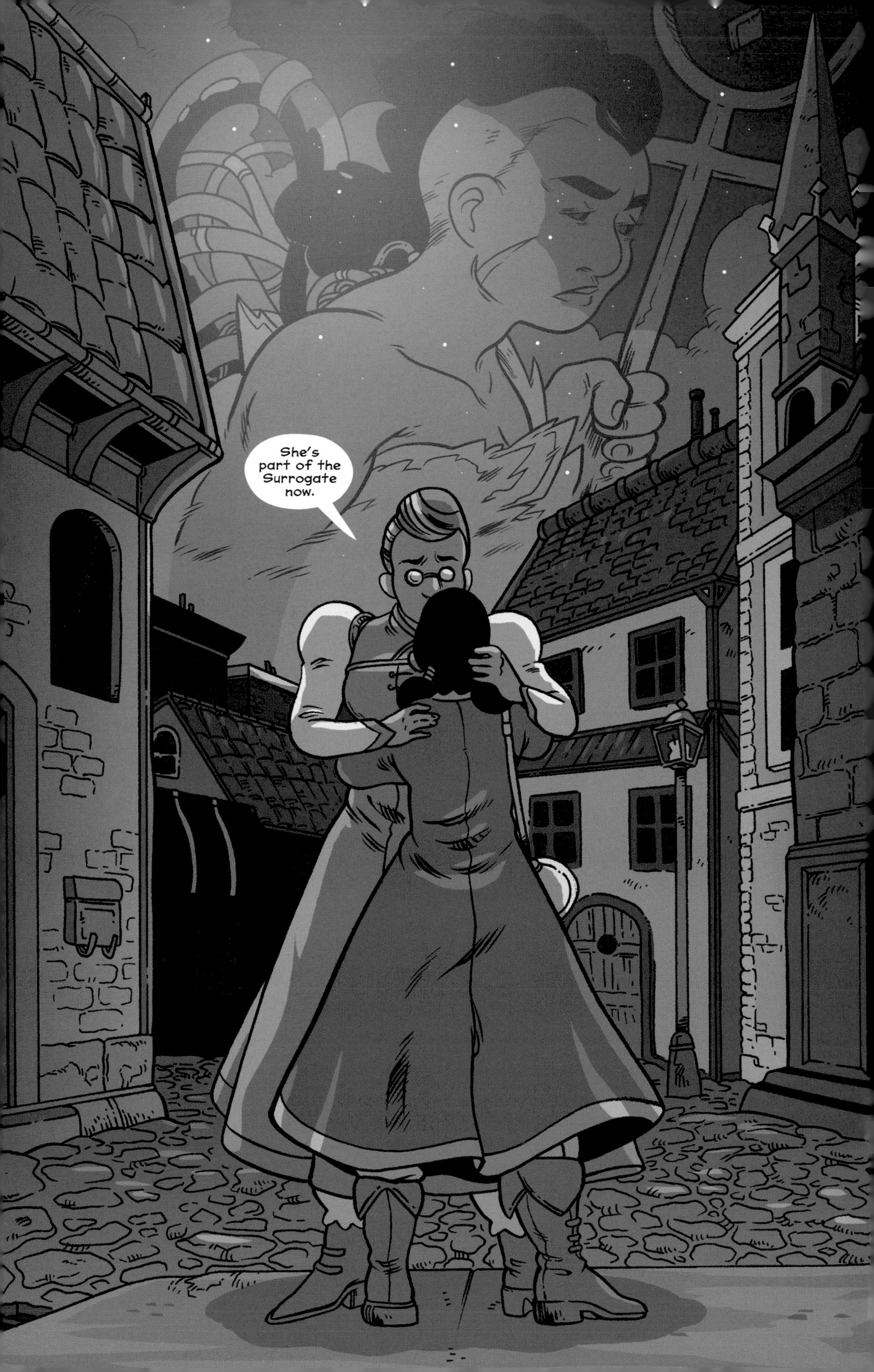
She's part of the Surrogate now.

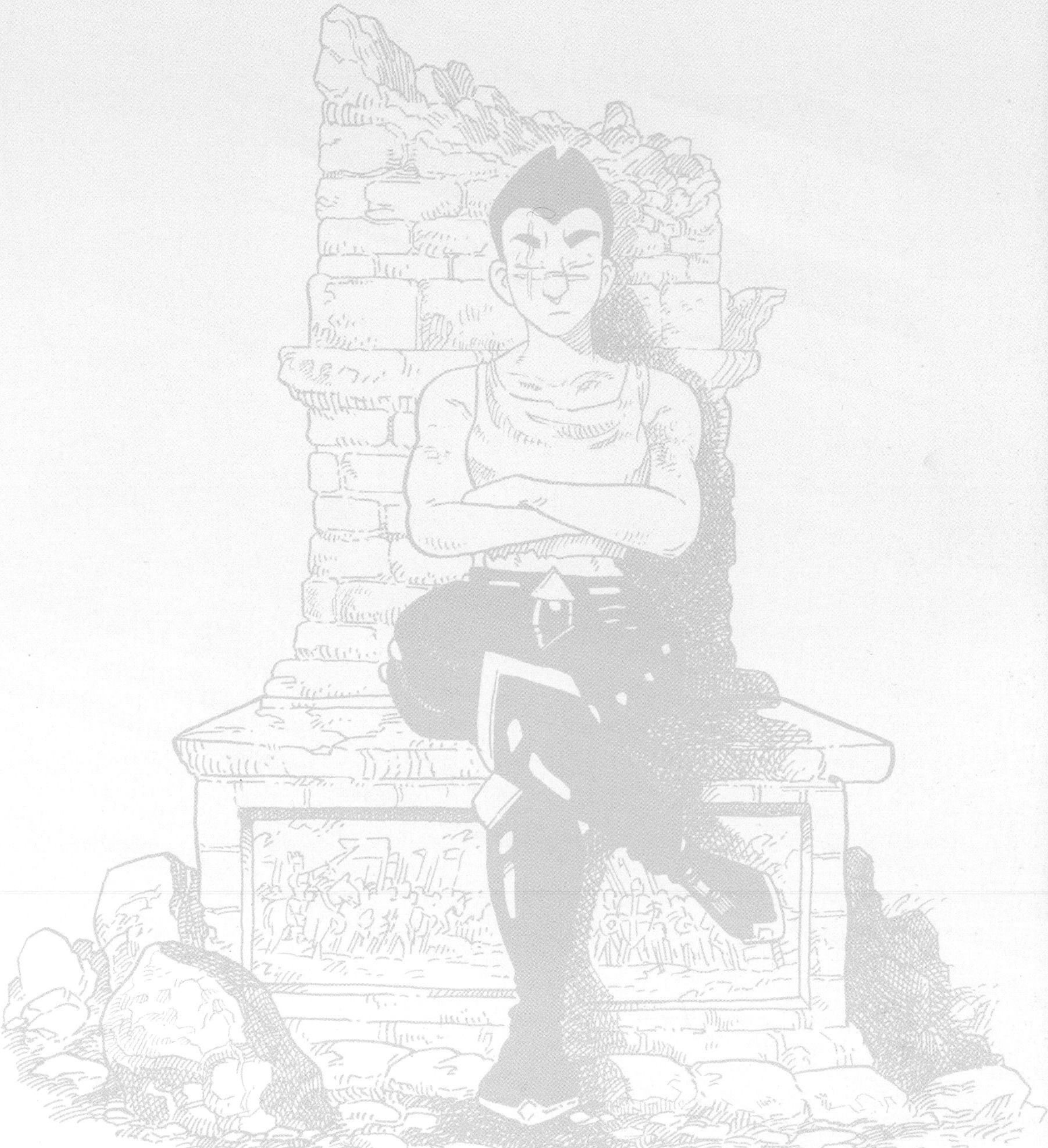

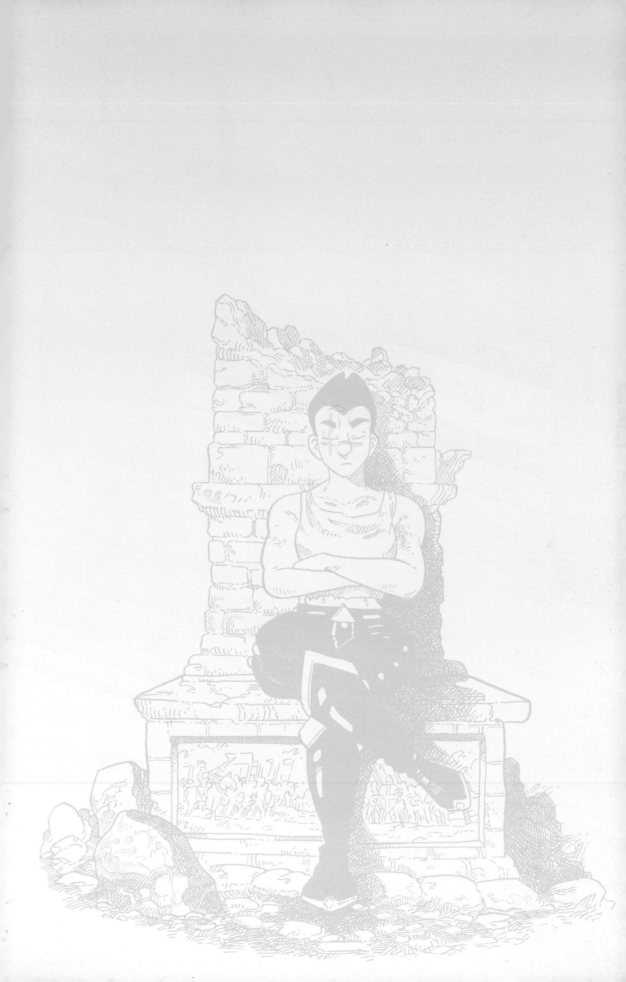

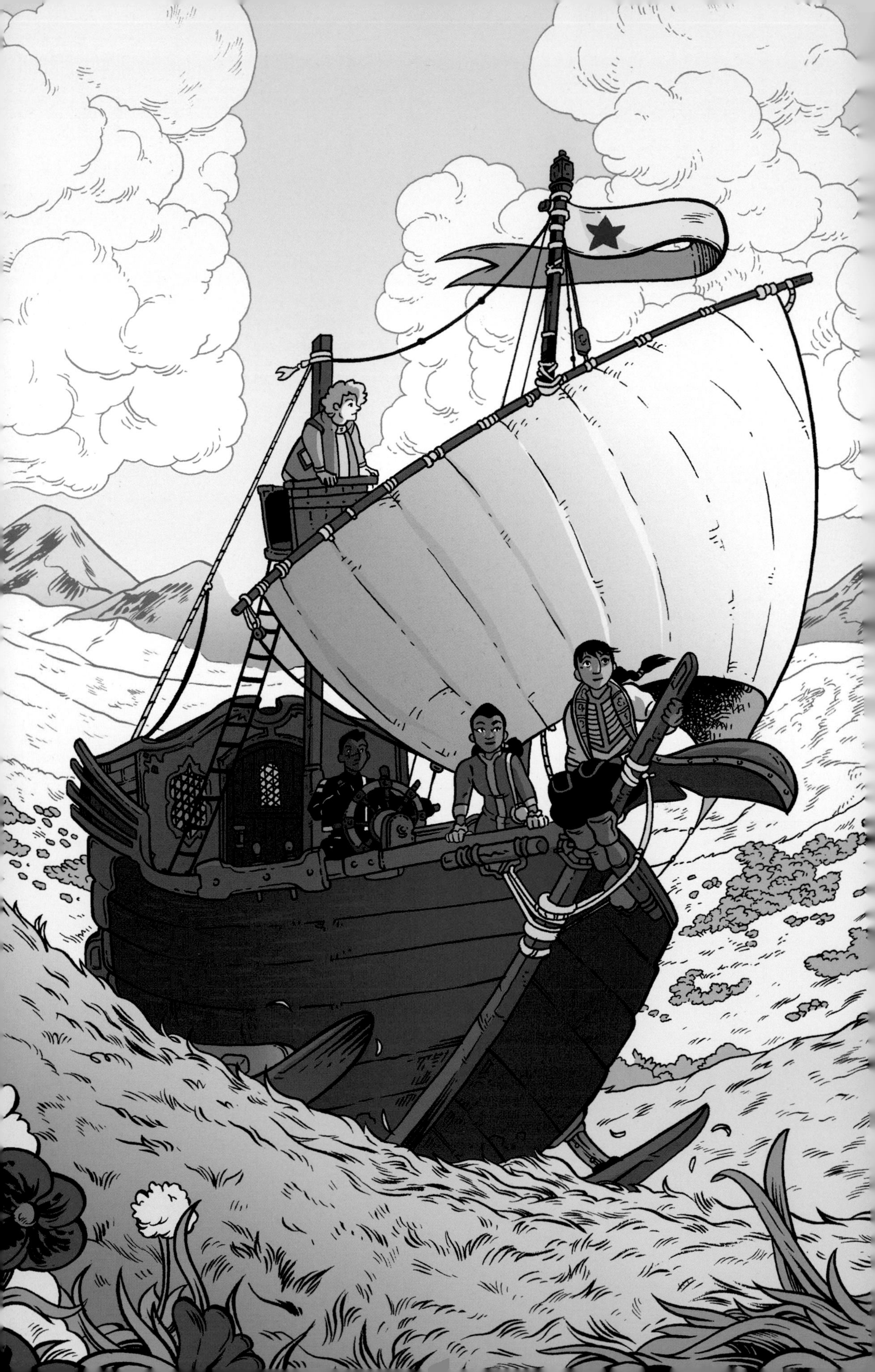

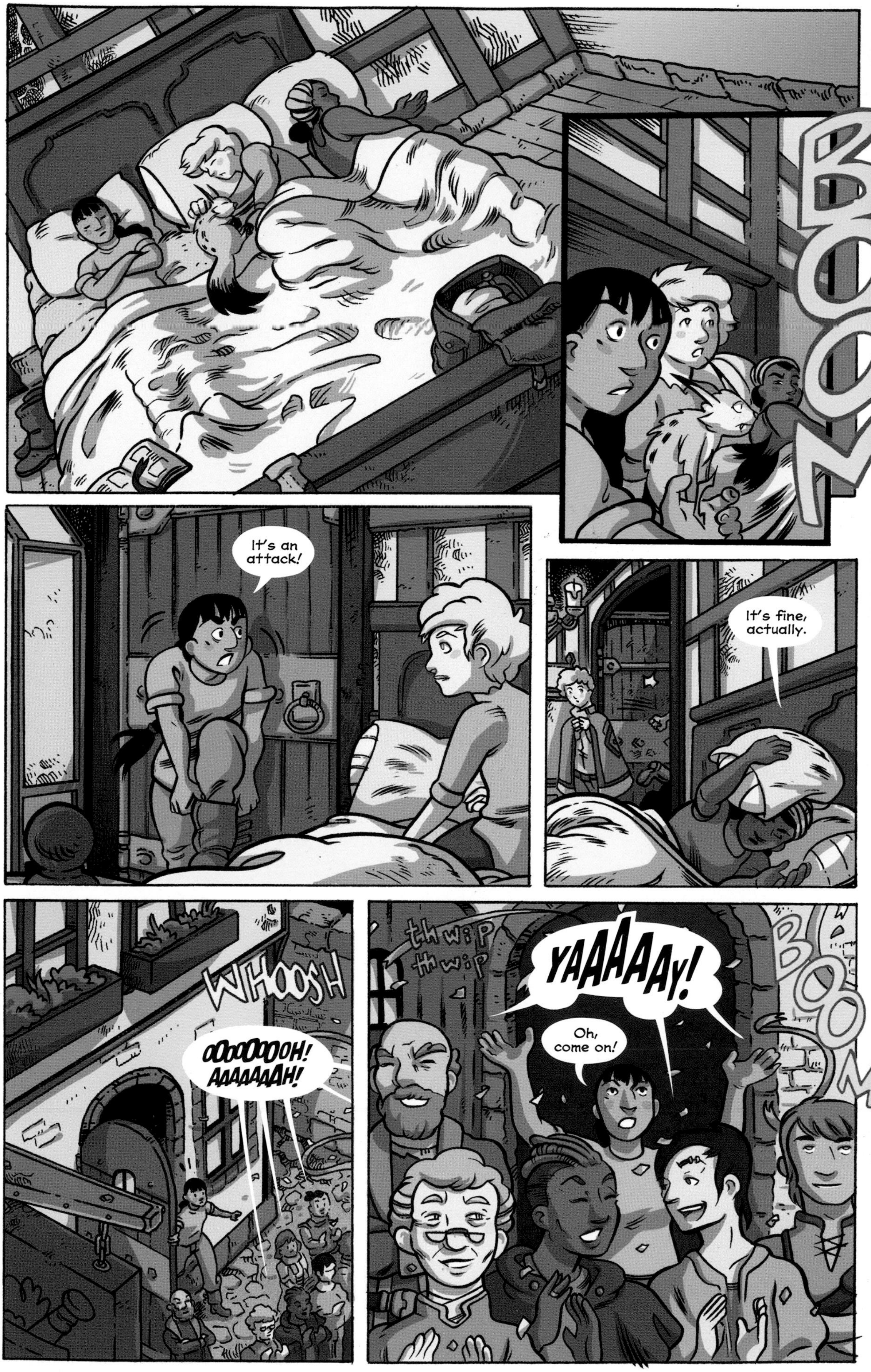

BOOOM
It's an attack!
It's fine, actually.
WHOOSH
OOOOOOOOH! AAAAAAAH!
thwip thwip
YAAAAAY!
Oh, come on!
BOOOM

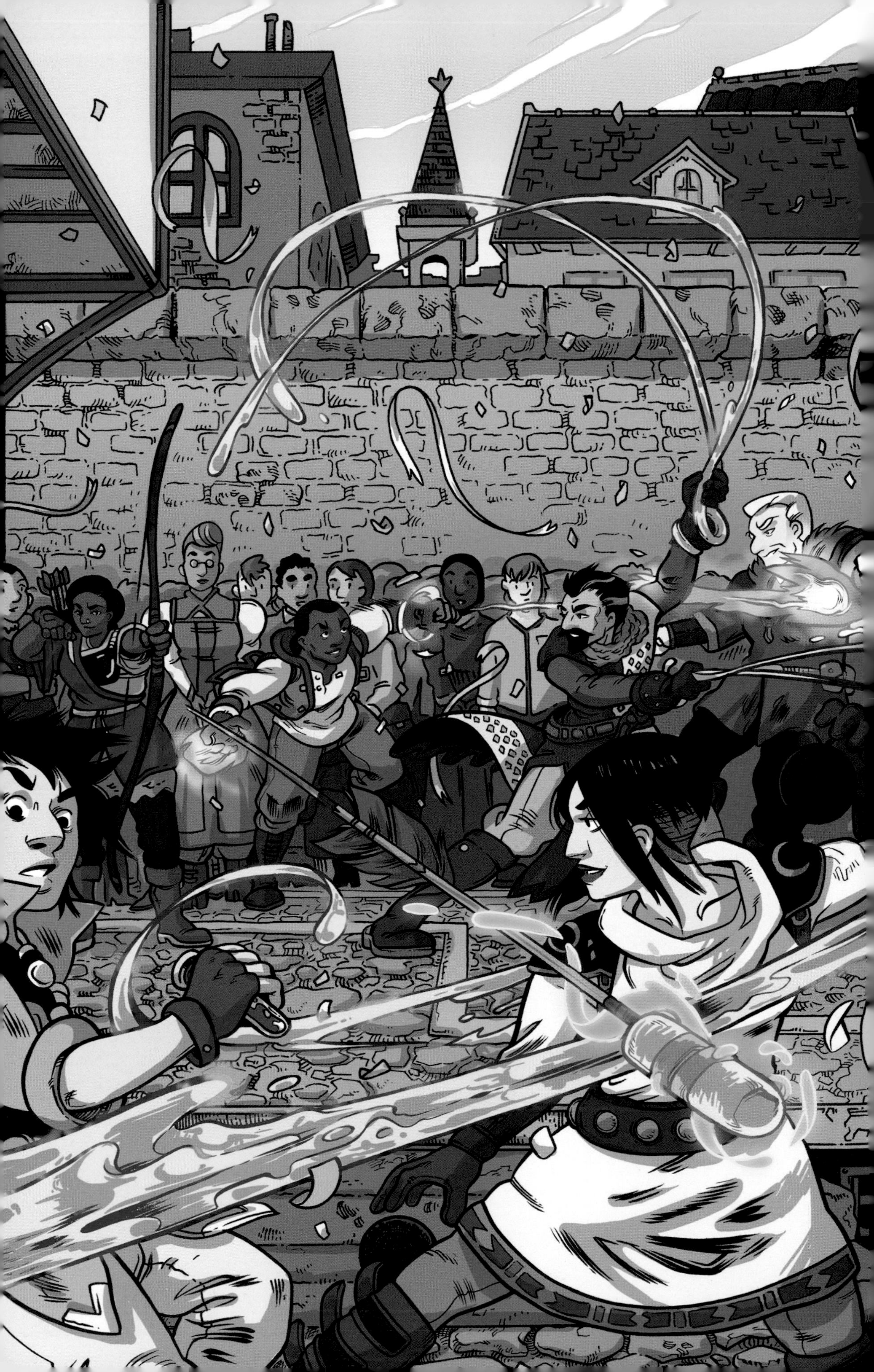

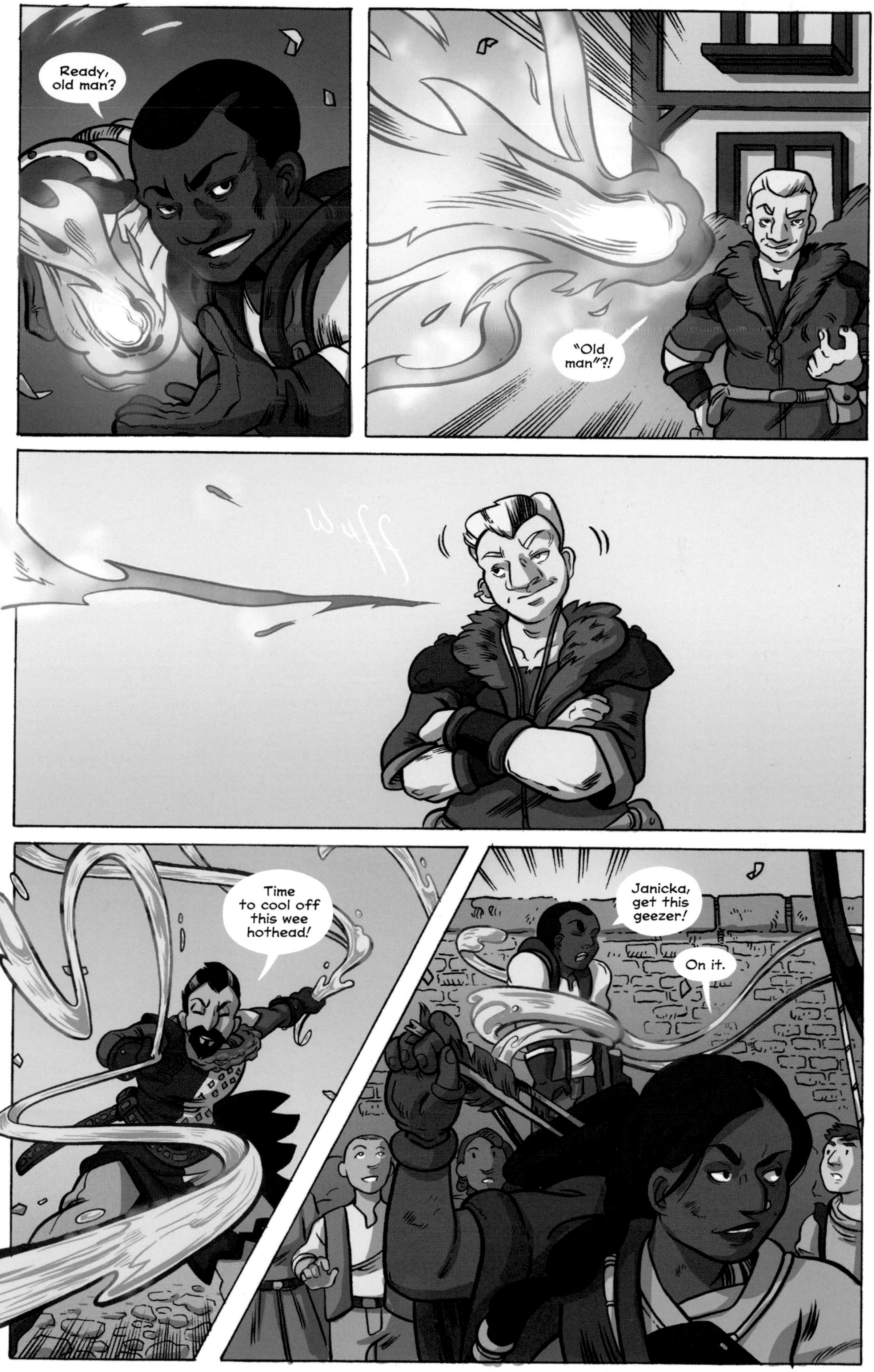
Ready, old man?
"Old man"?!
Time to cool off this wee hothead!
Janicka, get this geezer!
On it.

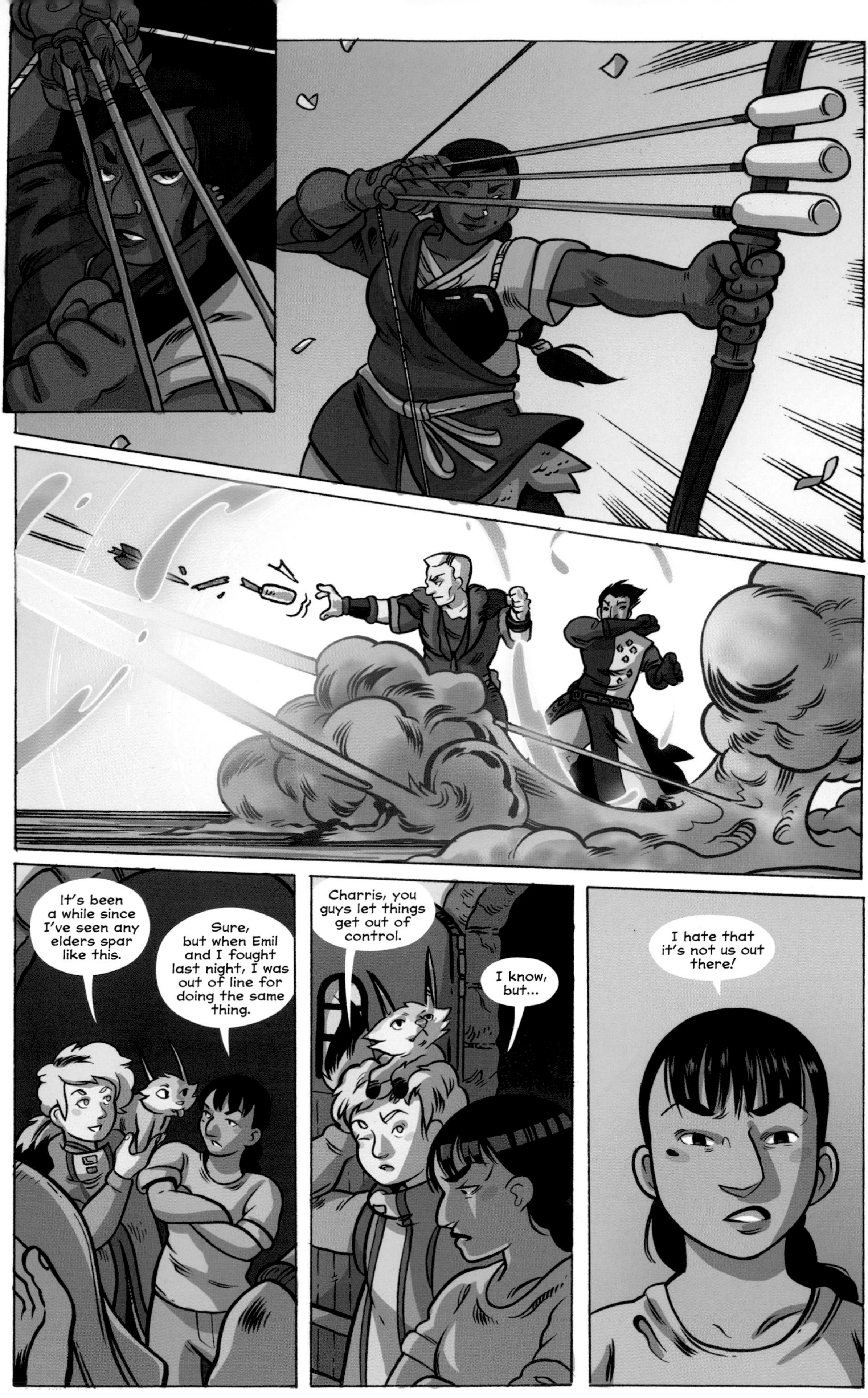
It's been a while since I've seen any elders spar like this.
Sure, but when Emil and I fought last night, I was out of line for doing the same thing.
Charris, you guys let things get out of control.
I know, but...
I hate that it's not us out there!

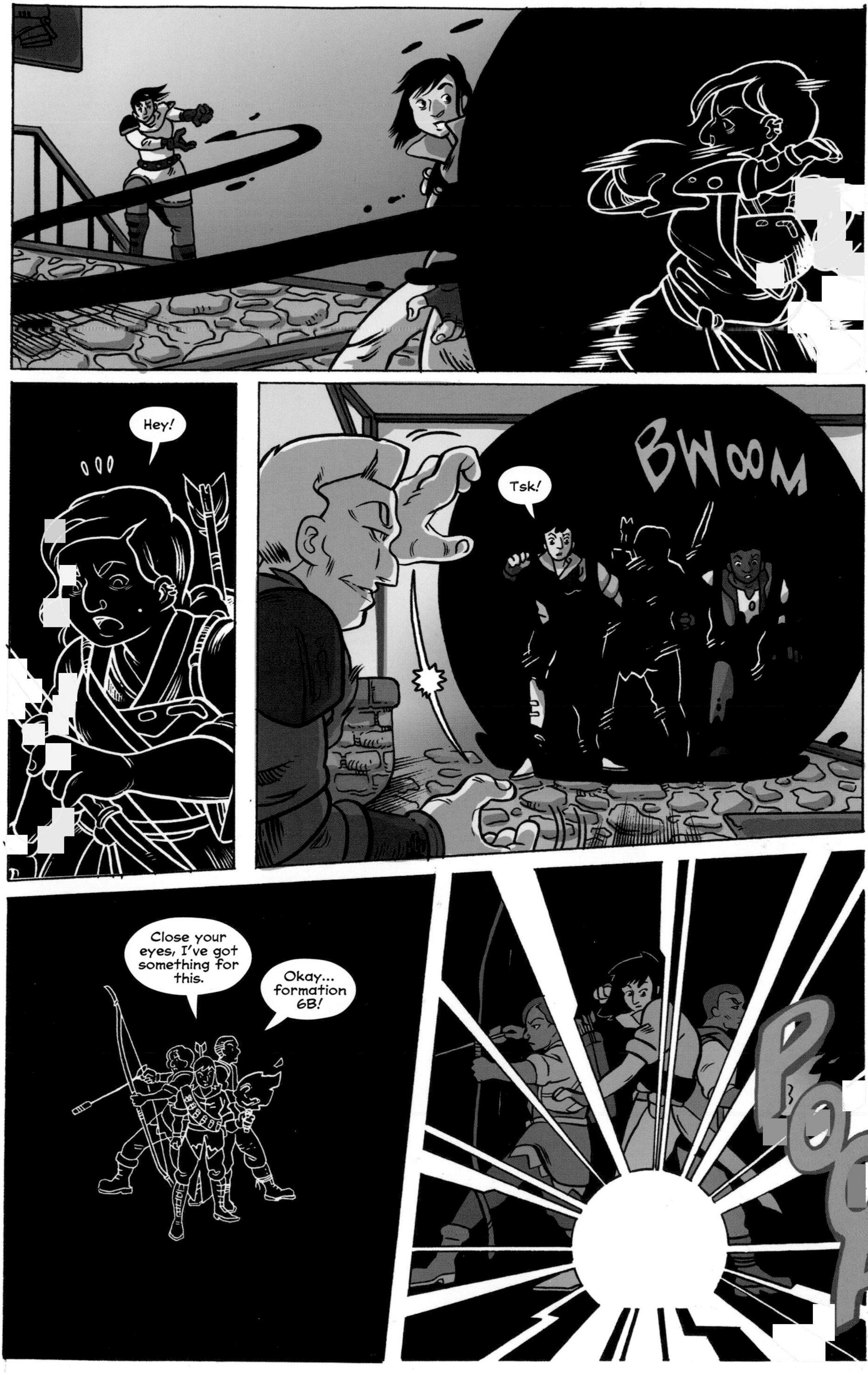
Hey!
BWOOM
Tsk!
Close your eyes, I've got something for this.
Okay... formation 6B!

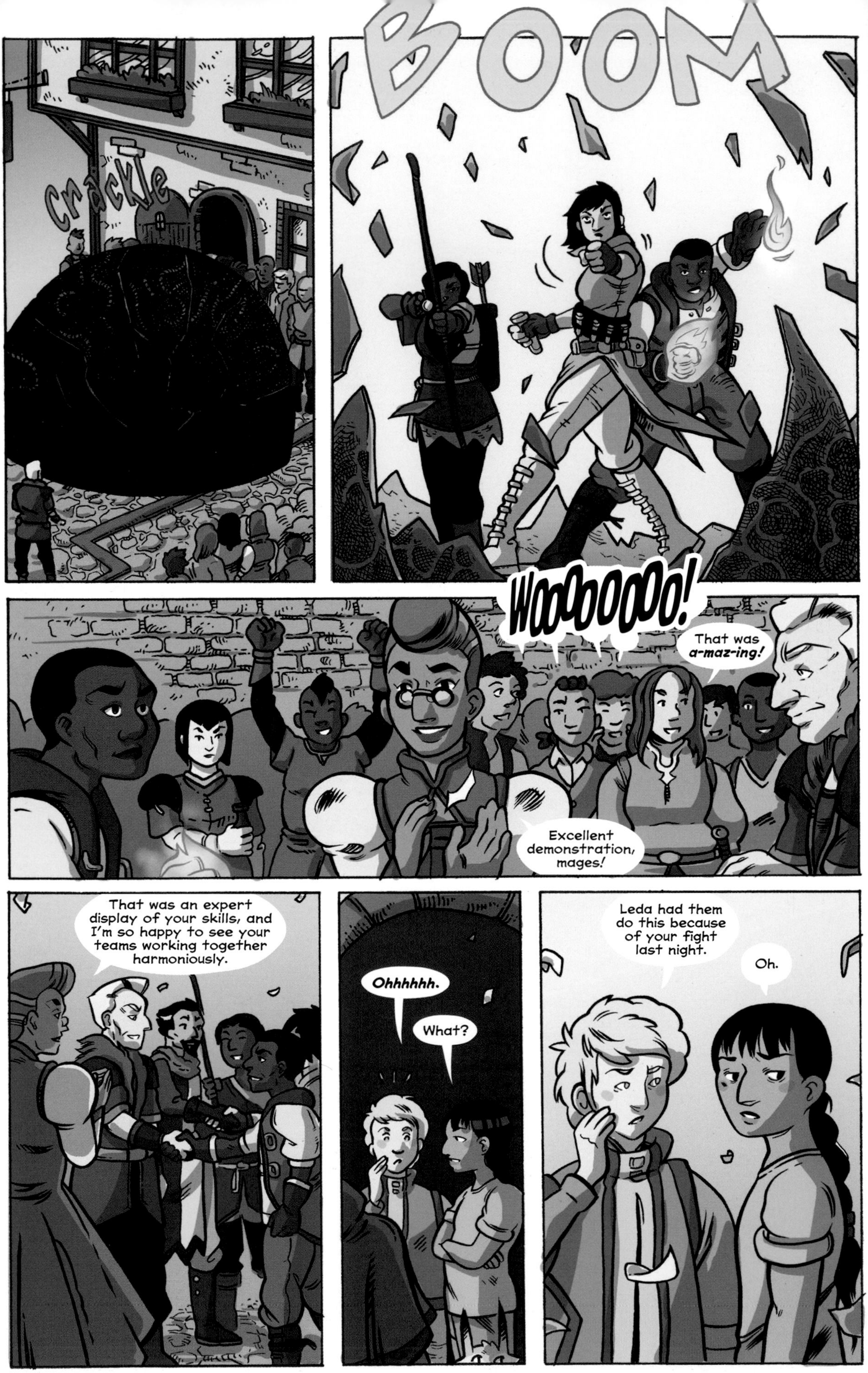
crackle
BOOM
WOOOOOOO!
That was a-maz-ing!
Excellent demonstration, mages!
That was an expert display of your skills, and I'm so happy to see your teams working together harmoniously.
Ohhhhhh.
What?
Leda had them do this because of your fight last night.
Oh.

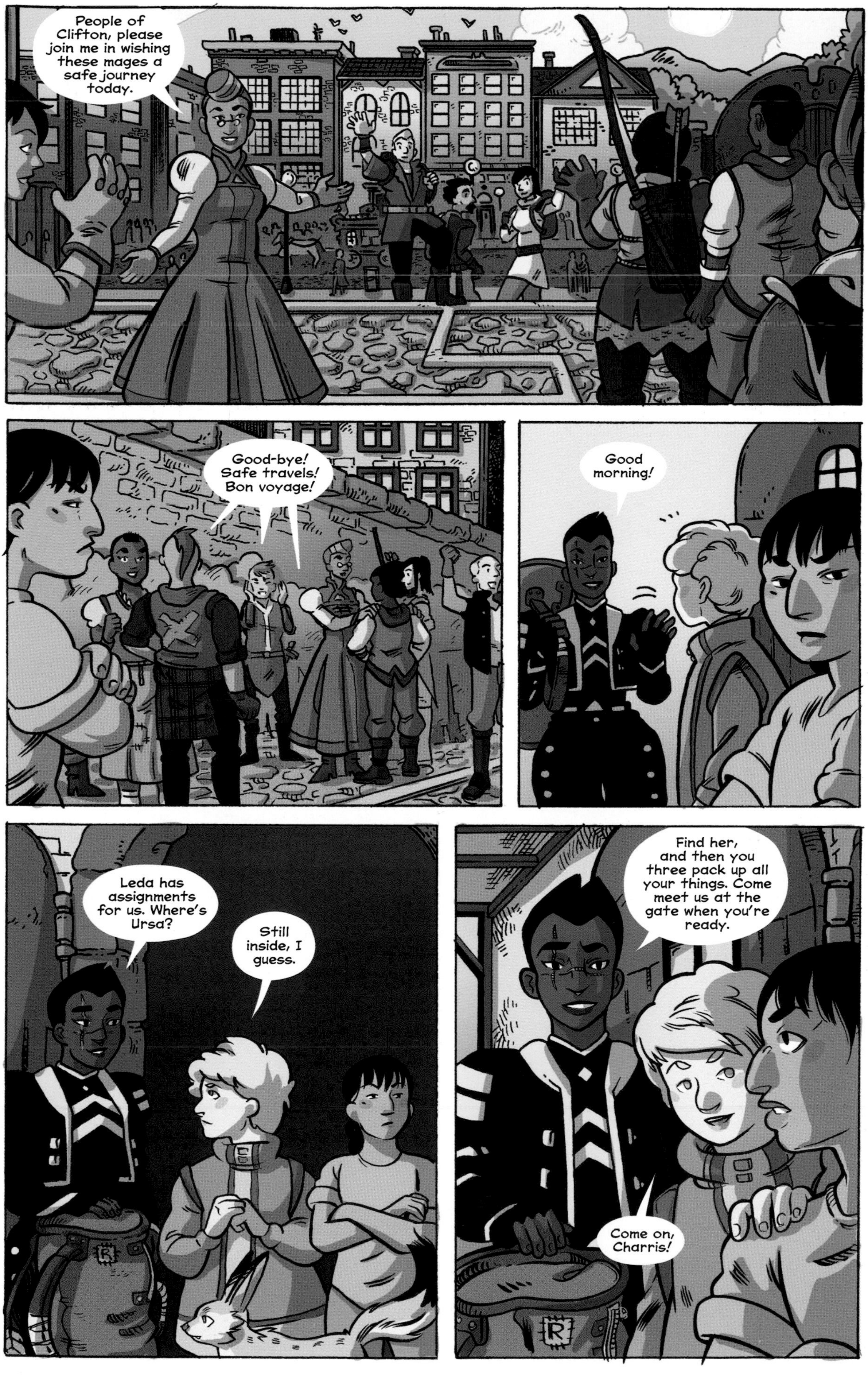
People of Clifton, please join me in wishing these mages a safe journey today.
Good-bye! Safe travels! Bon voyage!
Good morning!
Leda has assignments for us. Where's Ursa?
Still inside, I guess.
Find her, and then you three pack up all your things. Come meet us at the gate when you're ready.
Come on, Charris!

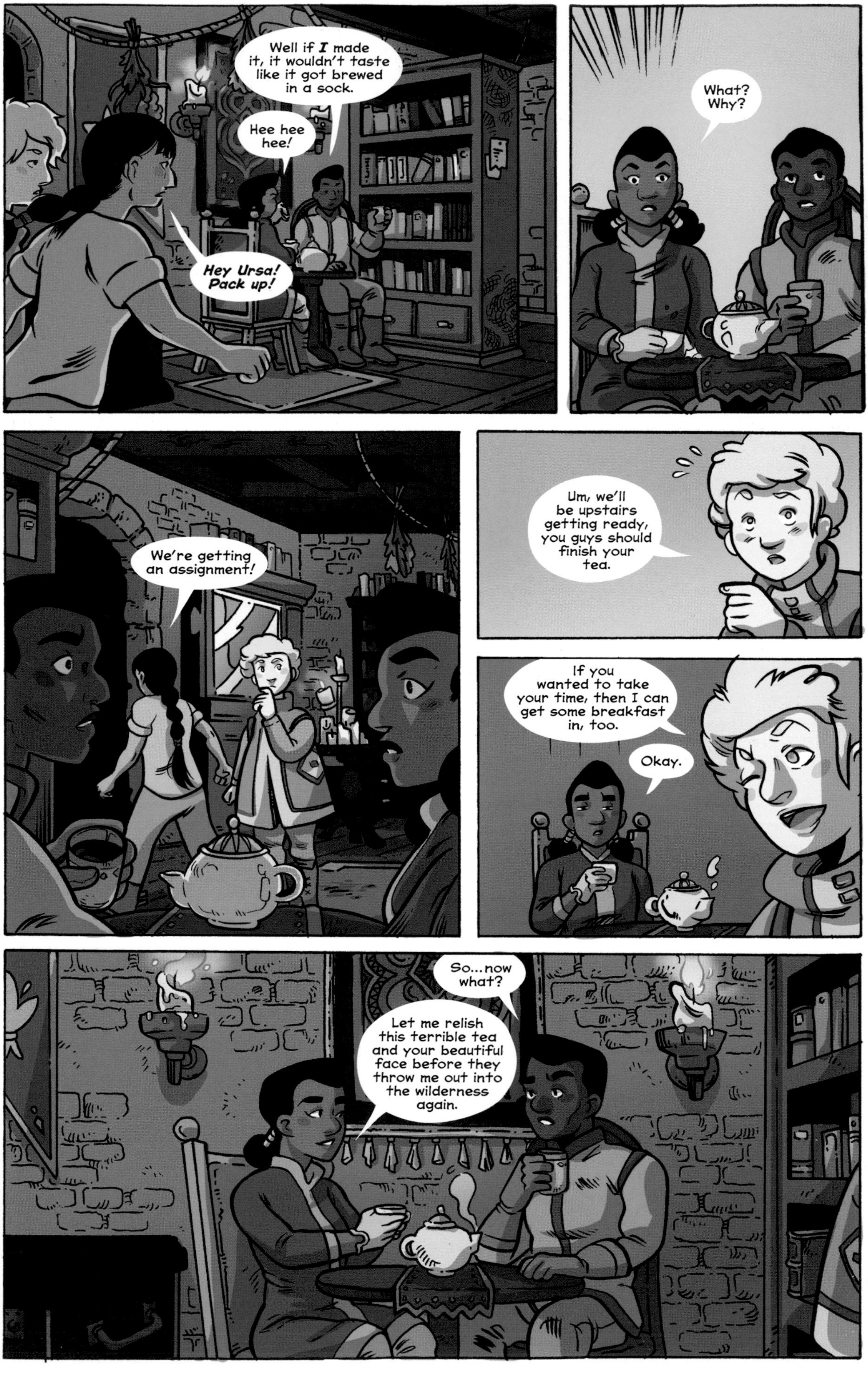
Well if *I* made it, it wouldn't taste like it got brewed in a sock.
Hee hee hee!
Hey Ursa! Pack up!
What? Why?
We're getting an assignment!
Um, we'll be upstairs getting ready, you guys should finish your tea.
If you wanted to take your time, then I can get some breakfast in, too.
Okay.
So...now what?
Let me relish this terrible tea and your beautiful face before they throw me out into the wilderness again.

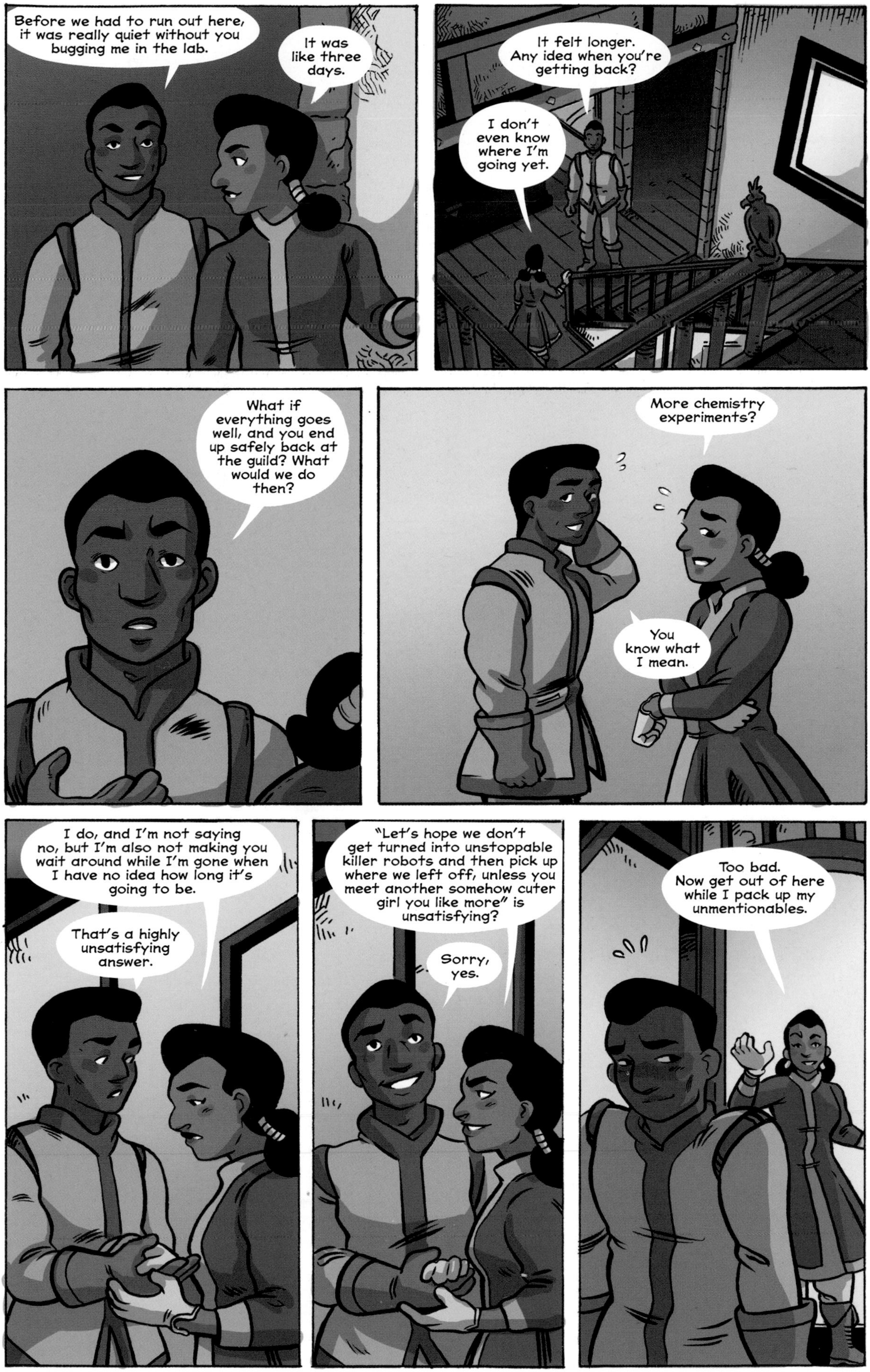
Before we had to run out here, it was really quiet without you bugging me in the lab.
It was like three days.
It felt longer. Any idea when you're getting back?
I don't even know where I'm going yet.
What if everything goes well, and you end up safely back at the guild? What would we do then?
More chemistry experiments?
You know what I mean.
I do, and I'm not saying no, but I'm also not making you wait around while I'm gone when I have no idea how long it's going to be.
That's a highly unsatisfying answer.
"Let's hope we don't get turned into unstoppable killer robots and then pick up where we left off, unless you meet another somehow cuter girl you like more" is unsatisfying?
Sorry, yes.
Too bad. Now get out of here while I pack up my unmentionables.

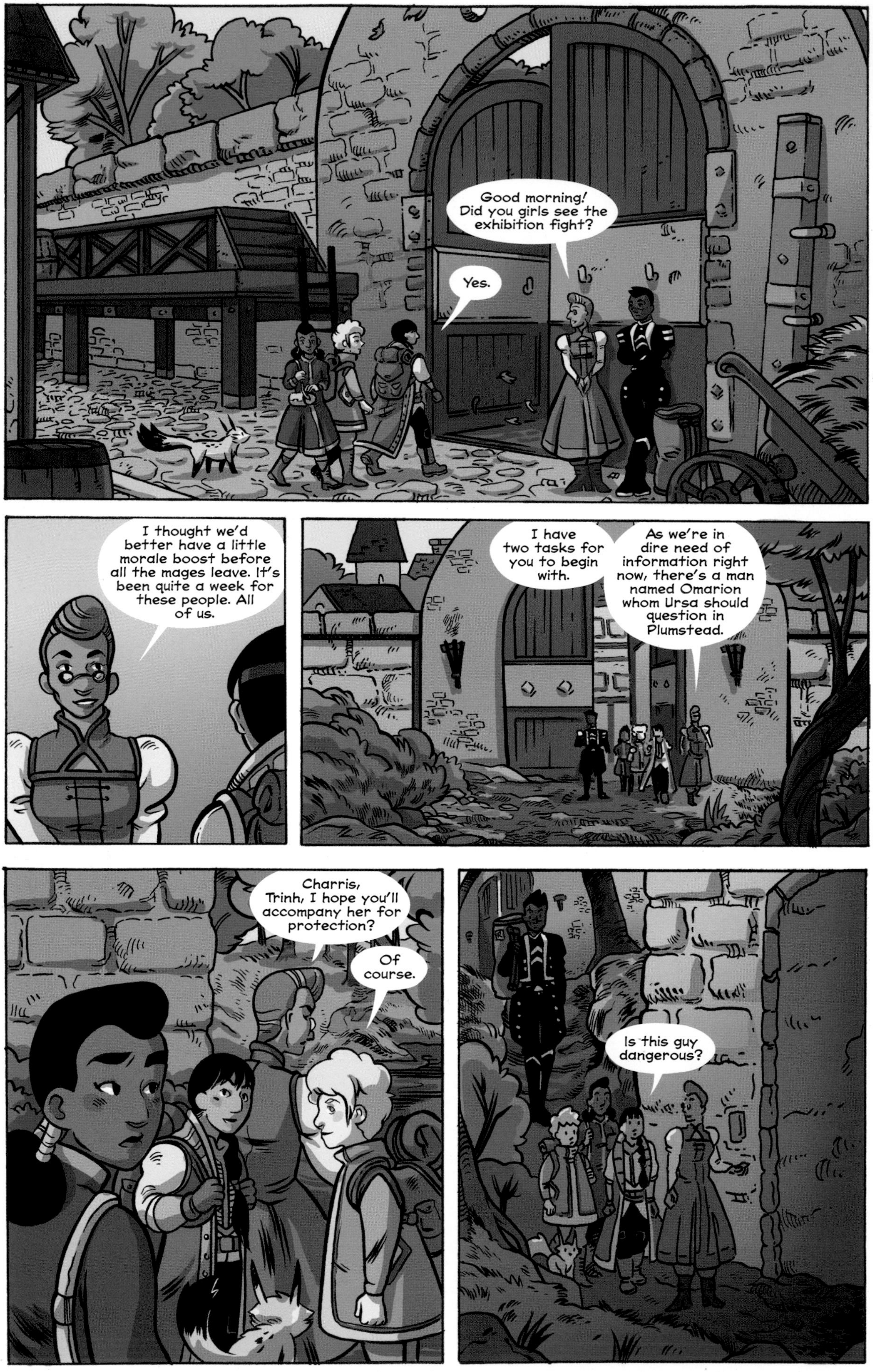
Good morning! Did you girls see the exhibition fight?
Yes.
I thought we'd better have a little morale boost before all the mages leave. It's been quite a week for these people. All of us.
I have two tasks for you to begin with.
As we're in dire need of information right now, there's a man named Omarion whom Ursa should question in Plumstead.
Charris, Trinh, I hope you'll accompany her for protection?
Of course.
Is this guy dangerous?

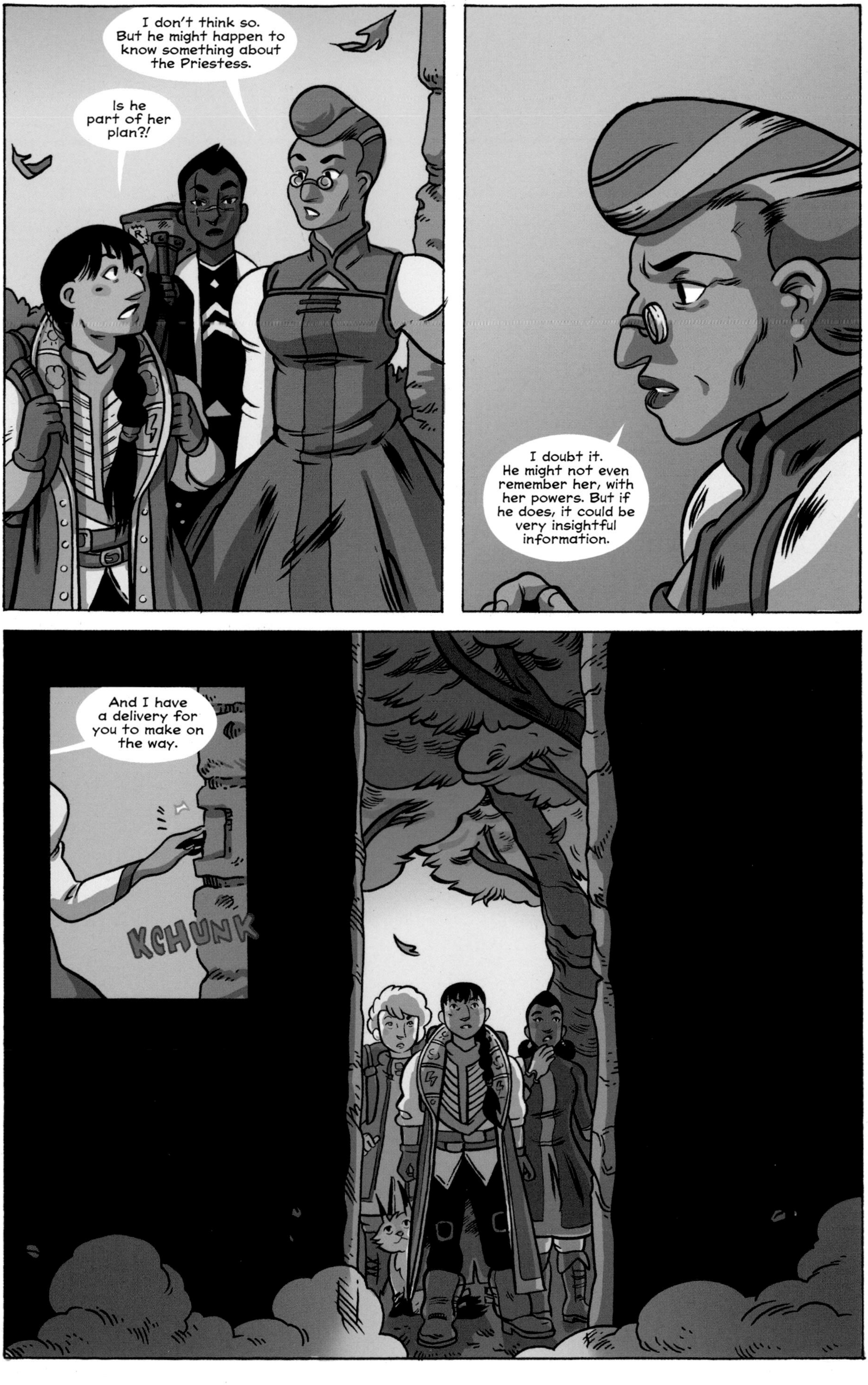
I don't think so. But he might happen to know something about the Priestess.
Is he part of her plan?!
I doubt it. He might not even remember her, with her powers. But if he does, it could be very insightful information.
And I have a delivery for you to make on the way.
KCHUNK

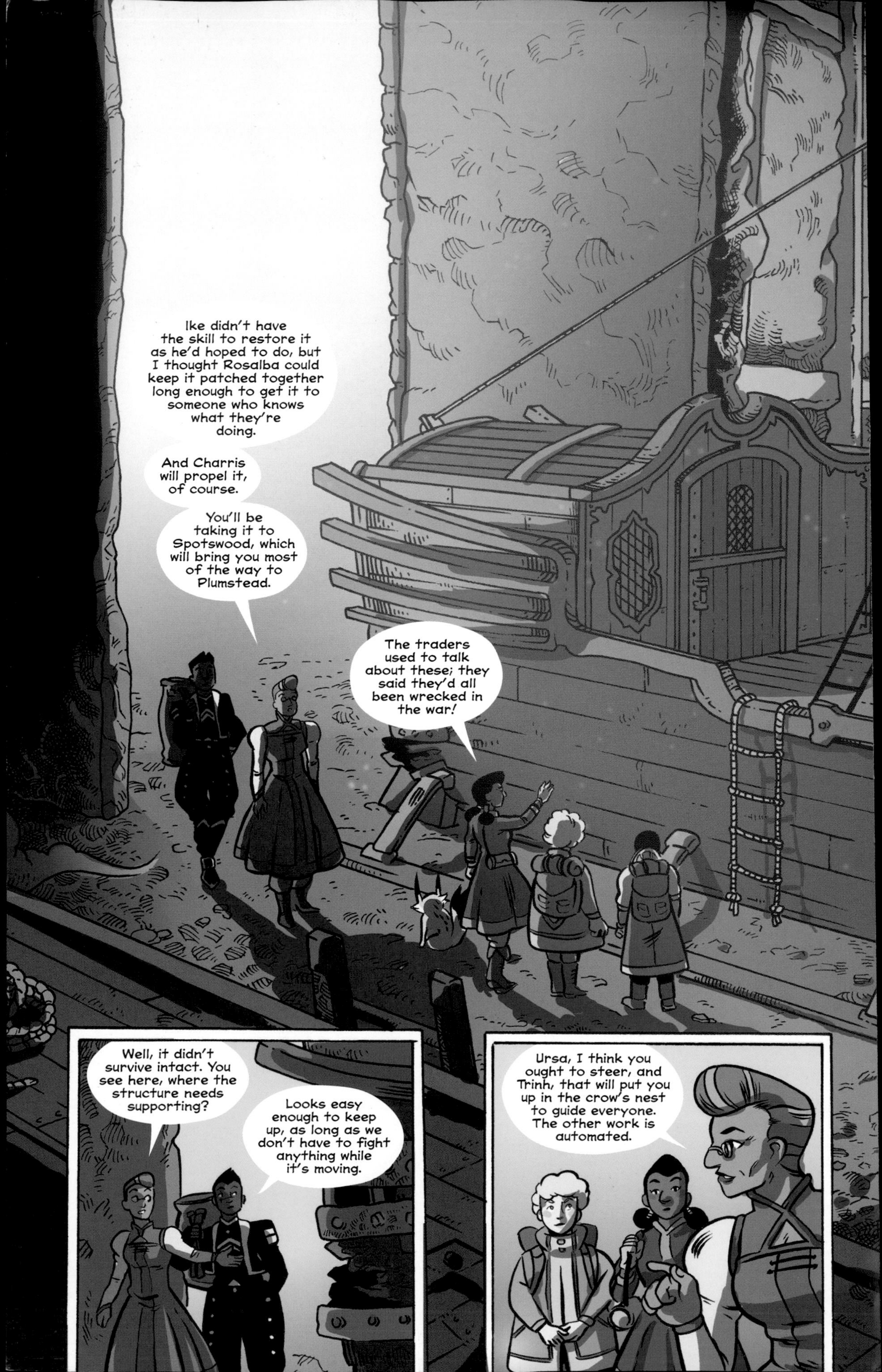

Ike didn't have the skill to restore it as he'd hoped to do, but I thought Rosalba could keep it patched together long enough to get it to someone who knows what they're doing.
And Charris will propel it, of course.
You'll be taking it to Spotswood, which will bring you most of the way to Plumstead.
The traders used to talk about these; they said they'd all been wrecked in the war!
Well, it didn't survive intact. You see here, where the structure needs supporting?
Looks easy enough to keep up, as long as we don't have to fight anything while it's moving.
Ursa, I think you ought to steer, and Trinh, that will put you up in the crow's nest to guide everyone. The other work is automated.

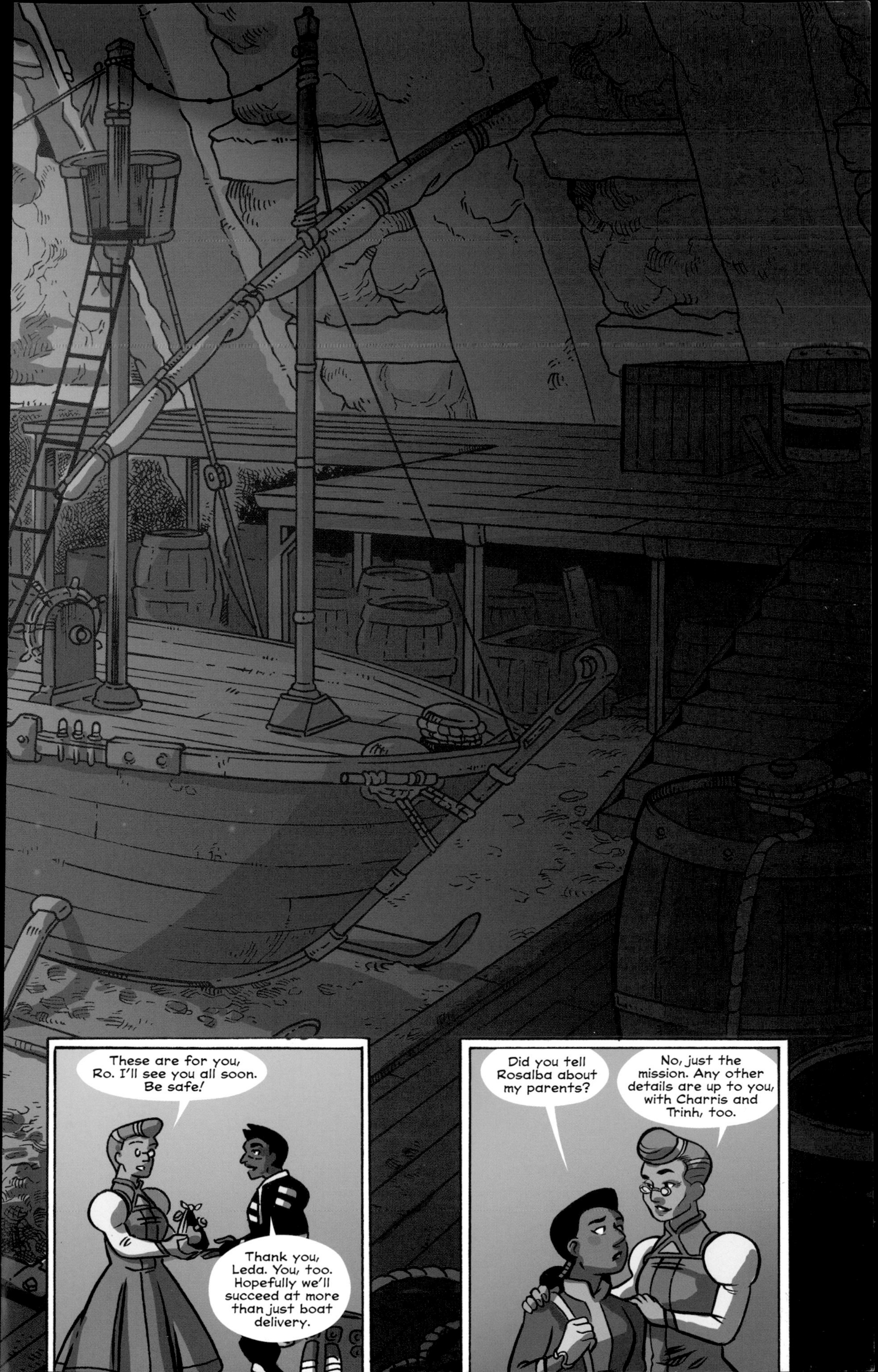
These are for you, Ro. I'll see you all soon. Be safe!
Thank you, Leda. You, too. Hopefully we'll succeed at more than just boat delivery.
Did you tell Rosalba about my parents?
No, just the mission. Any other details are up to you, with Charris and Trinh, too.

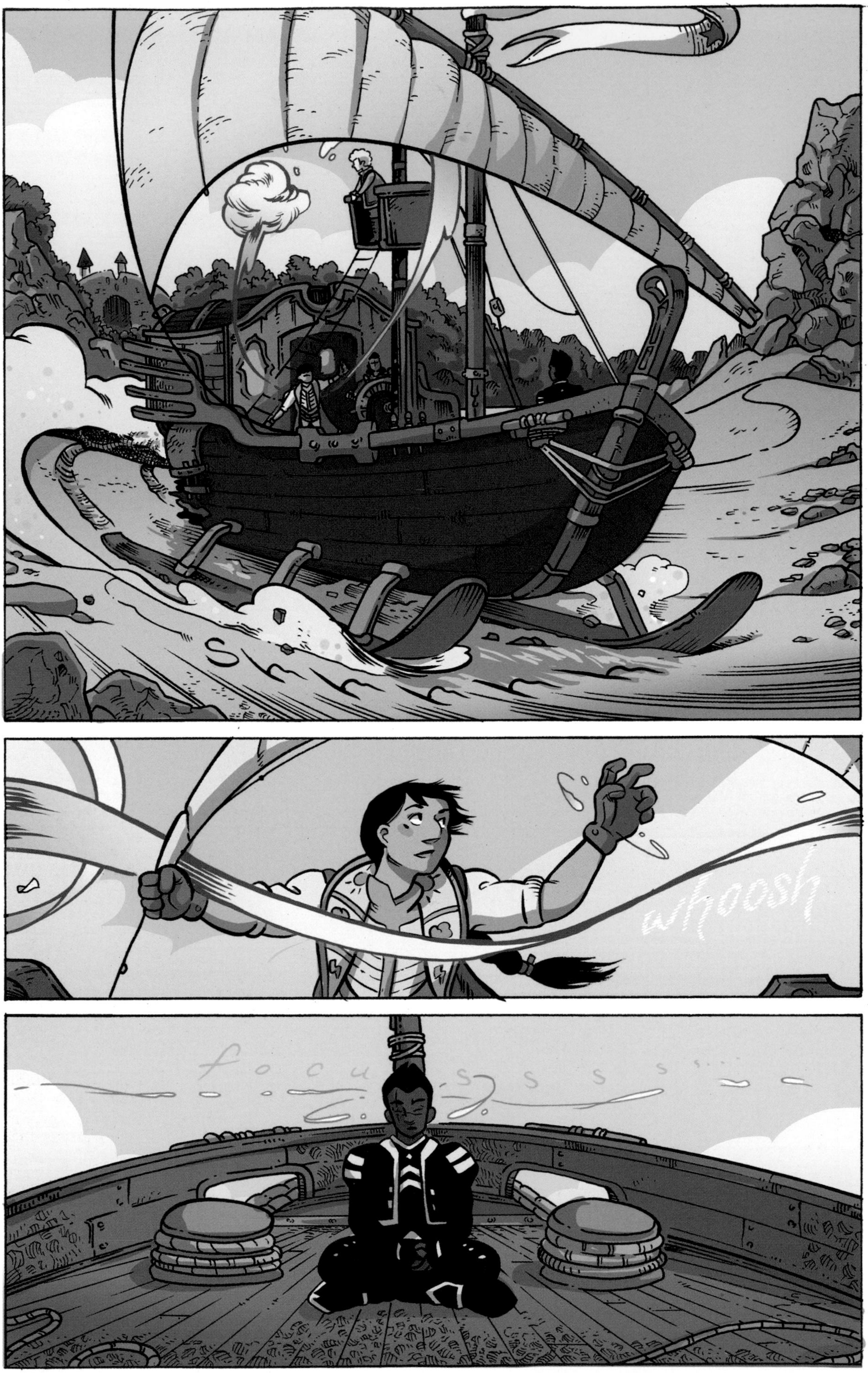
whoosh
focussss

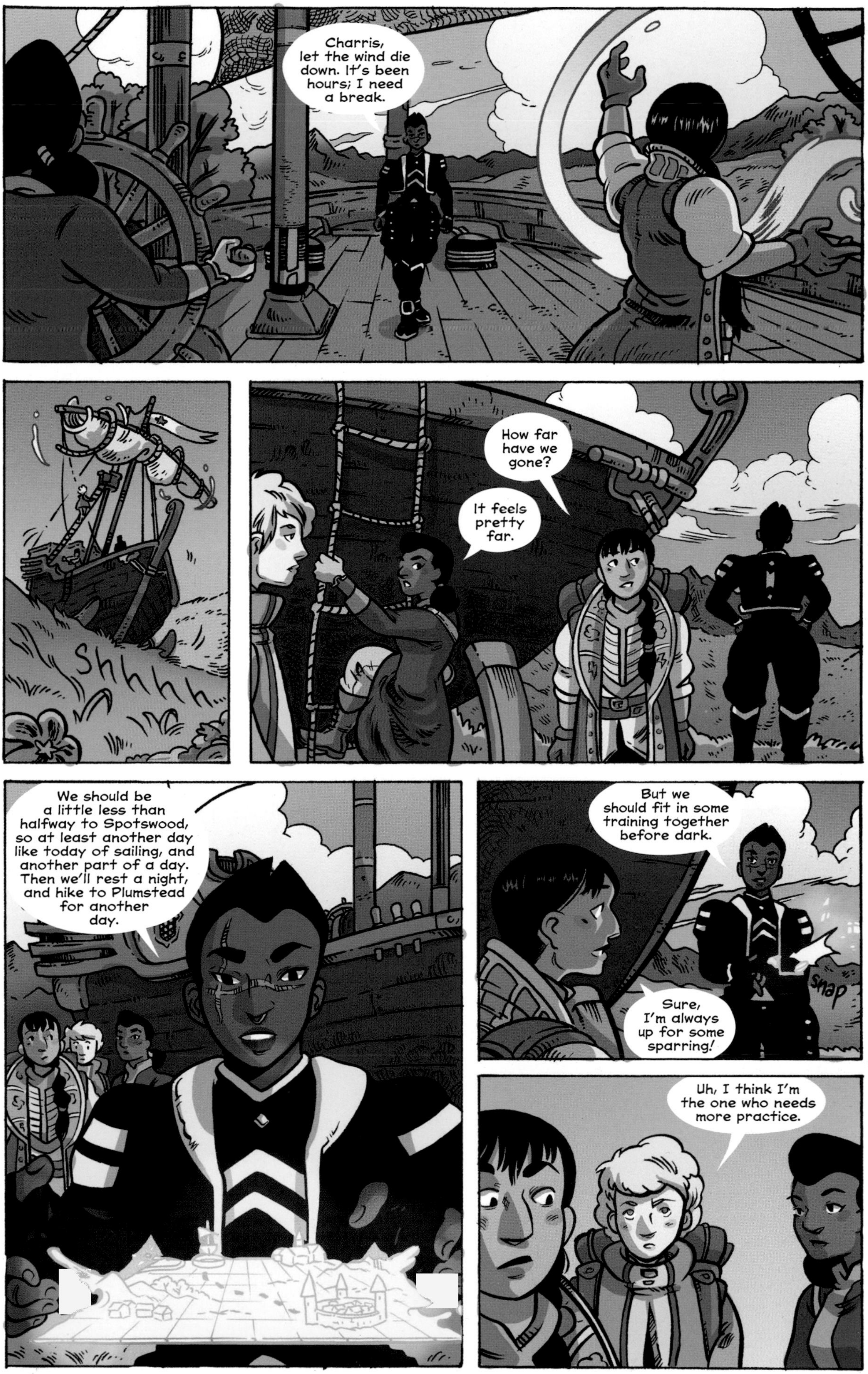
Charris, let the wind die down. It's been hours; I need a break.
Shhhhh
How far have we gone?
It feels pretty far.
We should be a little less than halfway to Spotswood, so at least another day like today of sailing, and another part of a day. Then we'll rest a night, and hike to Plumstead for another day.
But we should fit in some training together before dark.
snap
Sure, I'm always up for some sparring!
Uh, I think I'm the one who needs more practice.

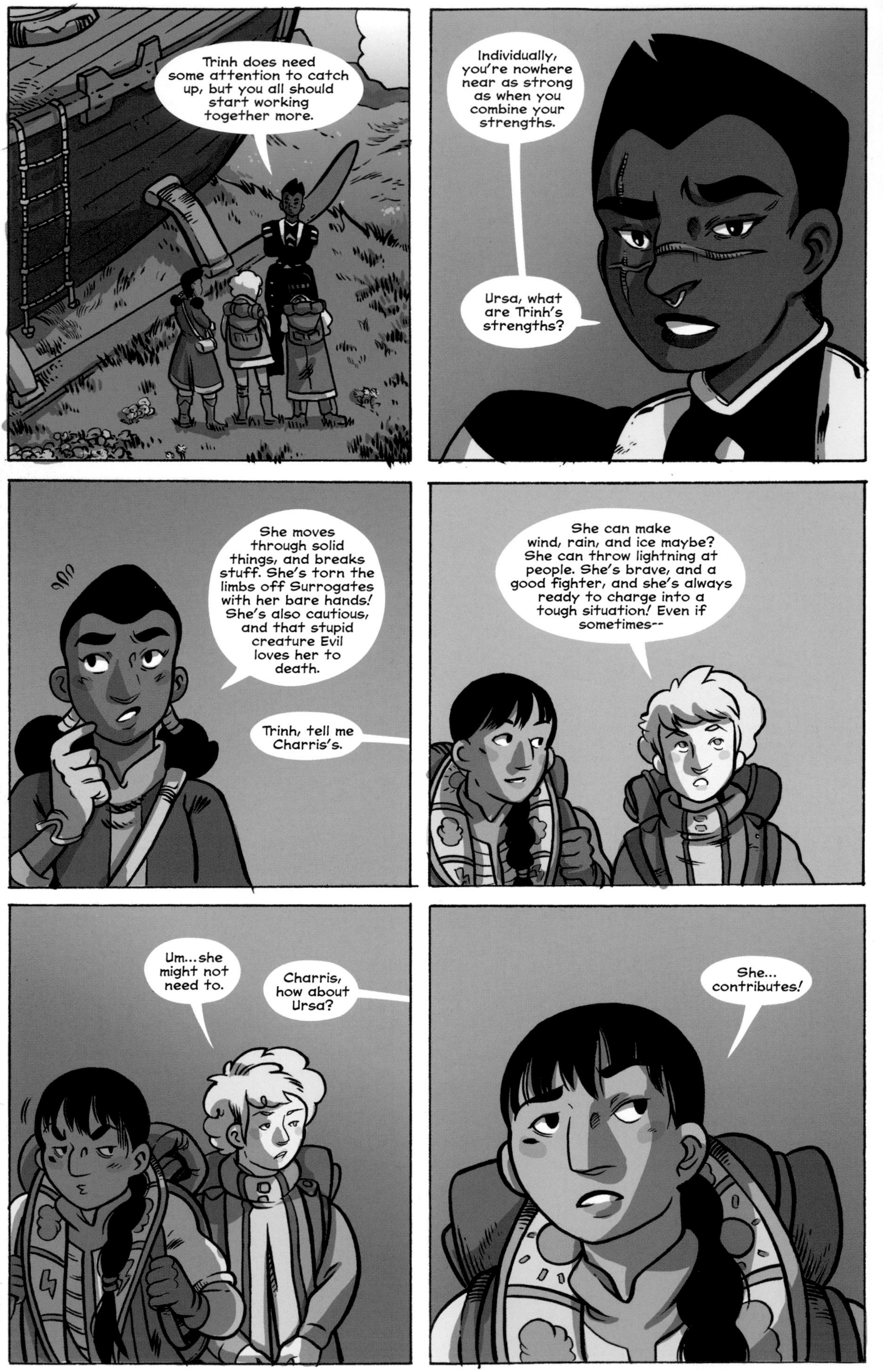
Trinh does need some attention to catch up, but you all should start working together more.
Individually, you're nowhere near as strong as when you combine your strengths.
Ursa, what are Trinh's strengths?
She moves through solid things, and breaks stuff. She's torn the limbs off Surrogates with her bare hands! She's also cautious, and that stupid creature Evil loves her to death.
Trinh, tell me Charris's.
She can make wind, rain, and ice maybe? She can throw lightning at people. She's brave, and a good fighter, and she's always ready to charge into a tough situation! Even if sometimes--
Um...she might not need to.
Charris, how about Ursa?
She... contributes!

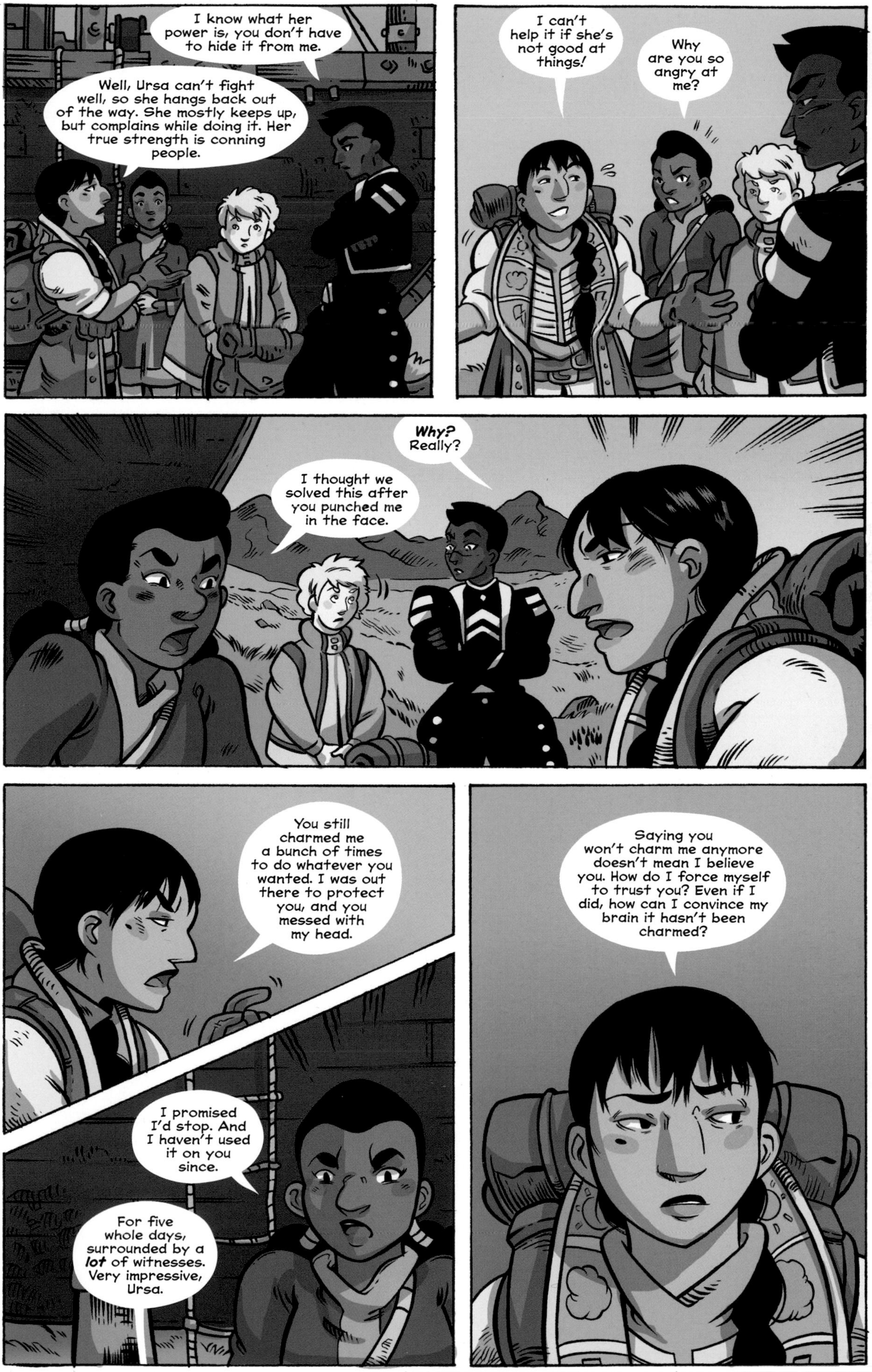
I know what her power is, you don't have to hide it from me.
Well, Ursa can't fight well, so she hangs back out of the way. She mostly keeps up, but complains while doing it. Her true strength is conning people.
I can't help it if she's not good at things!
Why are you so angry at me?
I thought we solved this after you punched me in the face.
Why? Really?
You still charmed me a bunch of times to do whatever you wanted. I was out there to protect you, and you messed with my head.
I promised I'd stop. And I haven't used it on you since.
For five whole days, surrounded by a *lot* of witnesses. Very impressive, Ursa.
Saying you won't charm me anymore doesn't mean I believe you. How do I force myself to trust you? Even if I did, how can I convince my brain it hasn't been charmed?

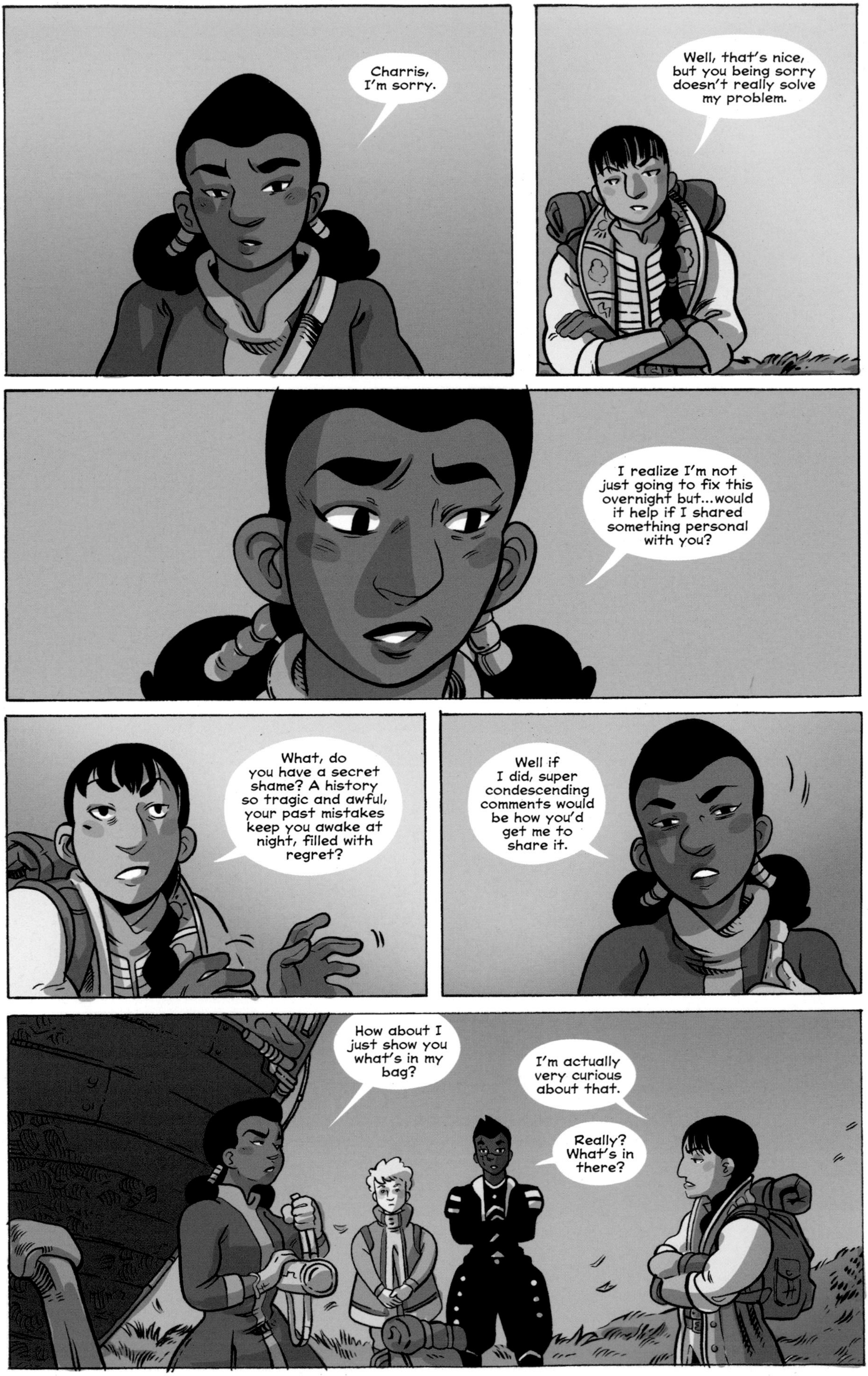
Charris, I'm sorry.
Well, that's nice, but you being sorry doesn't really solve my problem.
I realize I'm not just going to fix this overnight but...would it help if I shared something personal with you?
What, do you have a secret shame? A history so tragic and awful, your past mistakes keep you awake at night, filled with regret?
Well if I did, super condescending comments would be how you'd get me to share it.
How about I just show you what's in my bag?
I'm actually very curious about that.
Really? What's in there?

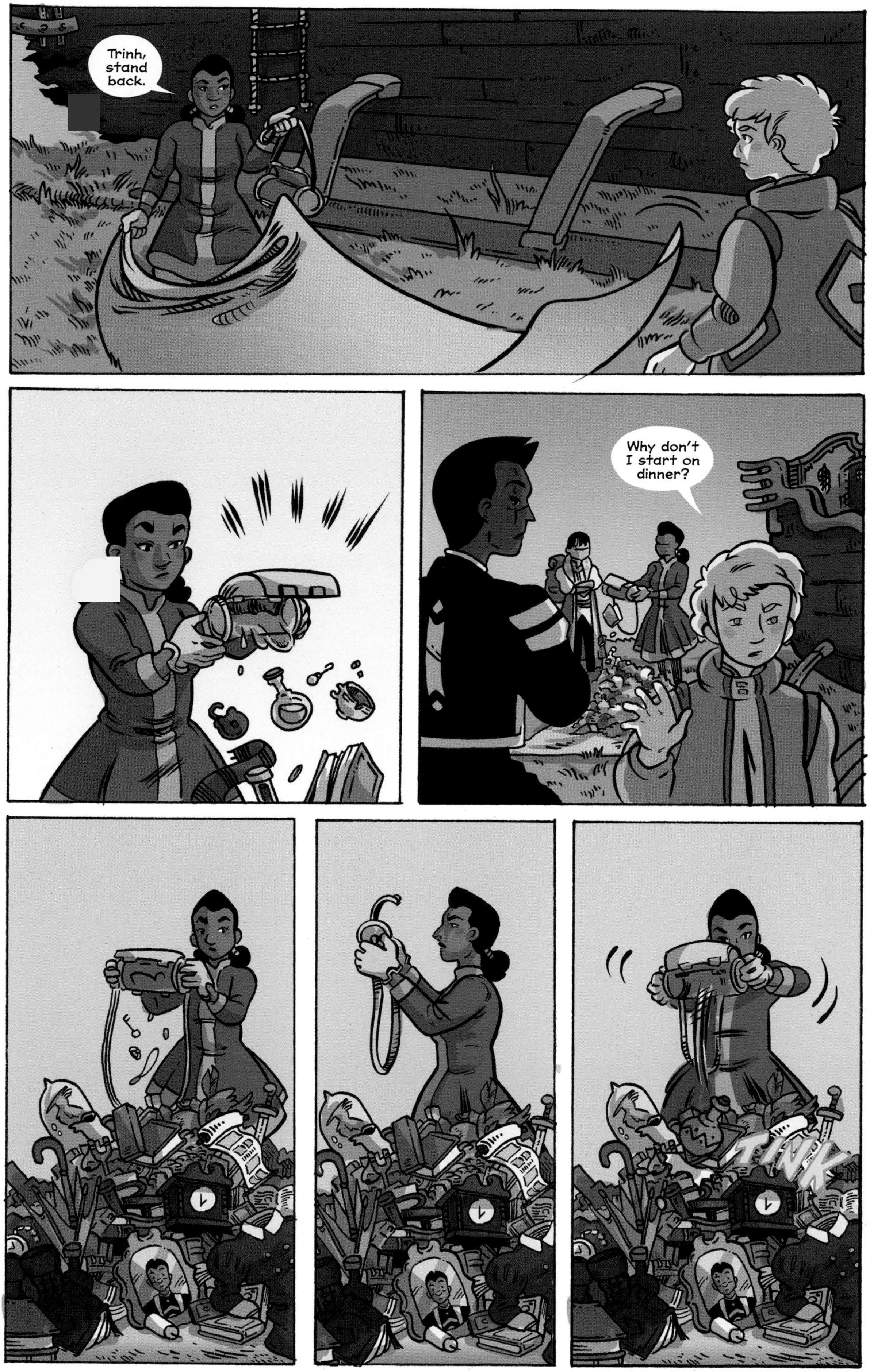
Trinh, stand back.
Why don't I start on dinner?
TINK

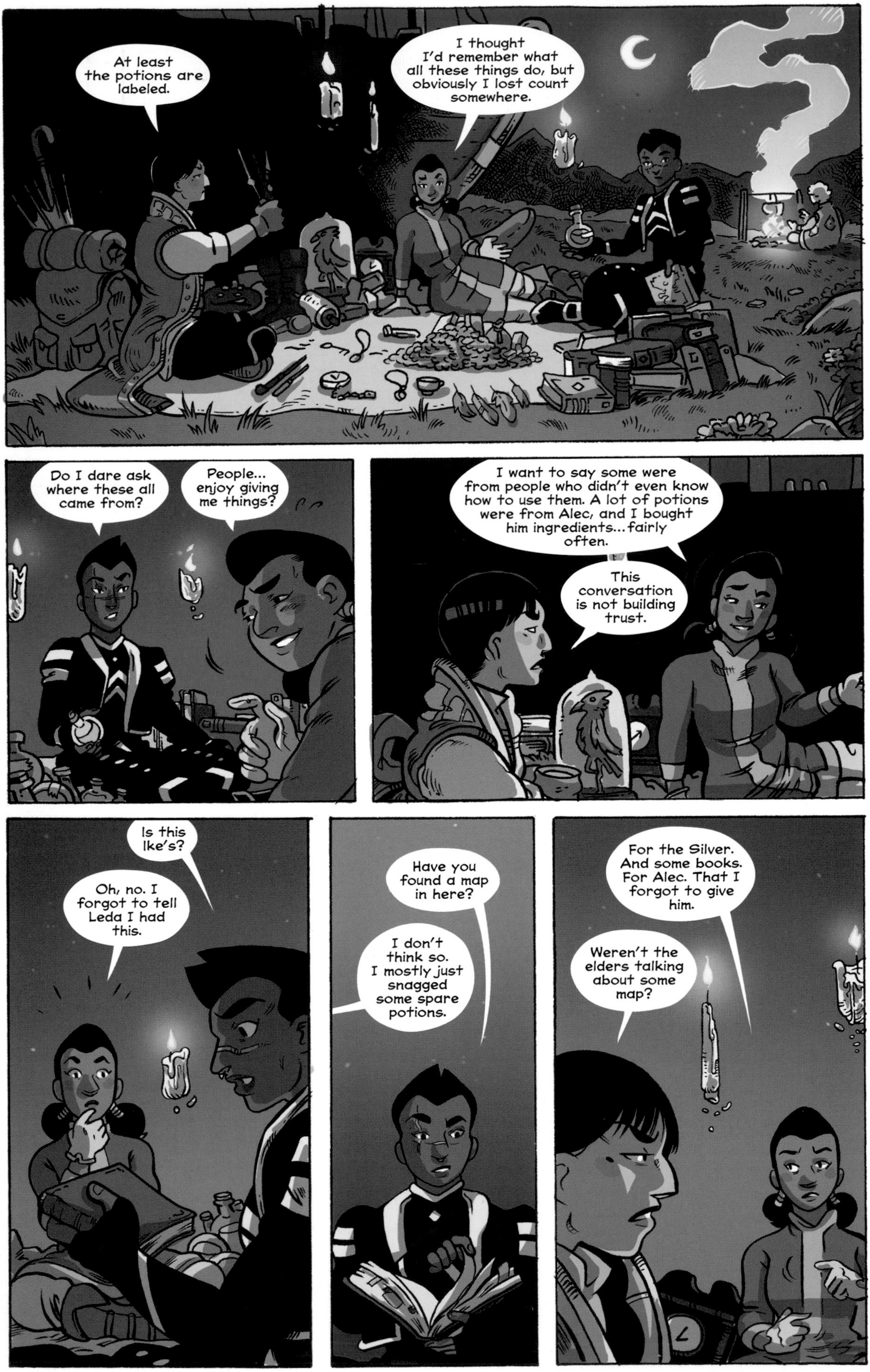
At least the potions are labeled.
I thought I'd remember what all these things do, but obviously I lost count somewhere.
Do I dare ask where these all came from?
People... enjoy giving me things?
I want to say some were from people who didn't even know how to use them. A lot of potions were from Alec, and I bought him ingredients...fairly often.
This conversation is not building trust.
Is this Ike's?
Oh, no. I forgot to tell Leda I had this.
Have you found a map in here?
I don't think so. I mostly just snagged some spare potions.
For the Silver. And some books. For Alec. That I forgot to give him.
Weren't the elders talking about some map?

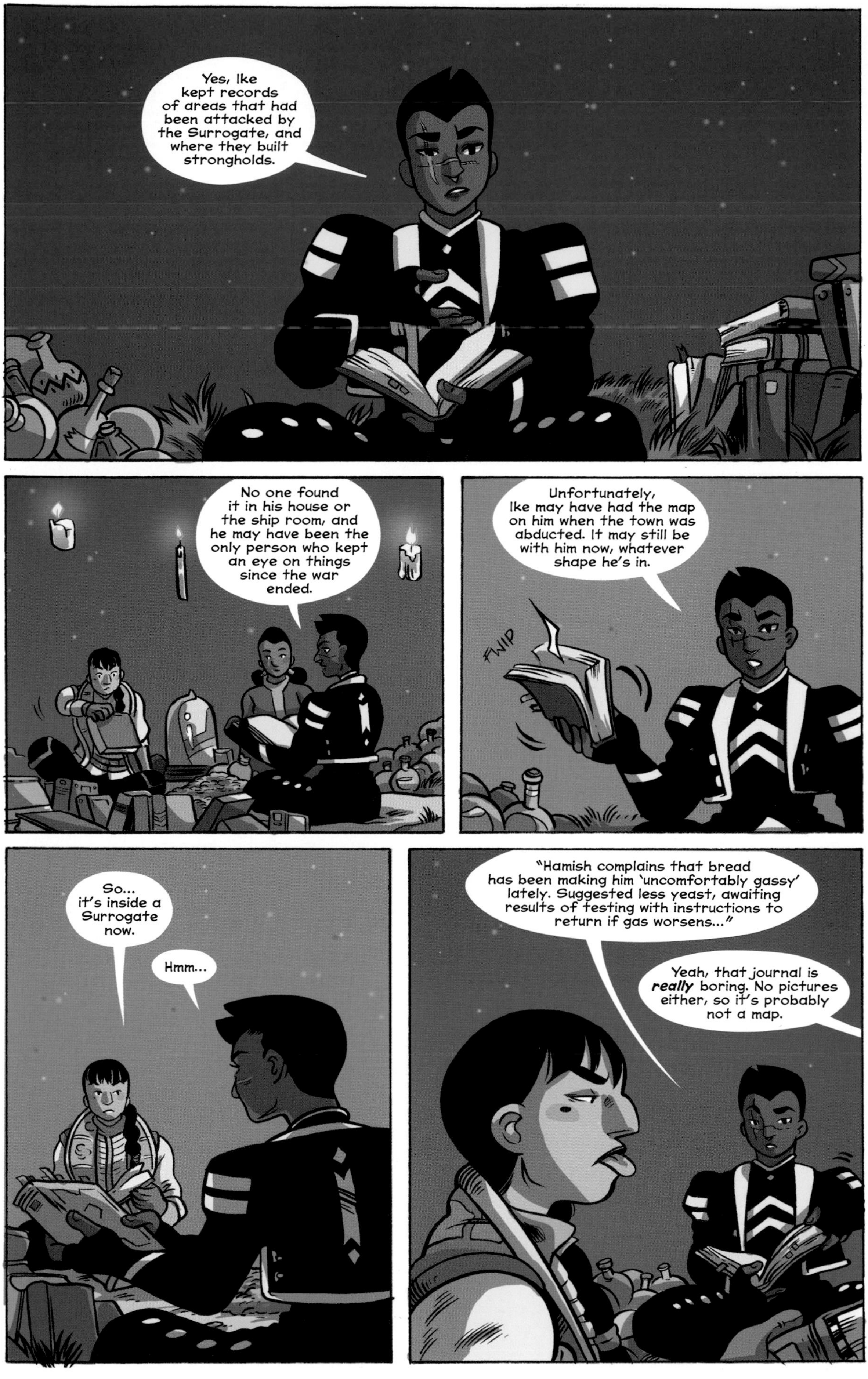
Yes, Ike kept records of areas that had been attacked by the Surrogate, and where they built strongholds.
No one found it in his house or the ship room, and he may have been the only person who kept an eye on things since the war ended.
Unfortunately, Ike may have had the map on him when the town was abducted. It may still be with him now, whatever shape he's in.
FWIP
So... it's inside a Surrogate now.
Hmm...
"Hamish complains that bread has been making him 'uncomfortably gassy' lately. Suggested less yeast, awaiting results of testing with instructions to return if gas worsens..."
Yeah, that journal is ***really*** boring. No pictures either, so it's probably not a map.

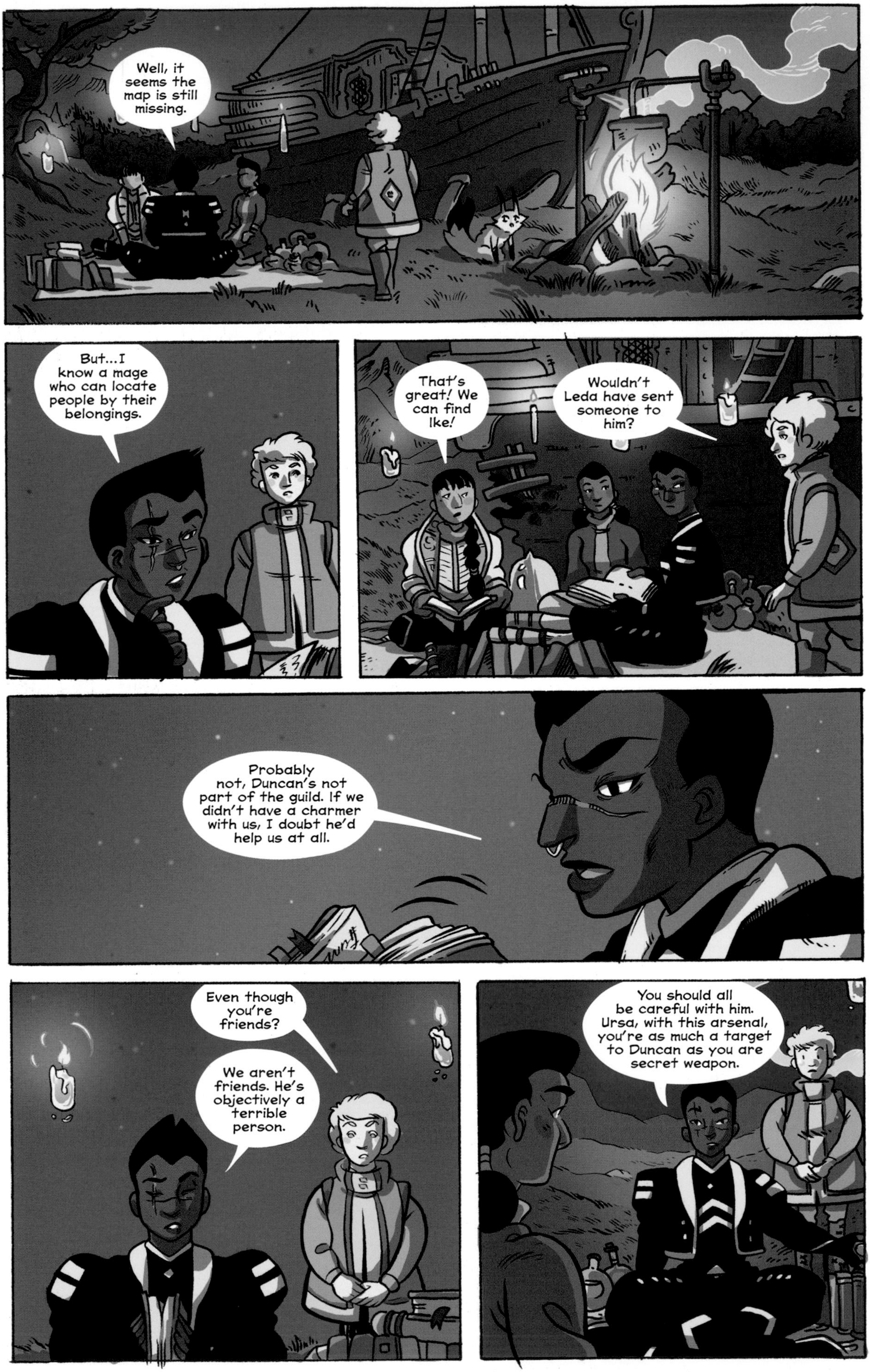
Well, it seems the map is still missing.
But...I know a mage who can locate people by their belongings.
That's great! We can find Ike!
Wouldn't Leda have sent someone to him?
Probably not, Duncan's not part of the guild. If we didn't have a charmer with us, I doubt he'd help us at all.
Even though you're friends?
We aren't friends. He's objectively a terrible person.
You should all be careful with him. Ursa, with this arsenal, you're as much a target to Duncan as you are secret weapon.

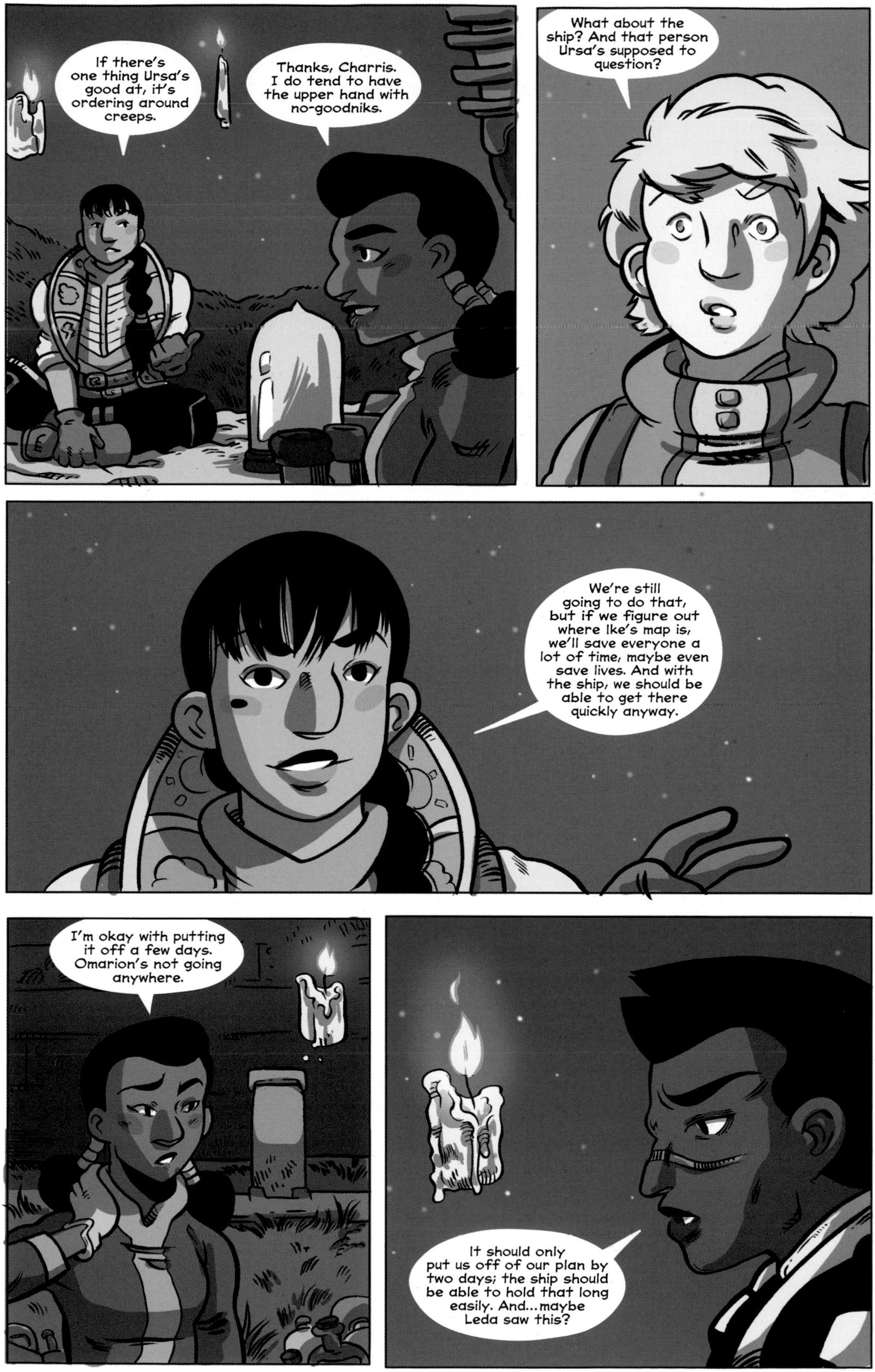
If there's one thing Ursa's good at, it's ordering around creeps.
Thanks, Charris. I do tend to have the upper hand with no-goodniks.
What about the ship? And that person Ursa's supposed to question?
We're still going to do that, but if we figure out where Ike's map is, we'll save everyone a lot of time, maybe even save lives. And with the ship, we should be able to get there quickly anyway.
I'm okay with putting it off a few days. Omarion's not going anywhere.
It should only put us off of our plan by two days; the ship should be able to hold that long easily. And...maybe Leda saw this?

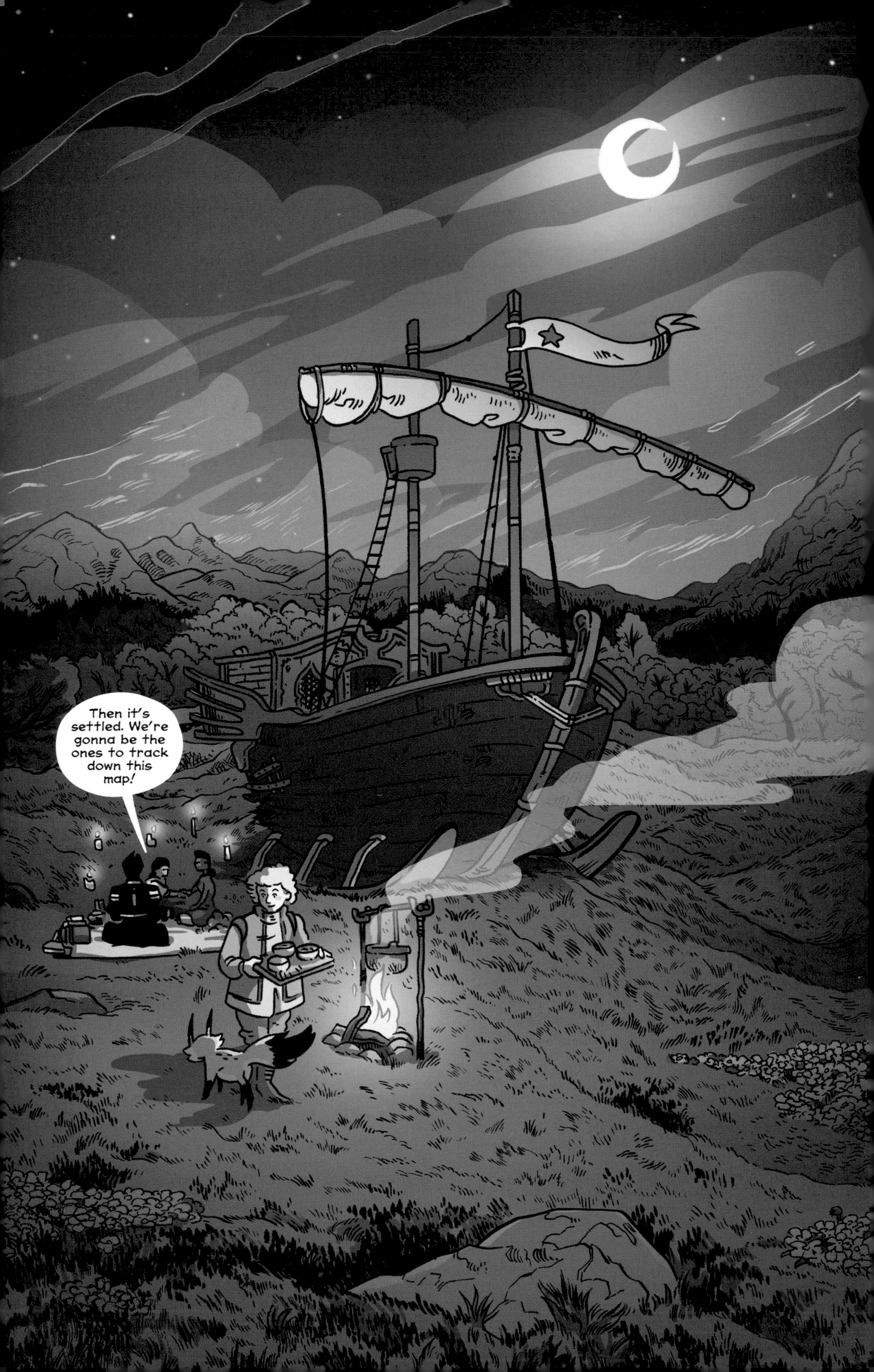
Then it's settled. We're gonna be the ones to track down this map!

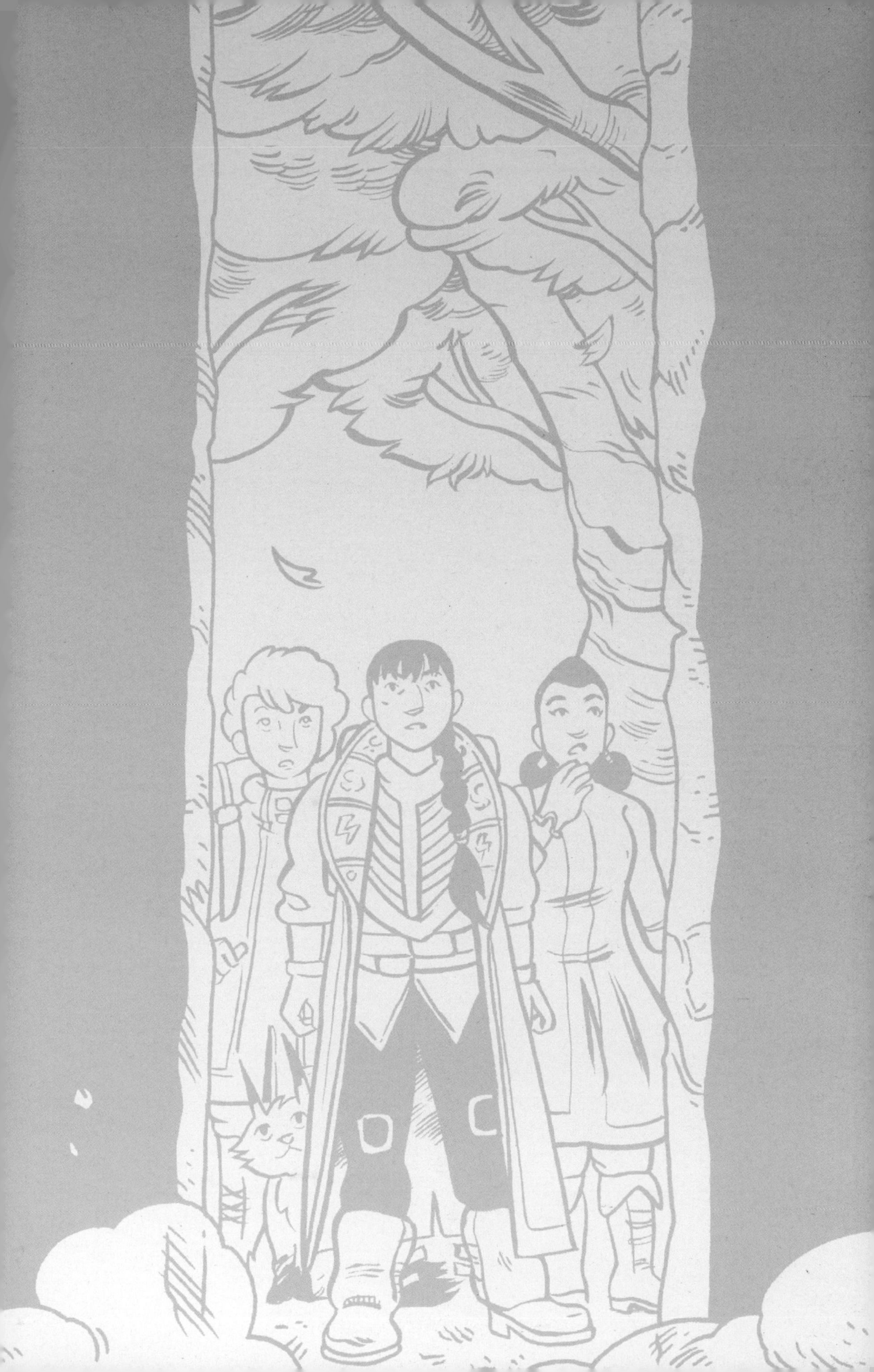

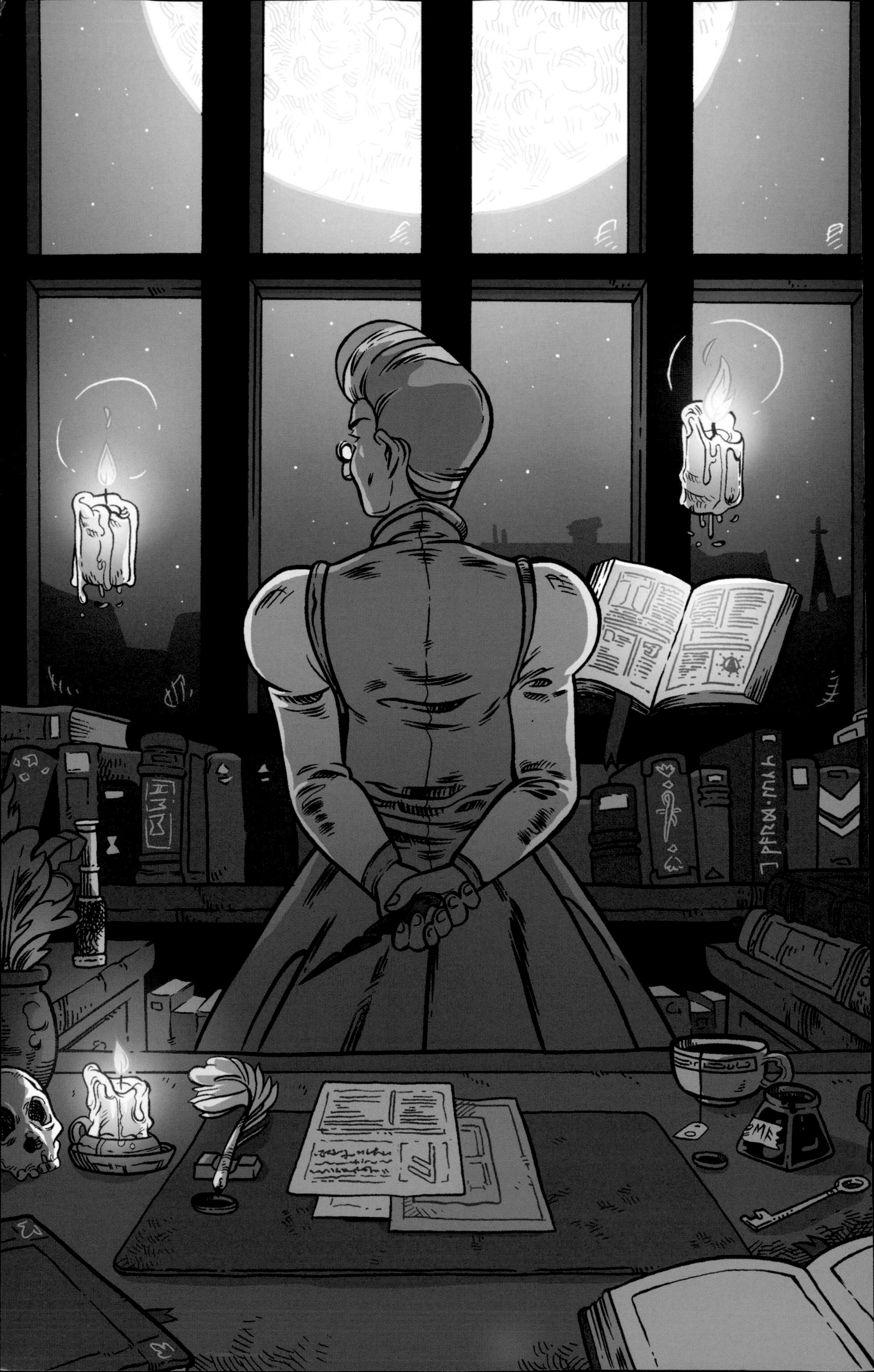

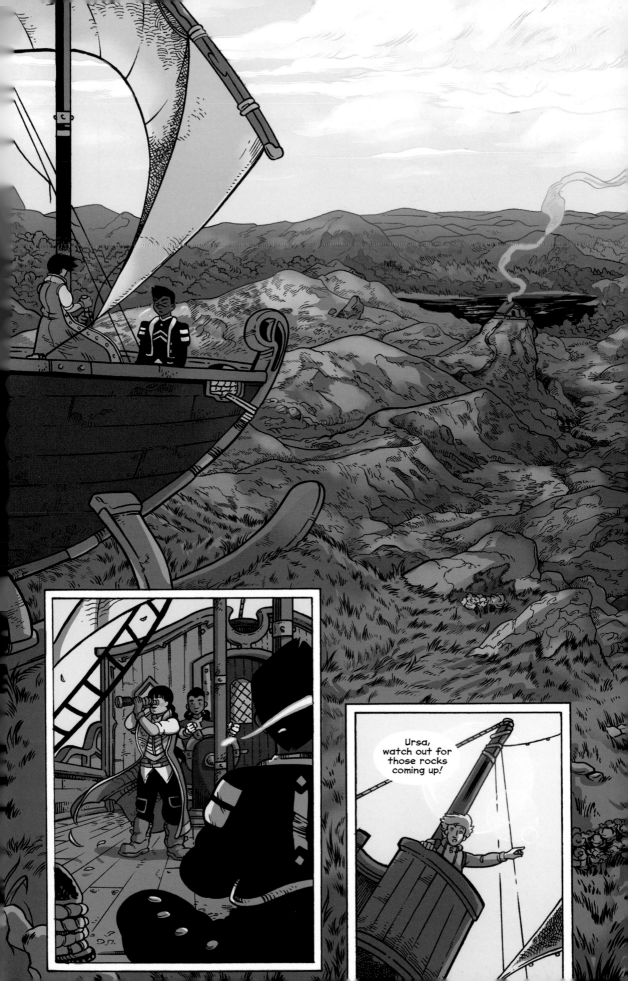

Ursa,
watch out for
those rocks
coming up!

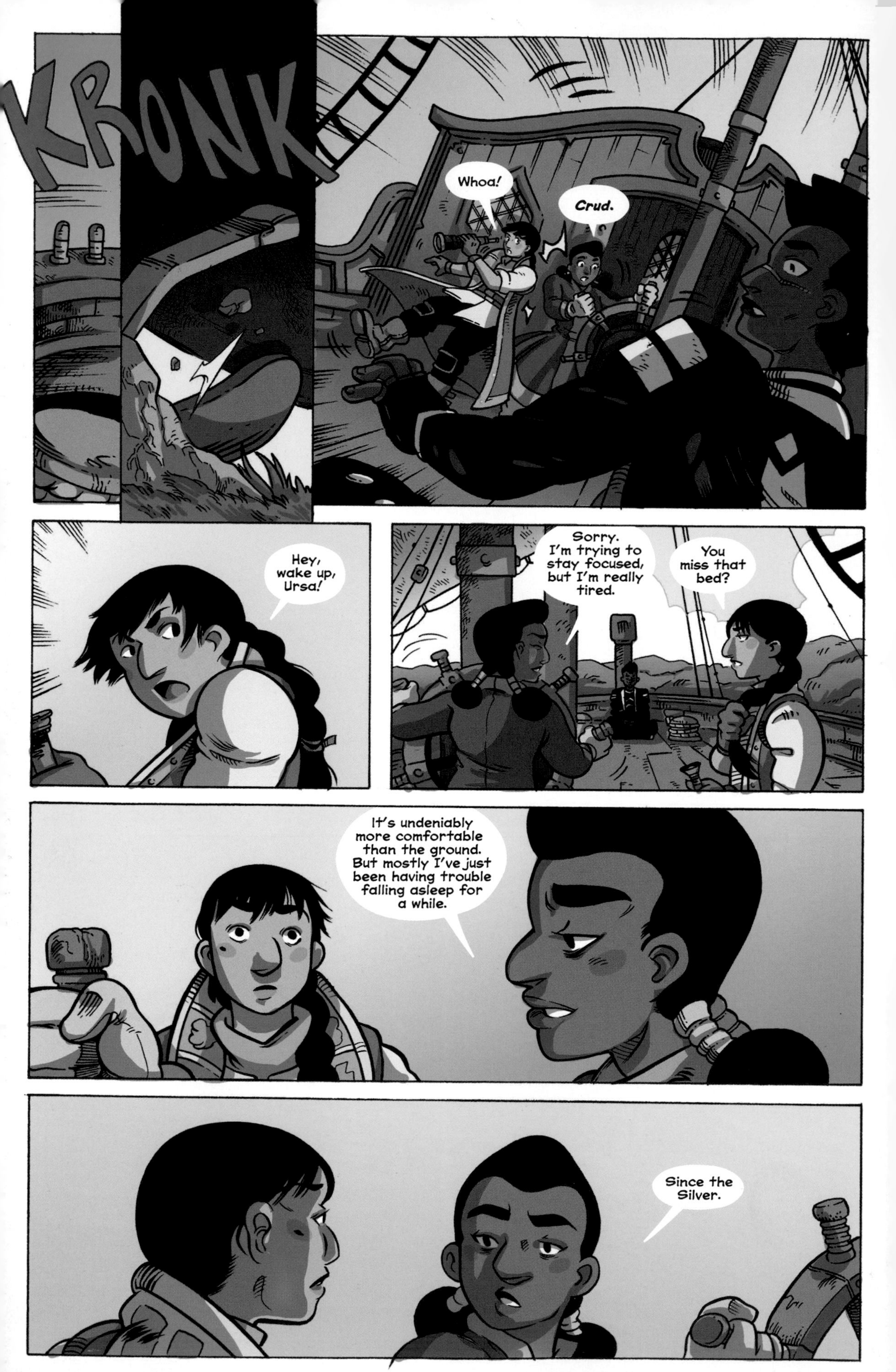
KRONK
Whoa!
Crud.
Hey, wake up, Ursa!
Sorry. I'm trying to stay focused, but I'm really tired.
You miss that bed?
It's undeniably more comfortable than the ground. But mostly I've just been having trouble falling asleep for a while.
Since the Silver.

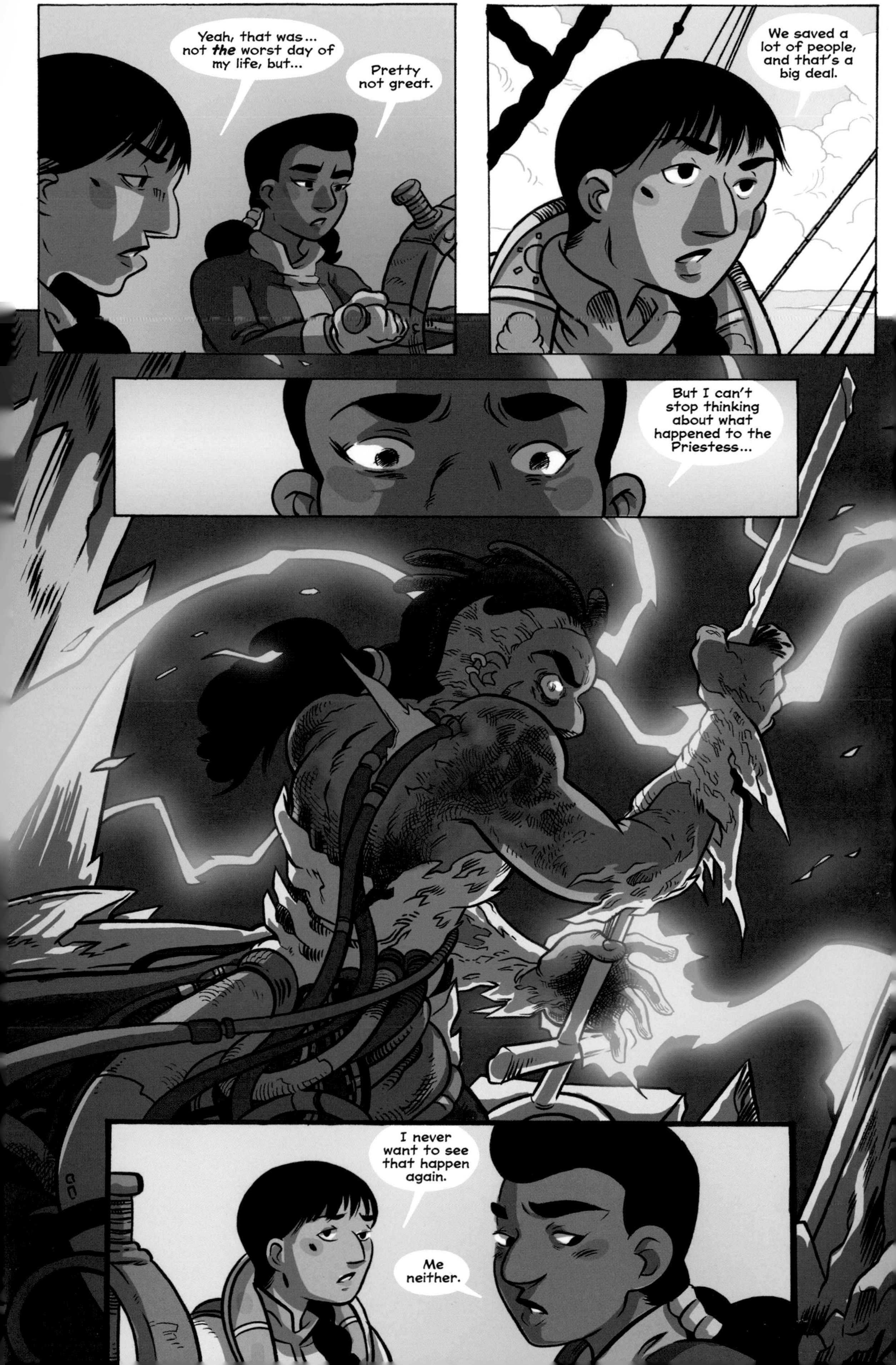
Yeah, that was... not *the* worst day of my life, but...
Pretty not great.
We saved a lot of people, and that's a big deal.
But I can't stop thinking about what happened to the Priestess...
I never want to see that happen again.
Me neither.

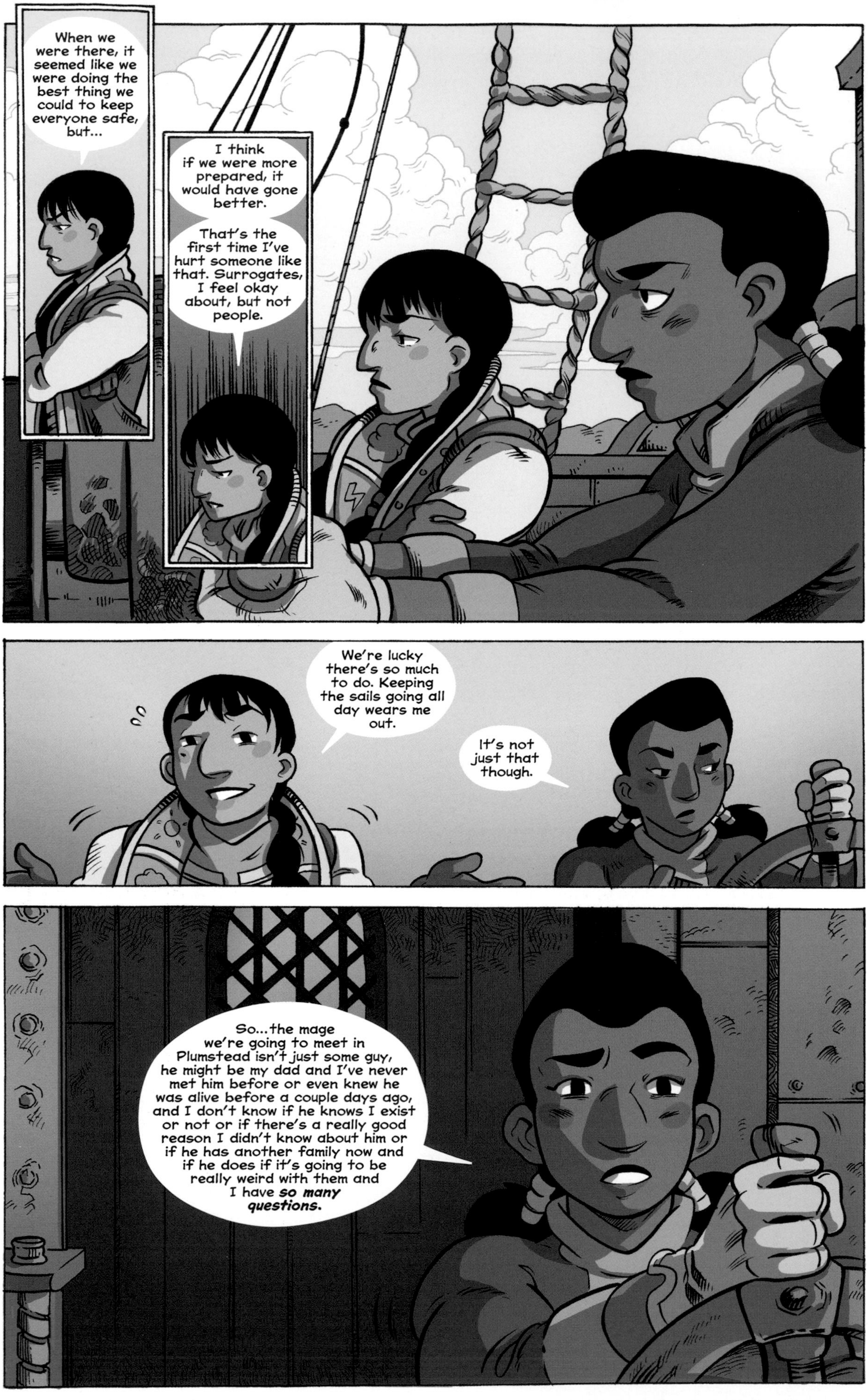

When we were there, it seemed like we were doing the best thing we could to keep everyone safe, but...
I think if we were more prepared, it would have gone better.
That's the first time I've hurt someone like that. Surrogates, I feel okay about, but not people.
We're lucky there's so much to do. Keeping the sails going all day wears me out.
It's not just that though.
So...the mage we're going to meet in Plumstead isn't just some guy, he might be my dad and I've never met him before or even knew he was alive before a couple days ago, and I don't know if he knows I exist or not or if there's a really good reason I didn't know about him or if he has another family now and if he does if it's going to be really weird with them and I have ***so many questions.***

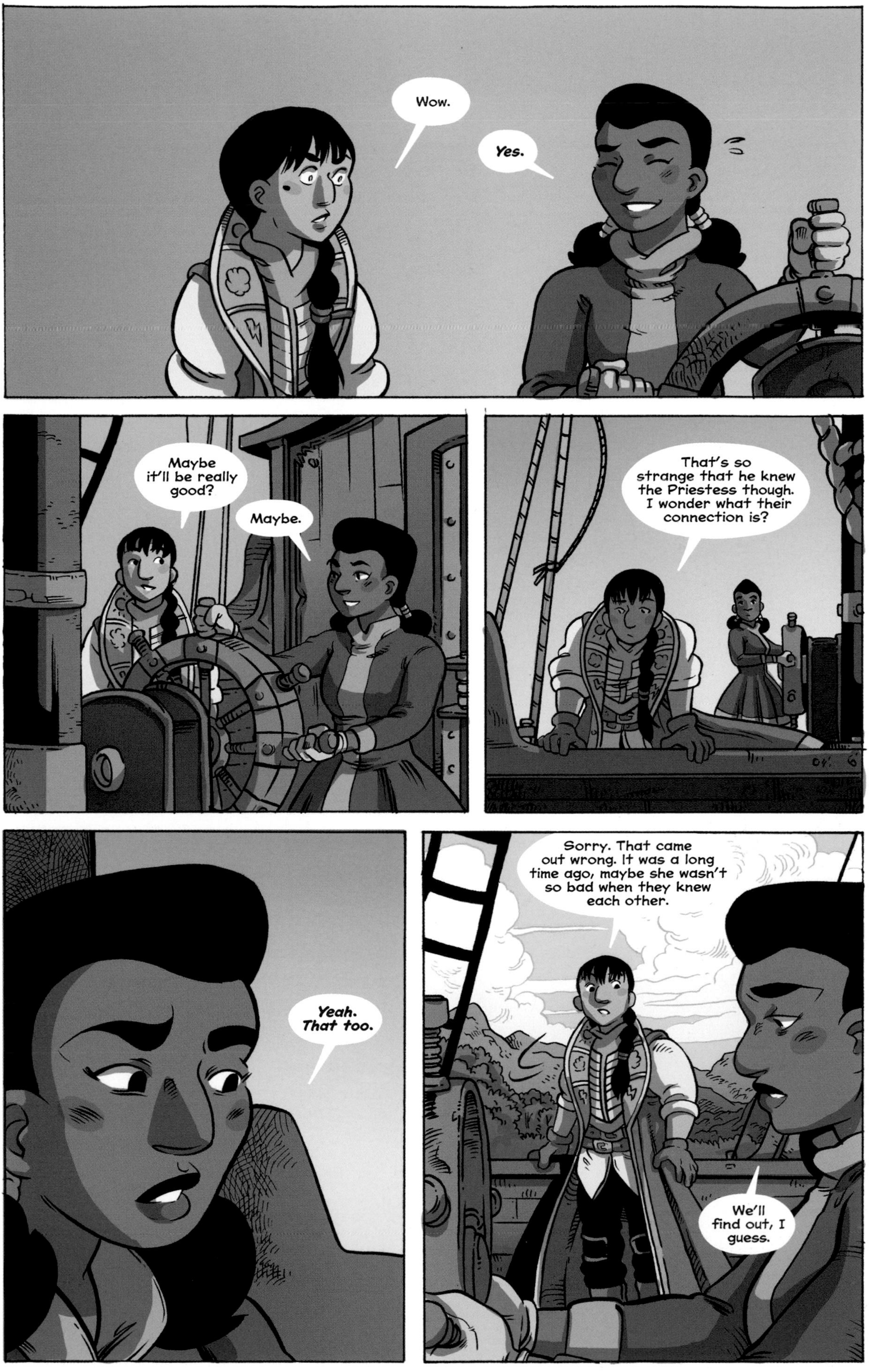
Wow.
Yes.
Maybe it'll be really good?
Maybe.
That's so strange that he knew the Priestess though. I wonder what their connection is?
Yeah. That too.
Sorry. That came out wrong. It was a long time ago, maybe she wasn't so bad when they knew each other.
We'll find out, I guess.

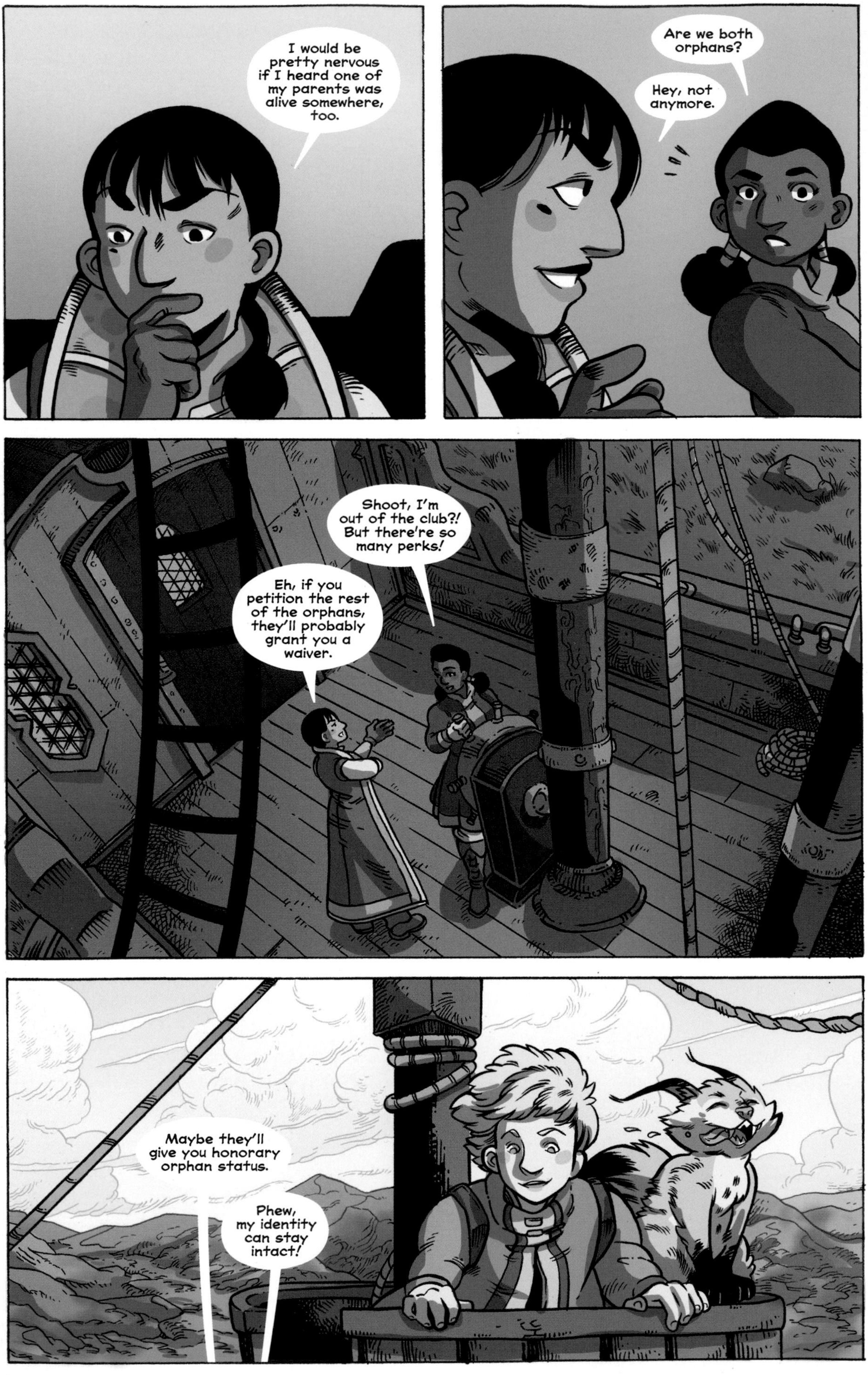
I would be pretty nervous if I heard one of my parents was alive somewhere, too.
Are we both orphans?
Hey, not anymore.
Shoot, I'm out of the club?! But there're so many perks!
Eh, if you petition the rest of the orphans, they'll probably grant you a waiver.
Maybe they'll give you honorary orphan status.
Phew, my identity can stay intact!

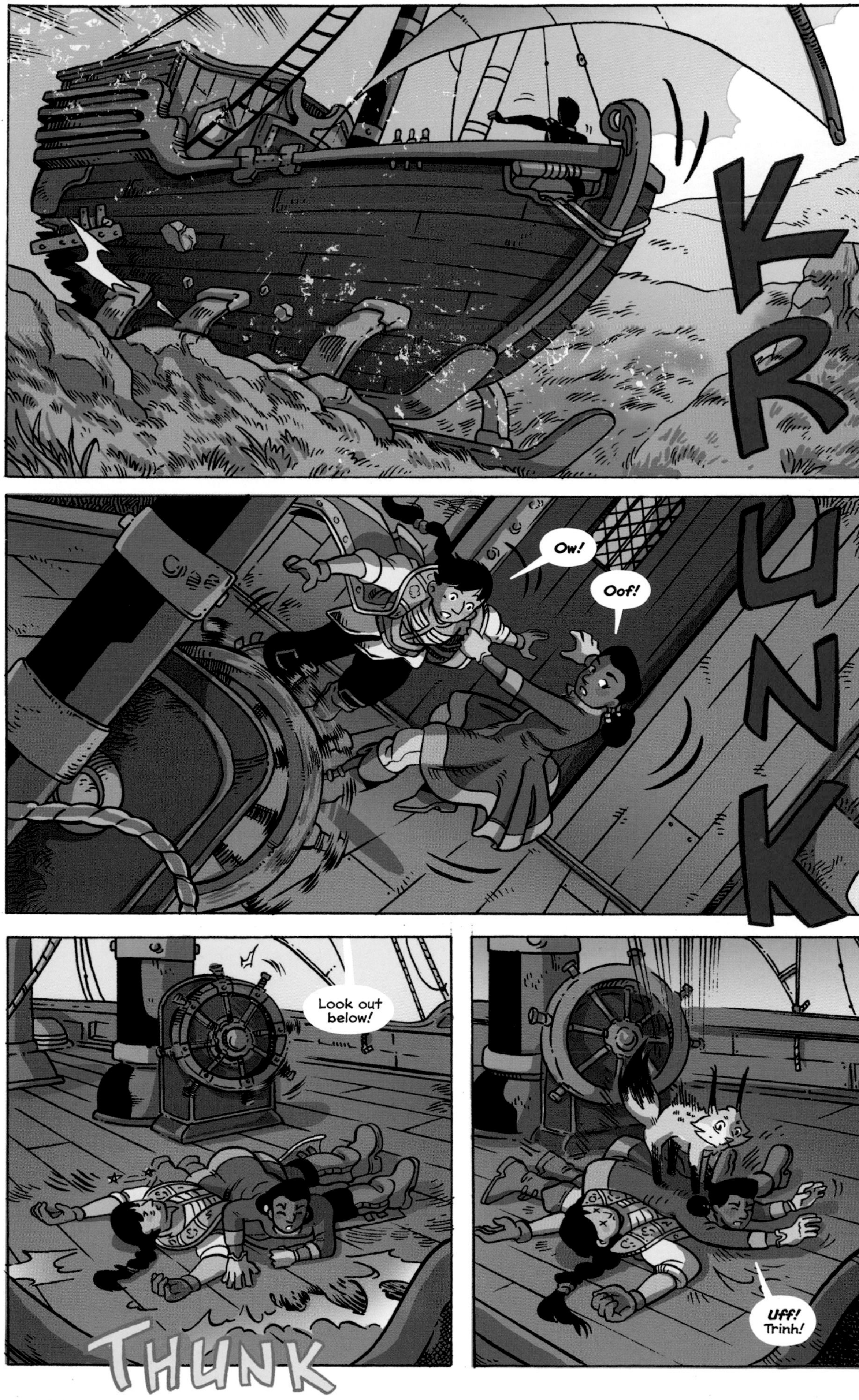
KRUNK
Ow!
Oof!
Look out below!
THUNK
Uff! Trinh!

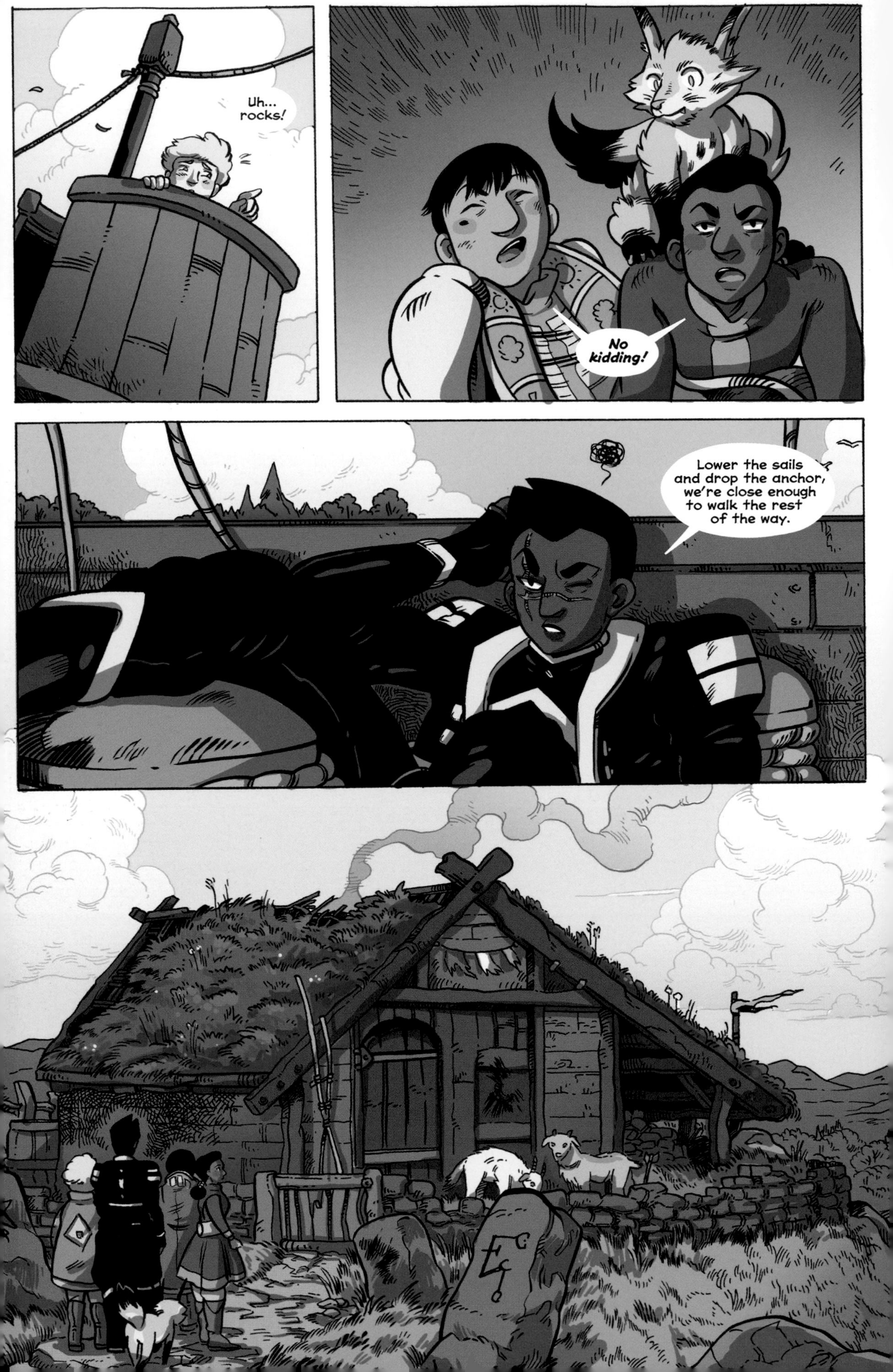
Uh... rocks!
No kidding!
Lower the sails and drop the anchor, we're close enough to walk the rest of the way.

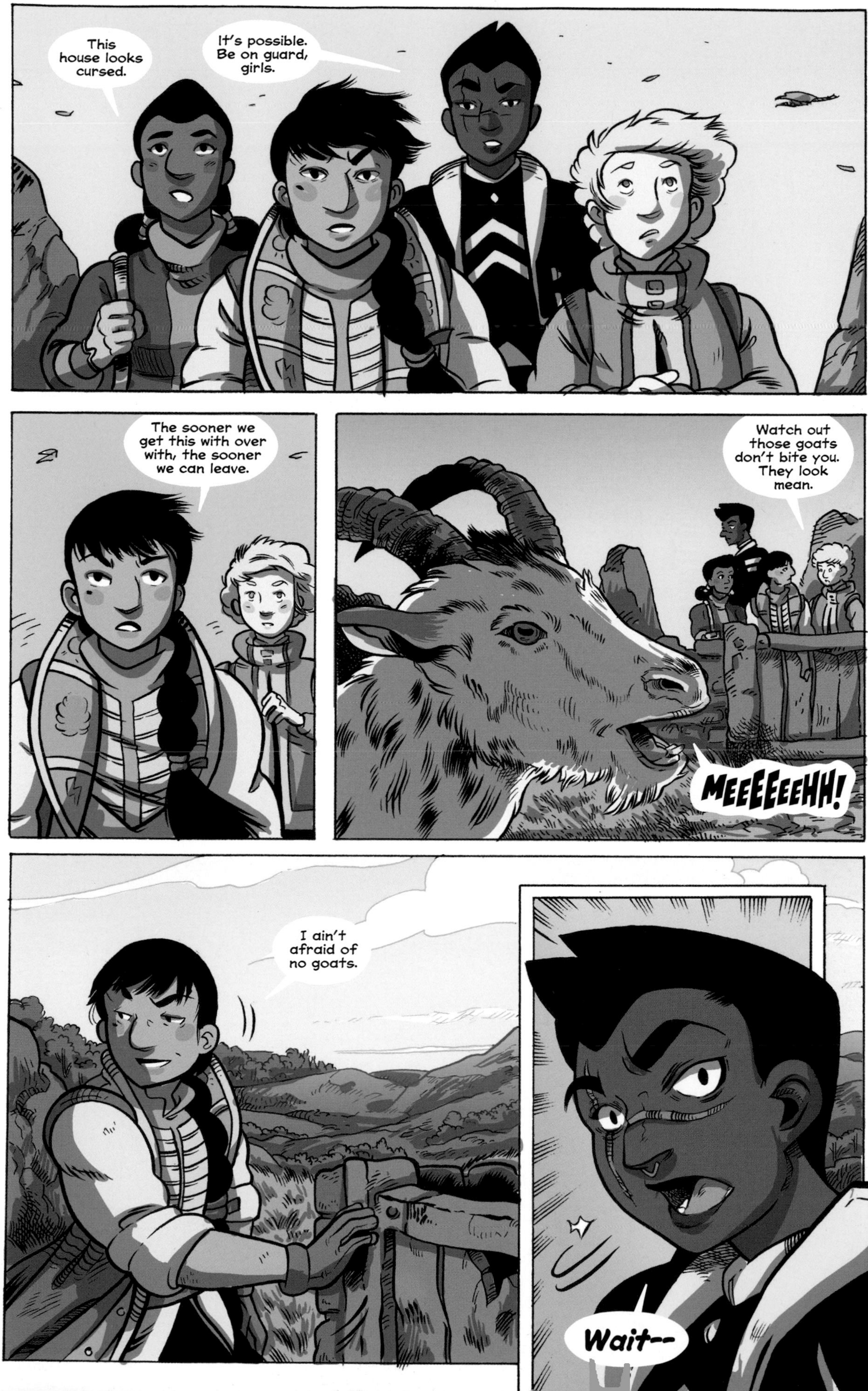
This house looks cursed.
It's possible. Be on guard, girls.
The sooner we get this with over with, the sooner we can leave.
Watch out those goats don't bite you. They look mean.
MEEEEEEHH!
I ain't afraid of no goats.
Wait--

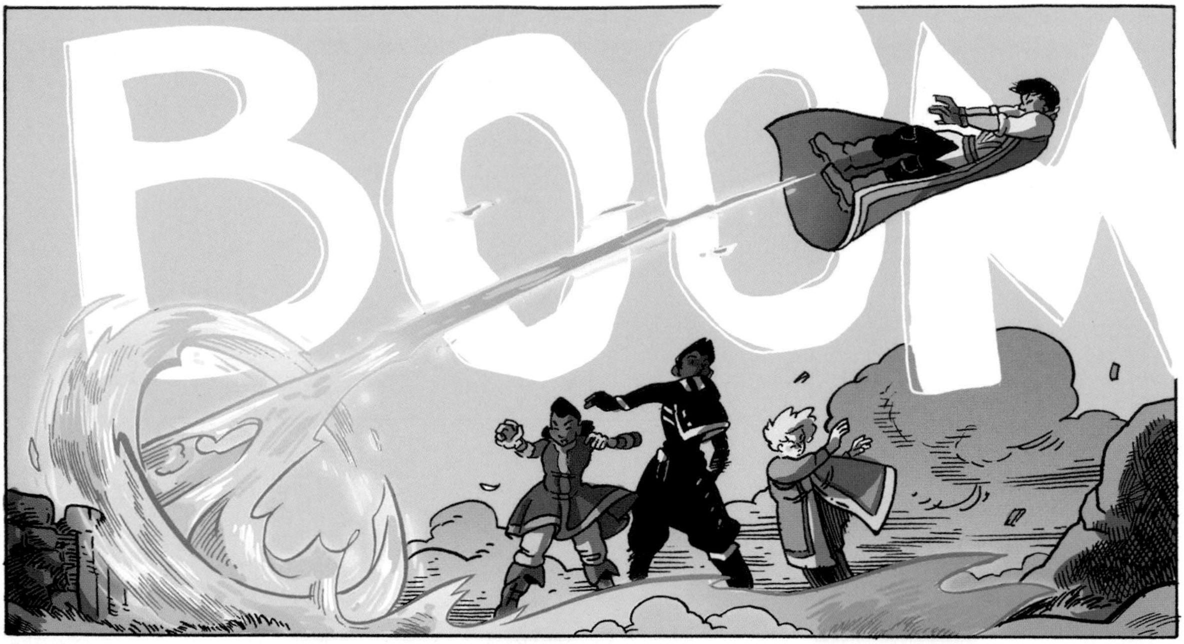
BOOM

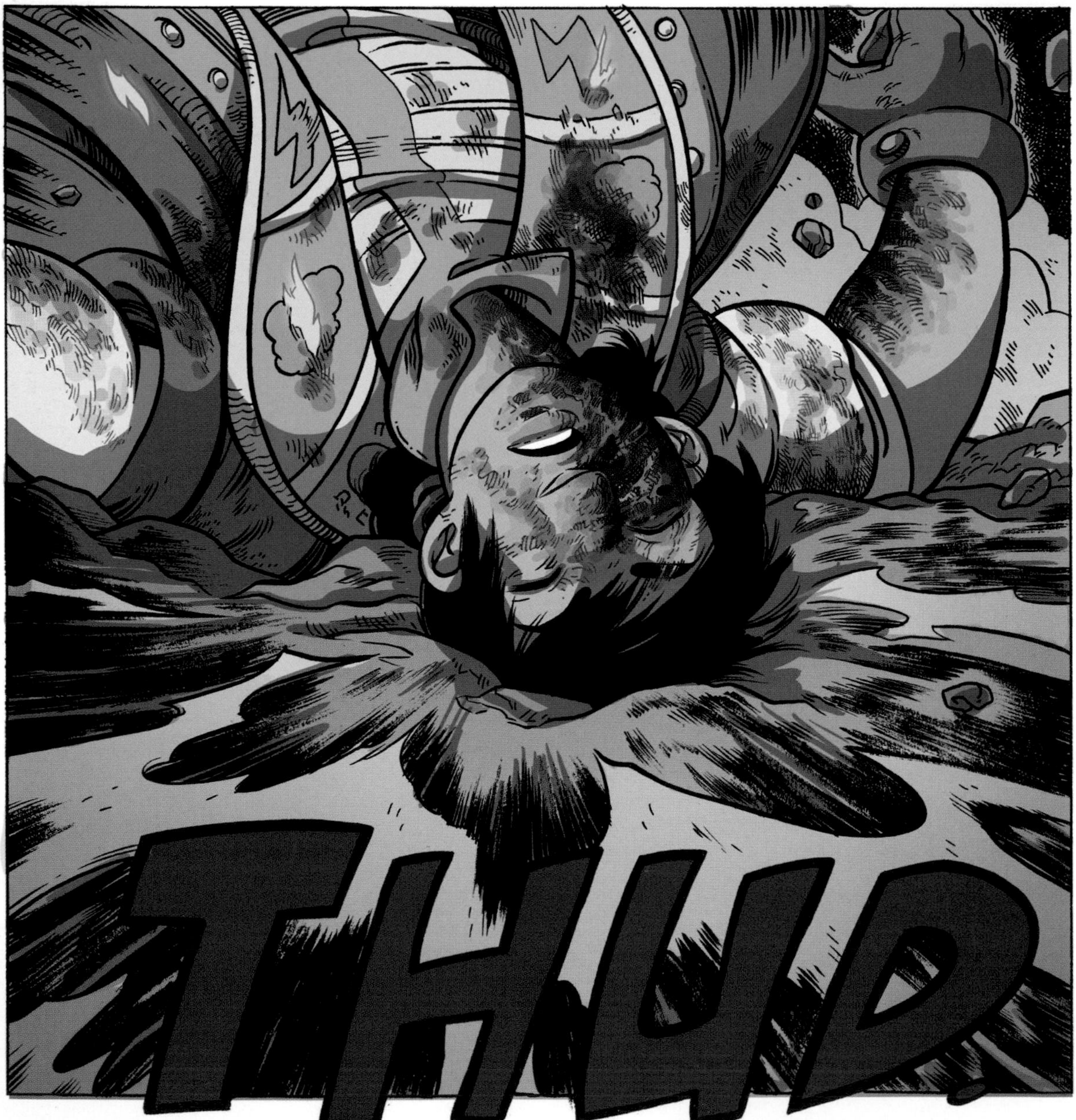
THUD

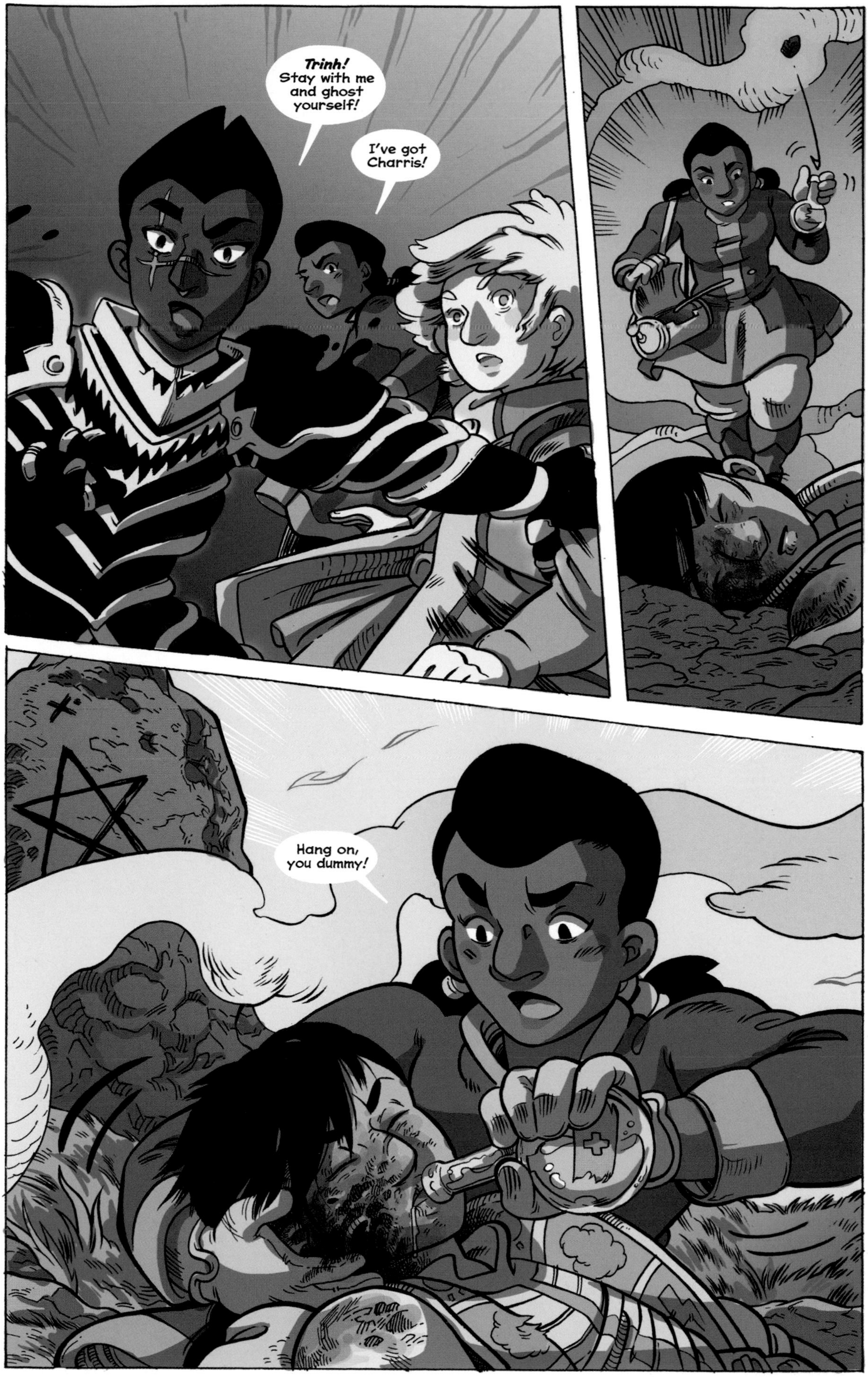
Trinh! Stay with me and ghost yourself!
I've got Charris!
Hang on, you dummy!

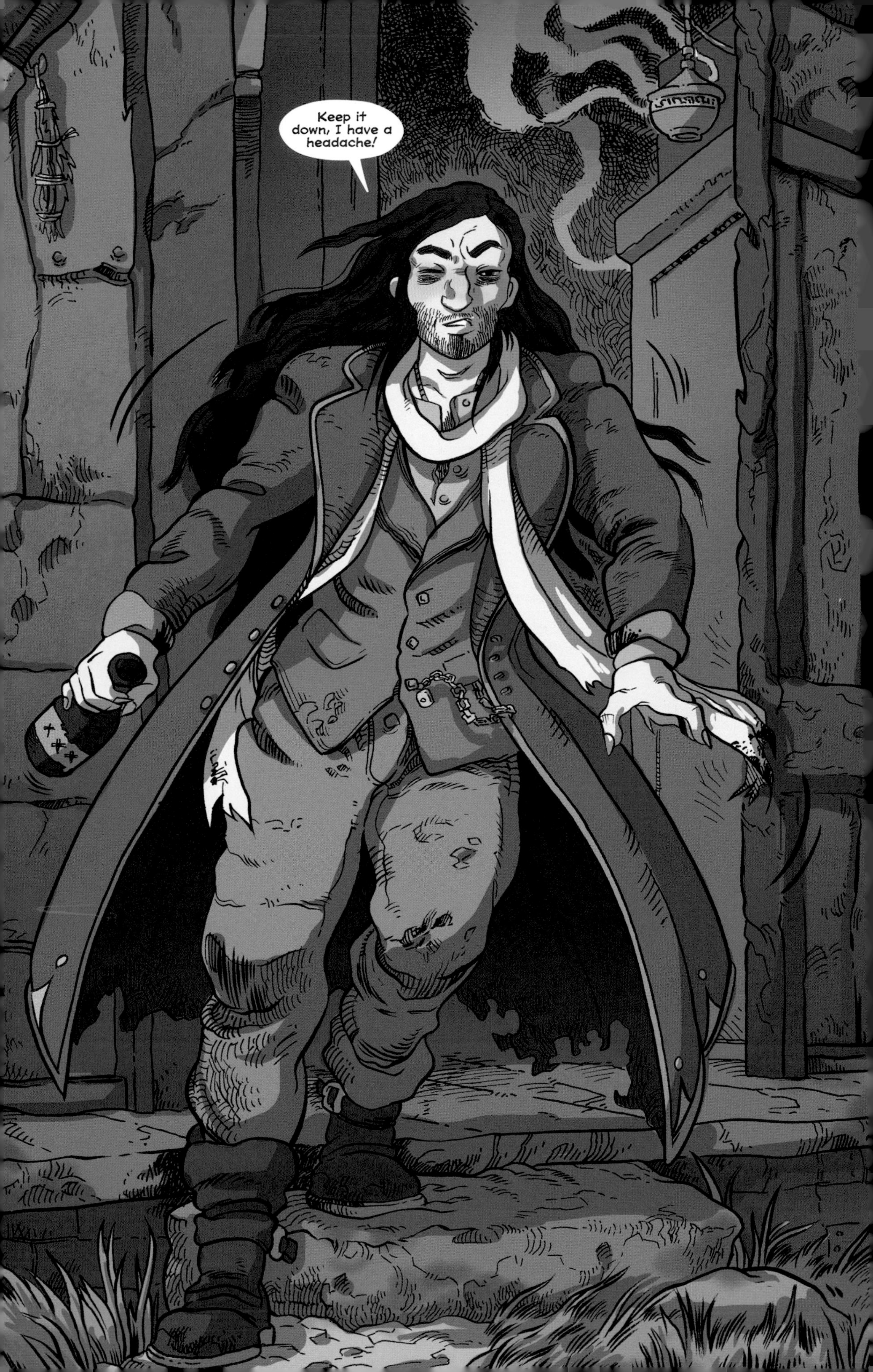
Keep it down, I have a headache!

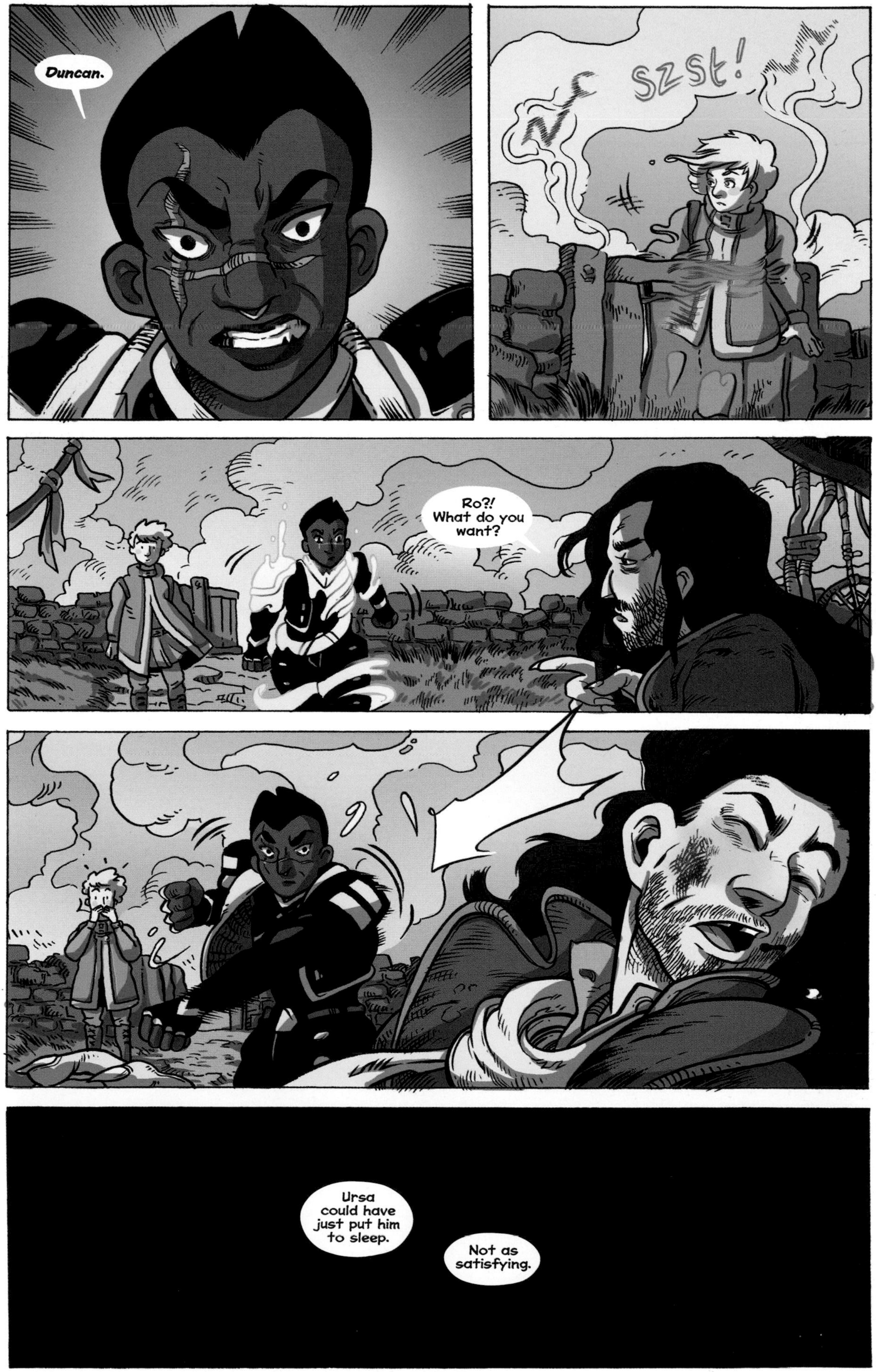
Duncan.
szst!
Ro?! What do you want?
Ursa could have just put him to sleep.
Not as satisfying.

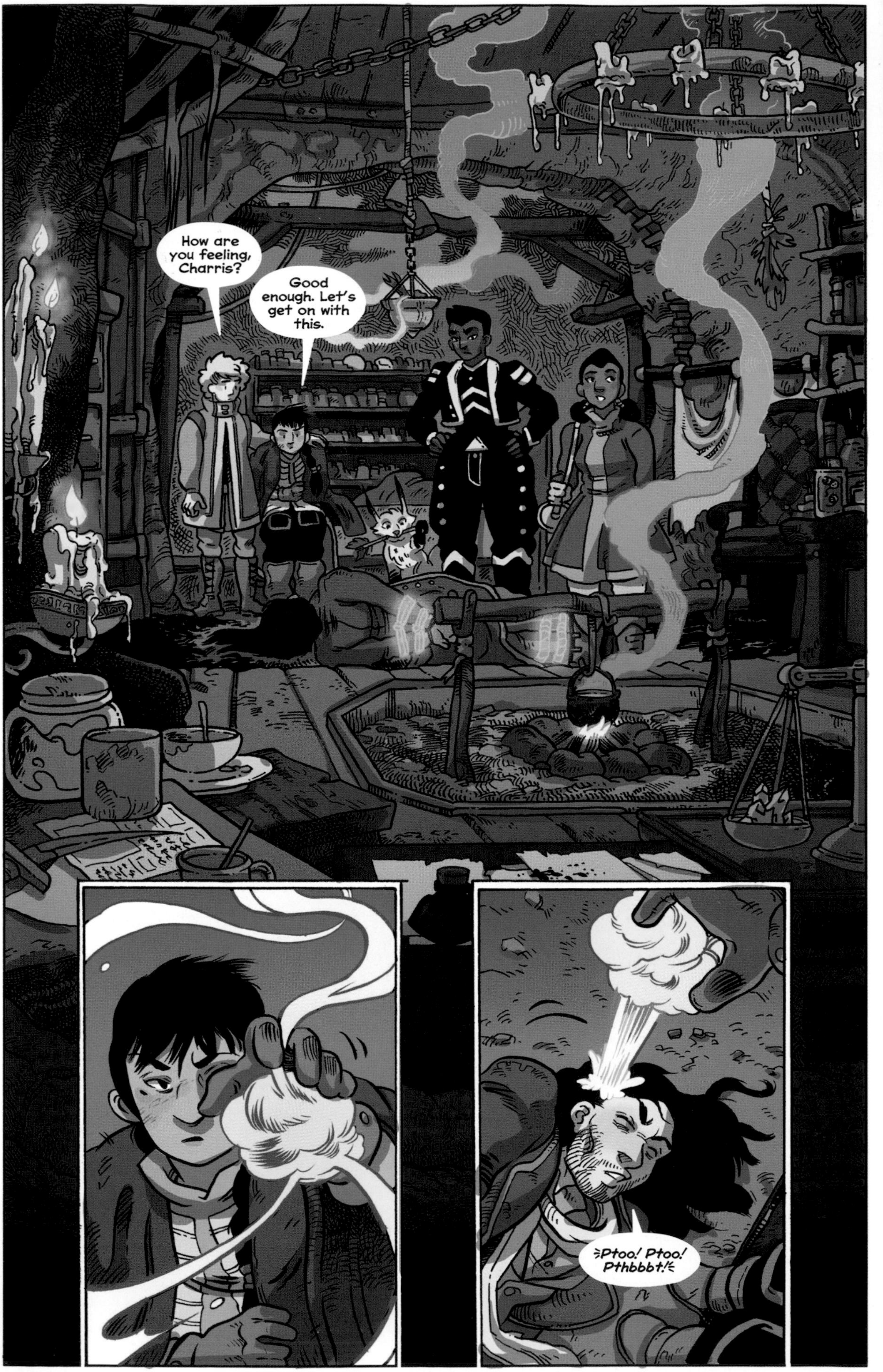
How are you feeling, Charris?
Good enough. Let's get on with this.
Ptoo! Ptoo! Pthbbbt!

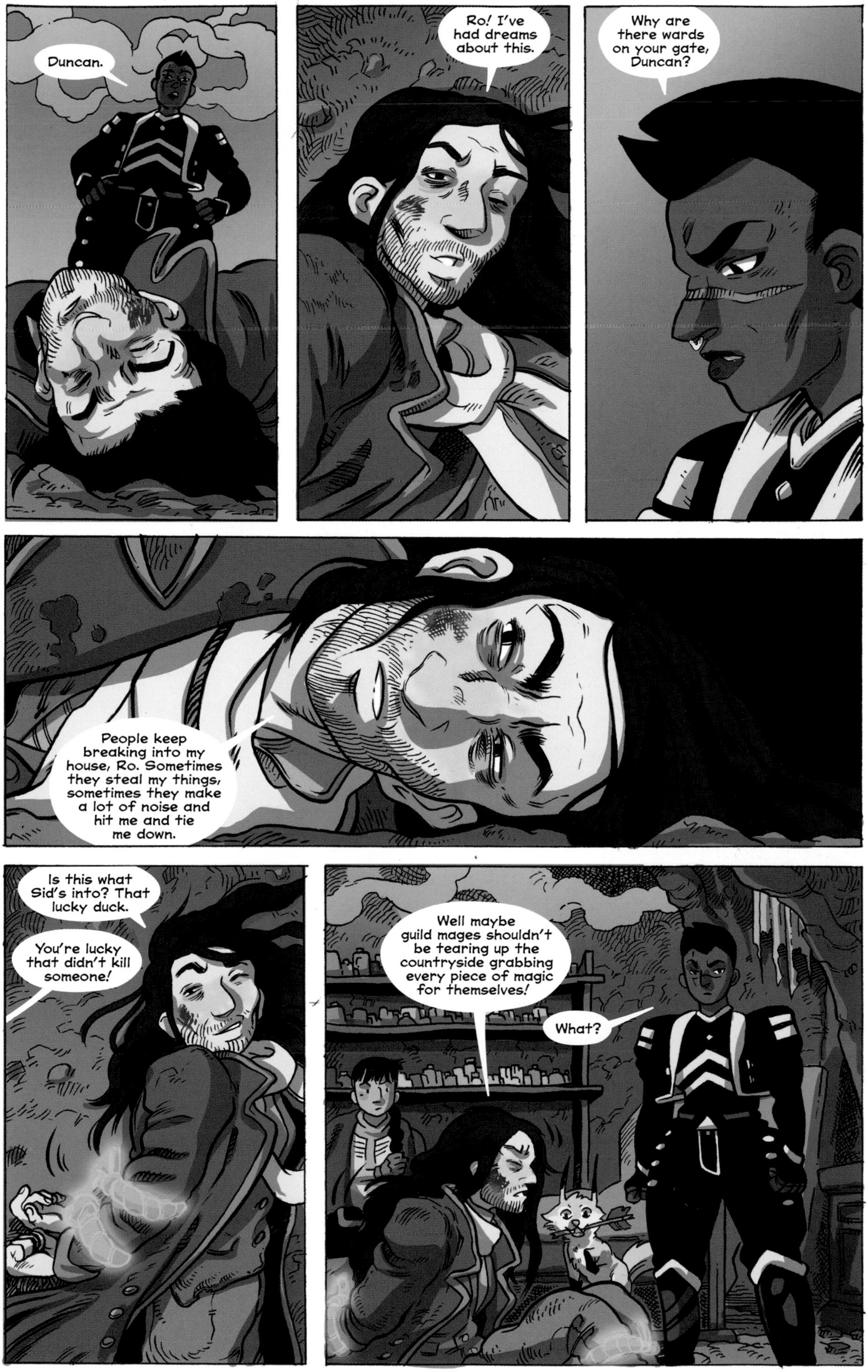
Duncan.
Ro! I've had dreams about this.
Why are there wards on your gate, Duncan?
People keep breaking into my house, Ro. Sometimes they steal my things, sometimes they make a lot of noise and hit me and tie me down.
Is this what Sid's into? That lucky duck.
You're lucky that didn't kill someone!
Well maybe guild mages shouldn't be tearing up the countryside grabbing every piece of magic for themselves!
What?

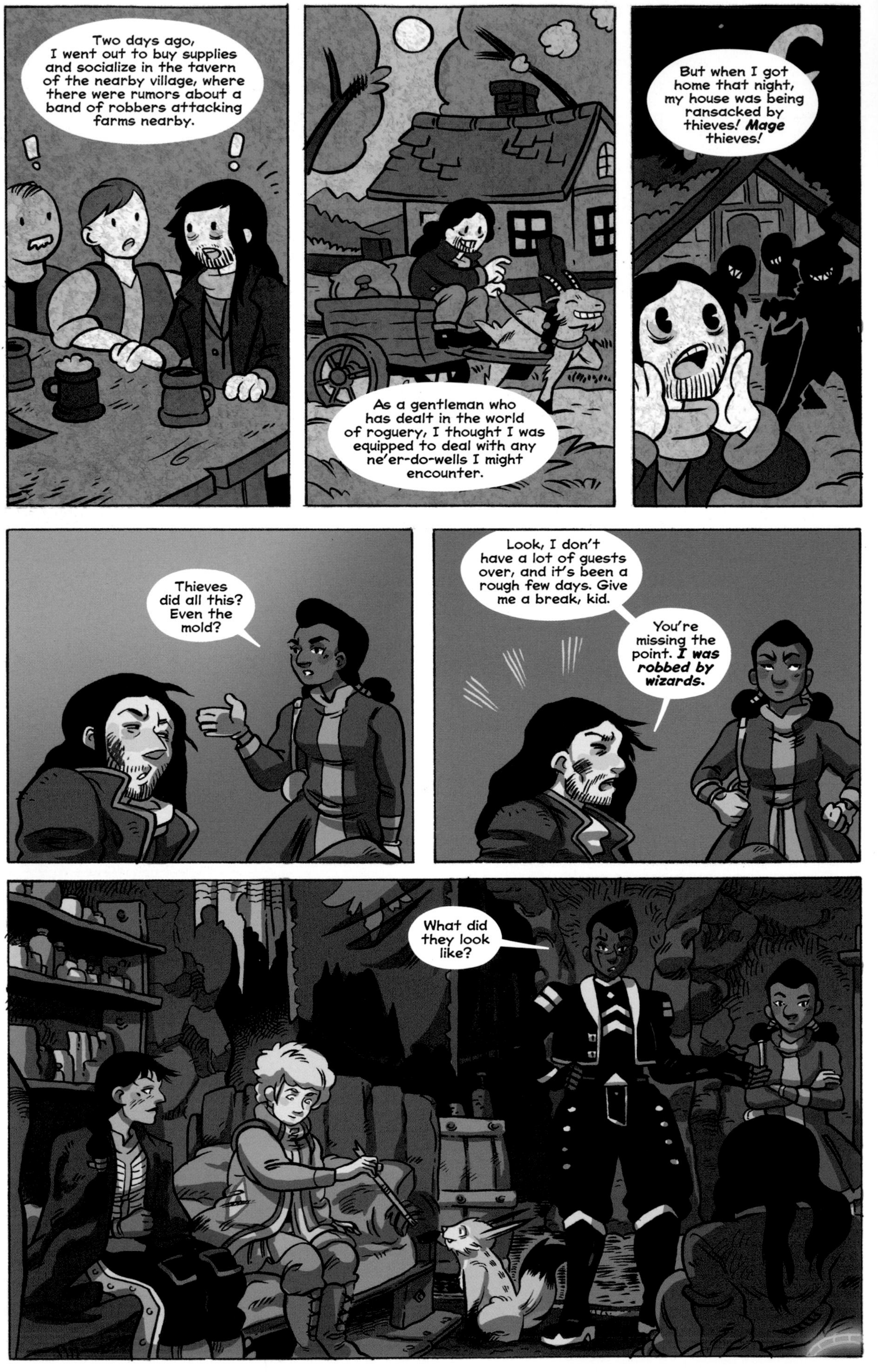
Two days ago, I went out to buy supplies and socialize in the tavern of the nearby village, where there were rumors about a band of robbers attacking farms nearby.
!
!
As a gentleman who has dealt in the world of roguery, I thought I was equipped to deal with any ne'er-do-wells I might encounter.
But when I got home that night, my house was being ransacked by thieves! *Mage* thieves!
Thieves did all this? Even the mold?
Look, I don't have a lot of guests over, and it's been a rough few days. Give me a break, kid.
You're missing the point. ***I was robbed by wizards.***
What did they look like?

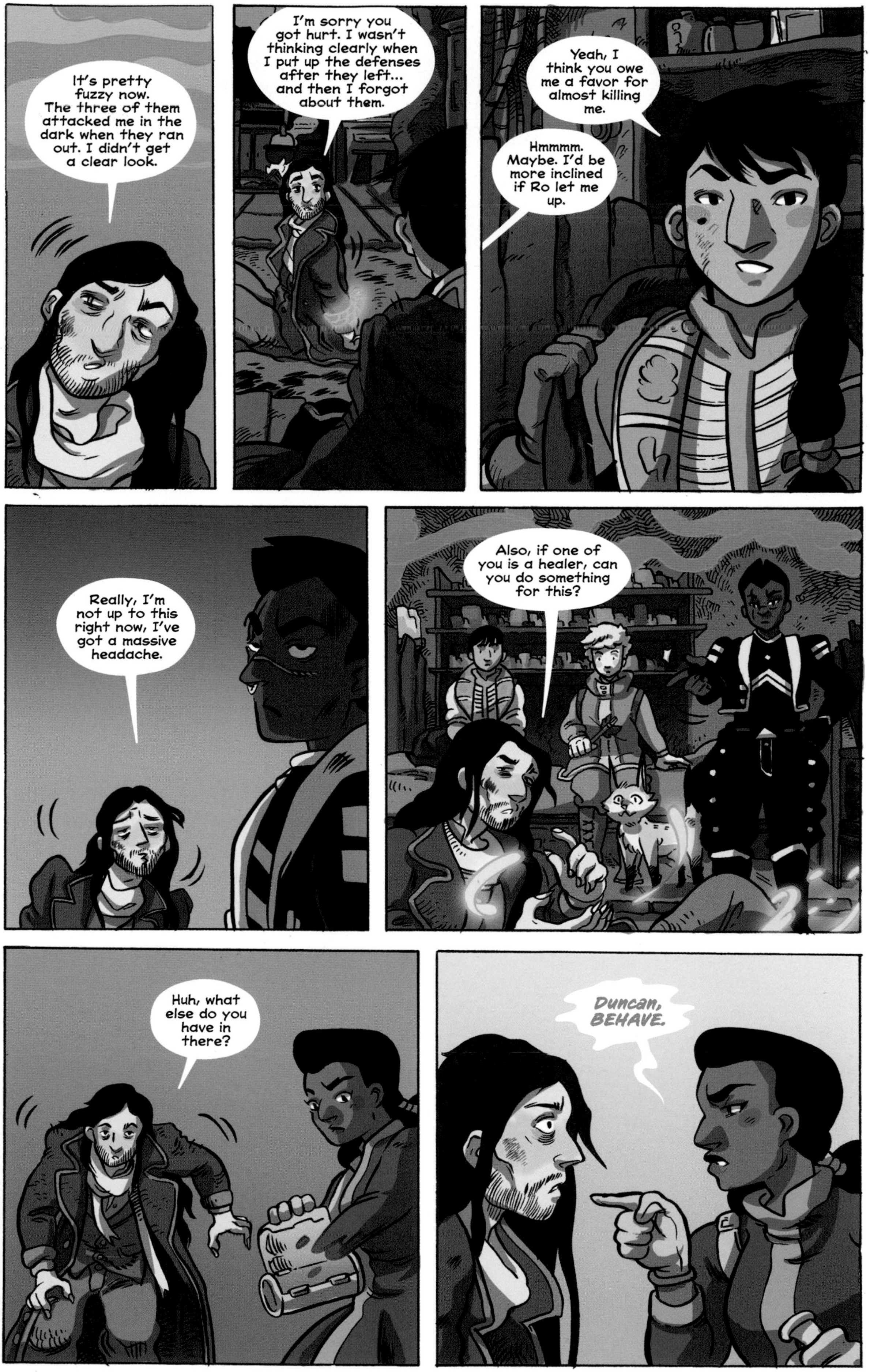
It's pretty fuzzy now. The three of them attacked me in the dark when they ran out. I didn't get a clear look.
I'm sorry you got hurt. I wasn't thinking clearly when I put up the defenses after they left... and then I forgot about them.
Yeah, I think you owe me a favor for almost killing me.
Hmmmm. Maybe. I'd be more inclined if Ro let me up.
Really, I'm not up to this right now, I've got a massive headache.
Also, if one of you is a healer, can you do something for this?
Huh, what else do you have in there?
Duncan, BEHAVE.

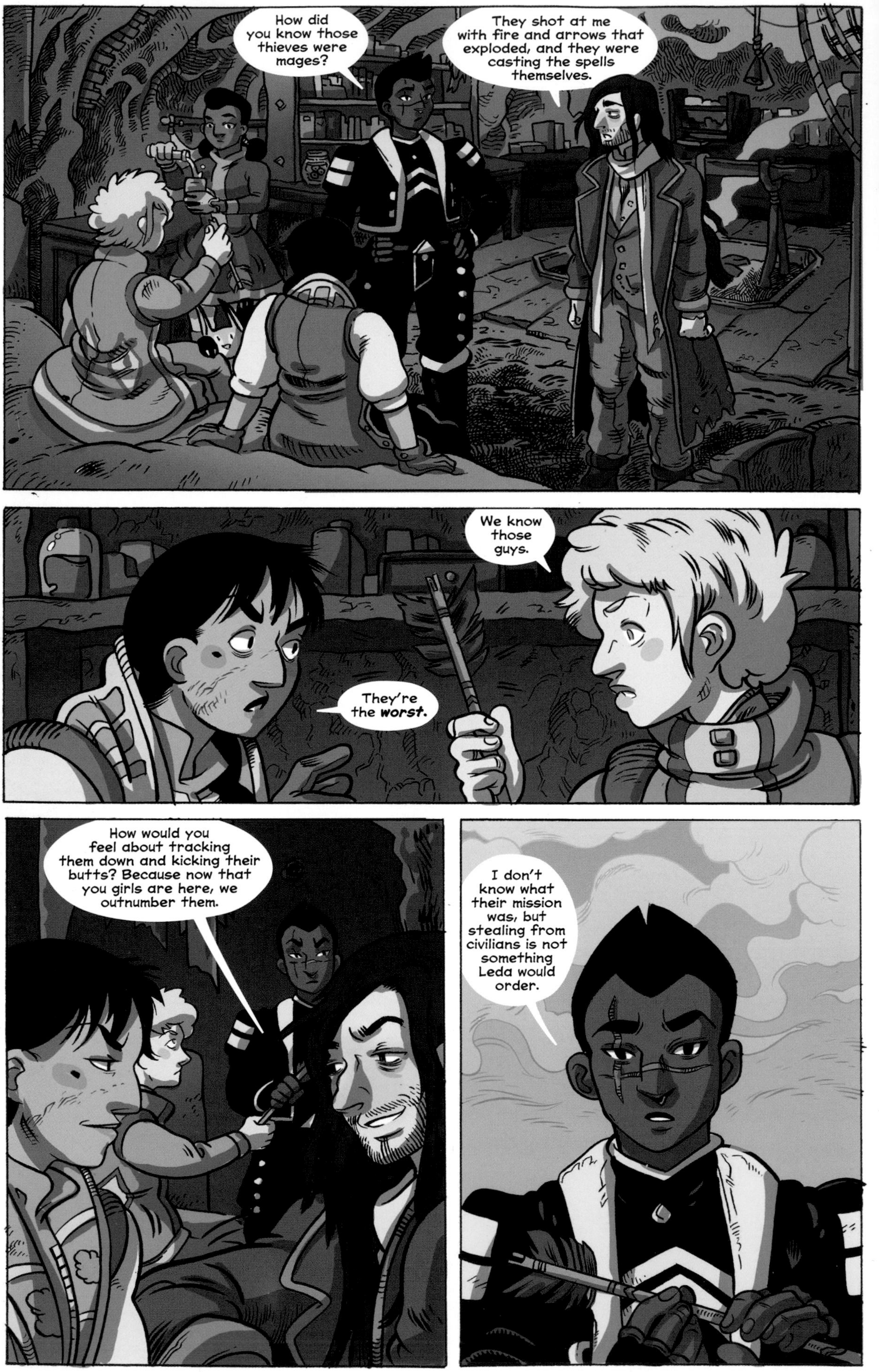
How did you know those thieves were mages?
They shot at me with fire and arrows that exploded, and they were casting the spells themselves.
We know those guys.
They're the *worst.*
How would you feel about tracking them down and kicking their butts? Because now that you girls are here, we outnumber them.
I don't know what their mission was, but stealing from civilians is not something Leda would order.

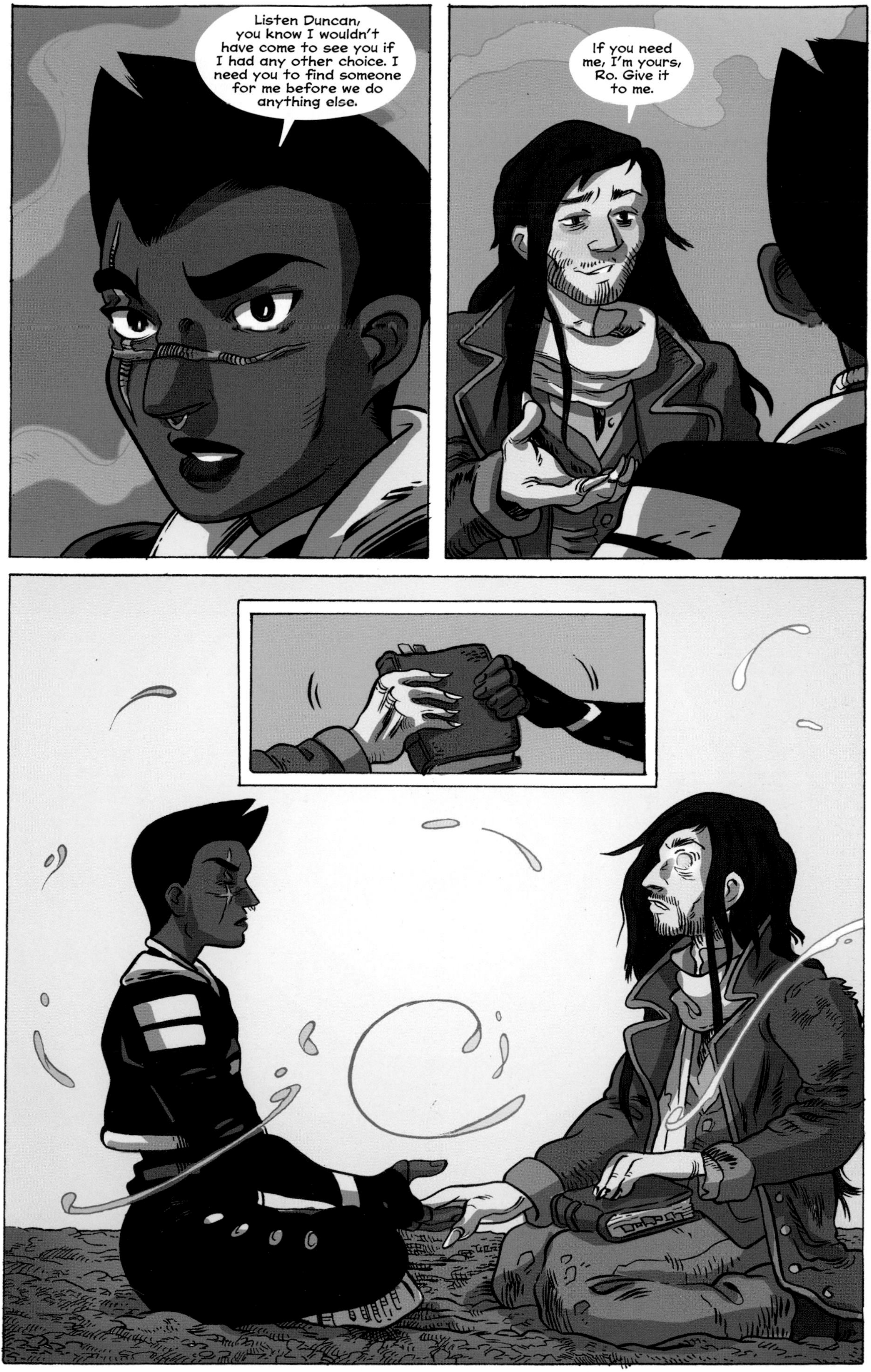
Listen Duncan, you know I wouldn't have come to see you if I had any other choice. I need you to find someone for me before we do anything else.
If you need me, I'm yours, Ro. Give it to me.

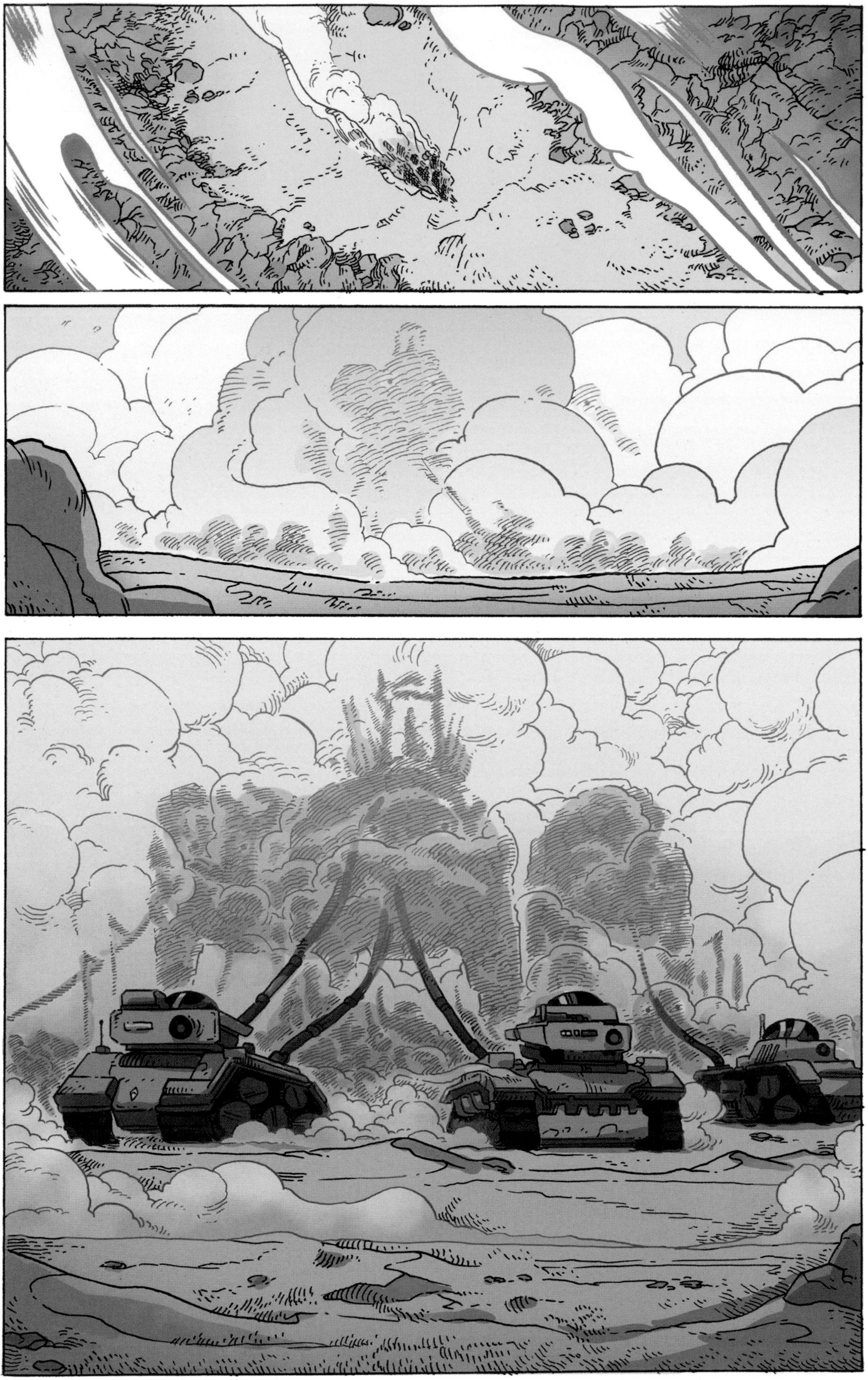

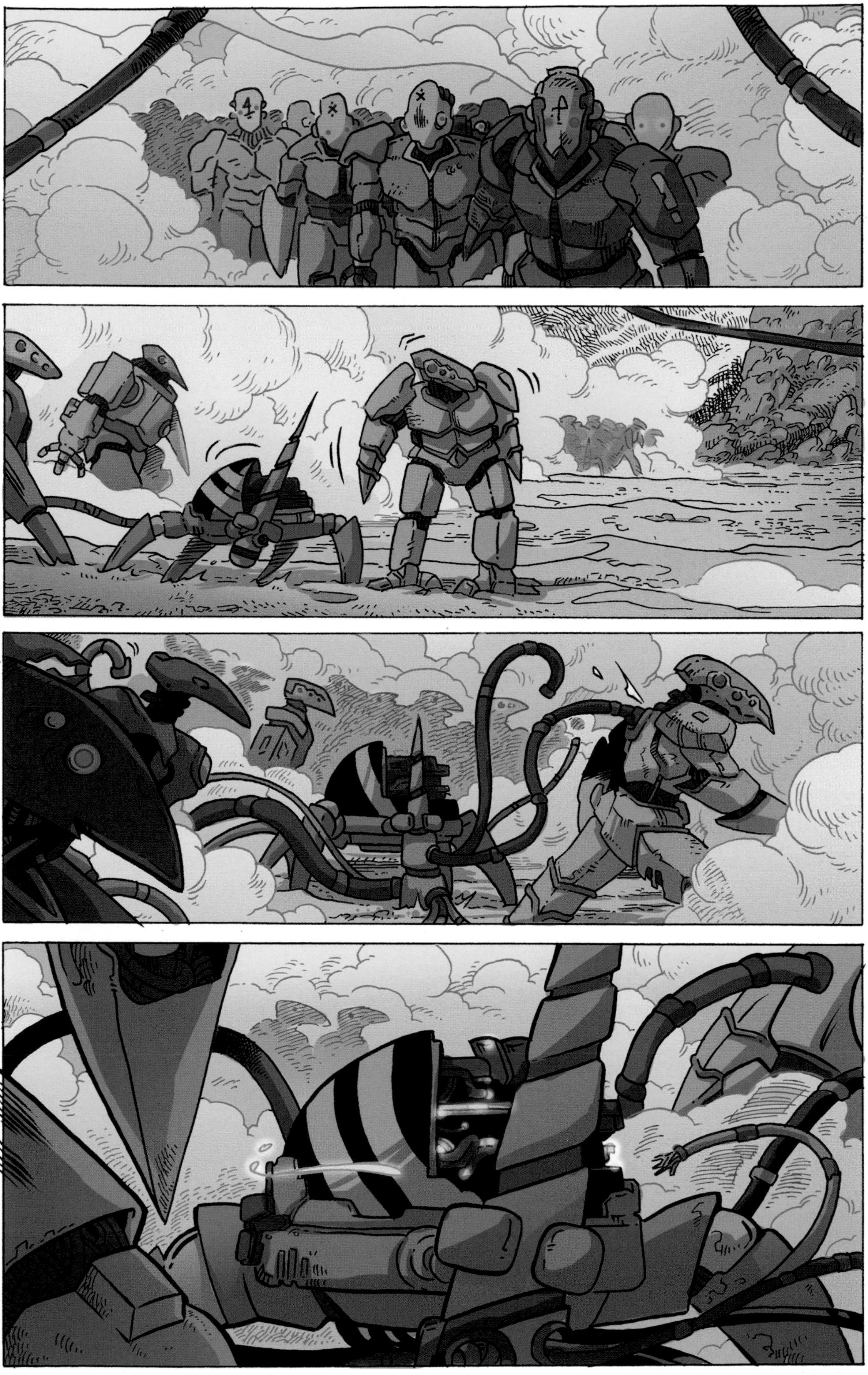

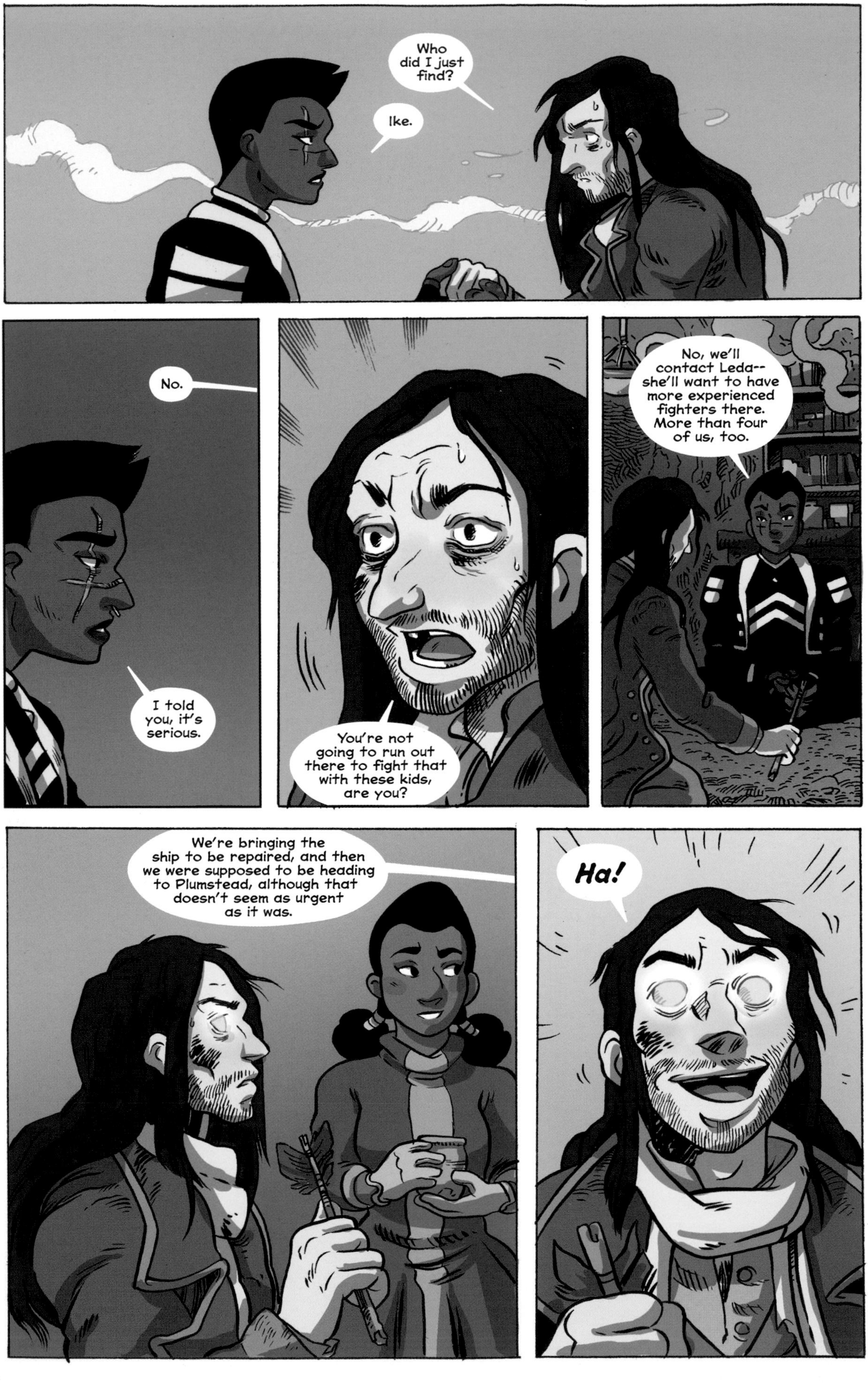
Who did I just find?
Ike.
No.
I told you, it's serious.
You're not going to run out there to fight that with these kids, are you?
No, we'll contact Leda-- she'll want to have more experienced fighters there. More than four of us, too.
We're bringing the ship to be repaired, and then we were supposed to be heading to Plumstead, although that doesn't seem as urgent as it was.
Ha!

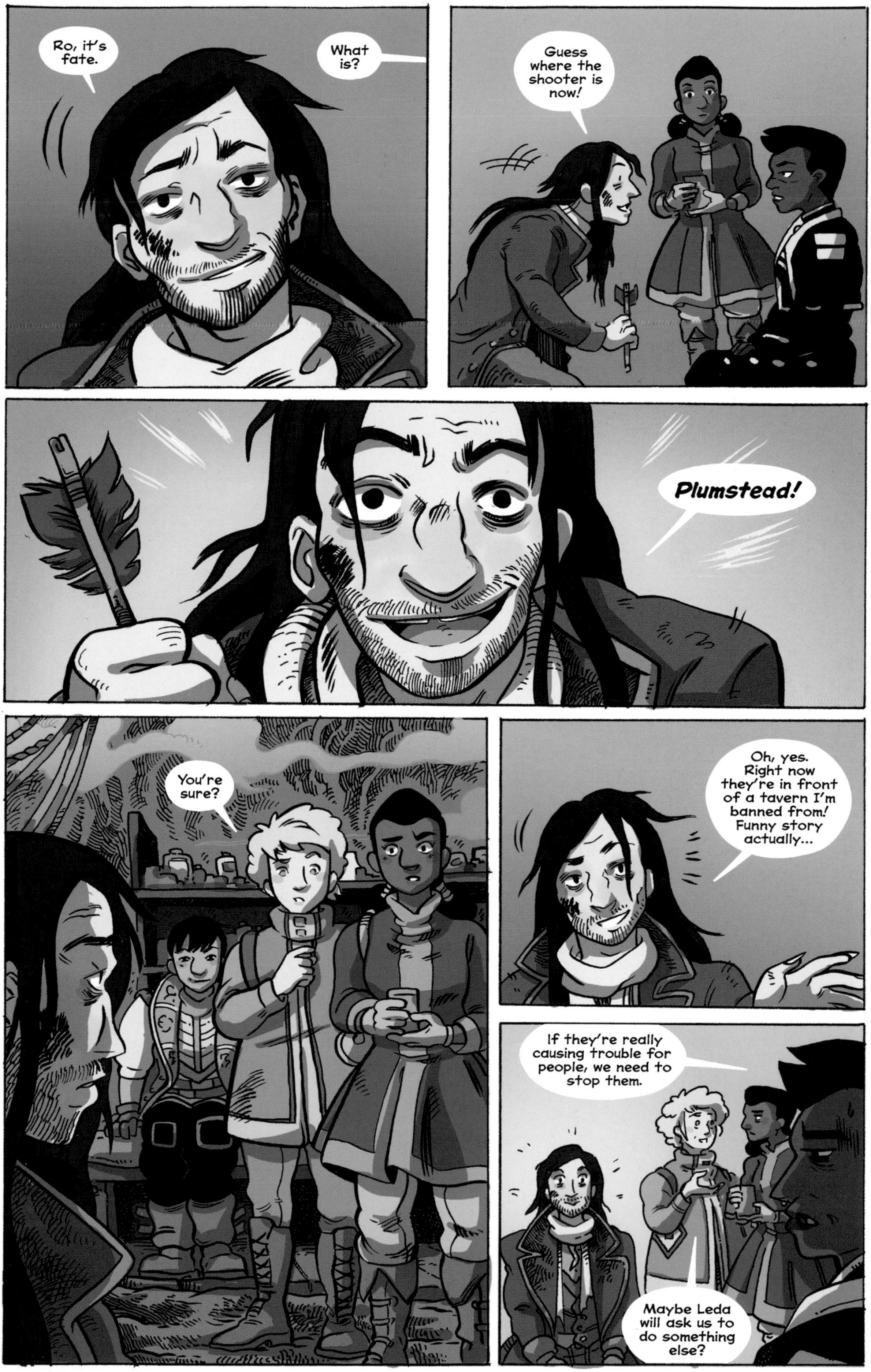
Ro, it's fate.
What is?
Guess where the shooter is now!
Plumstead!
You're sure?
Oh, yes. Right now they're in front of a tavern I'm banned from! Funny story actually...
If they're really causing trouble for people, we need to stop them.
Maybe Leda will ask us to do something else?

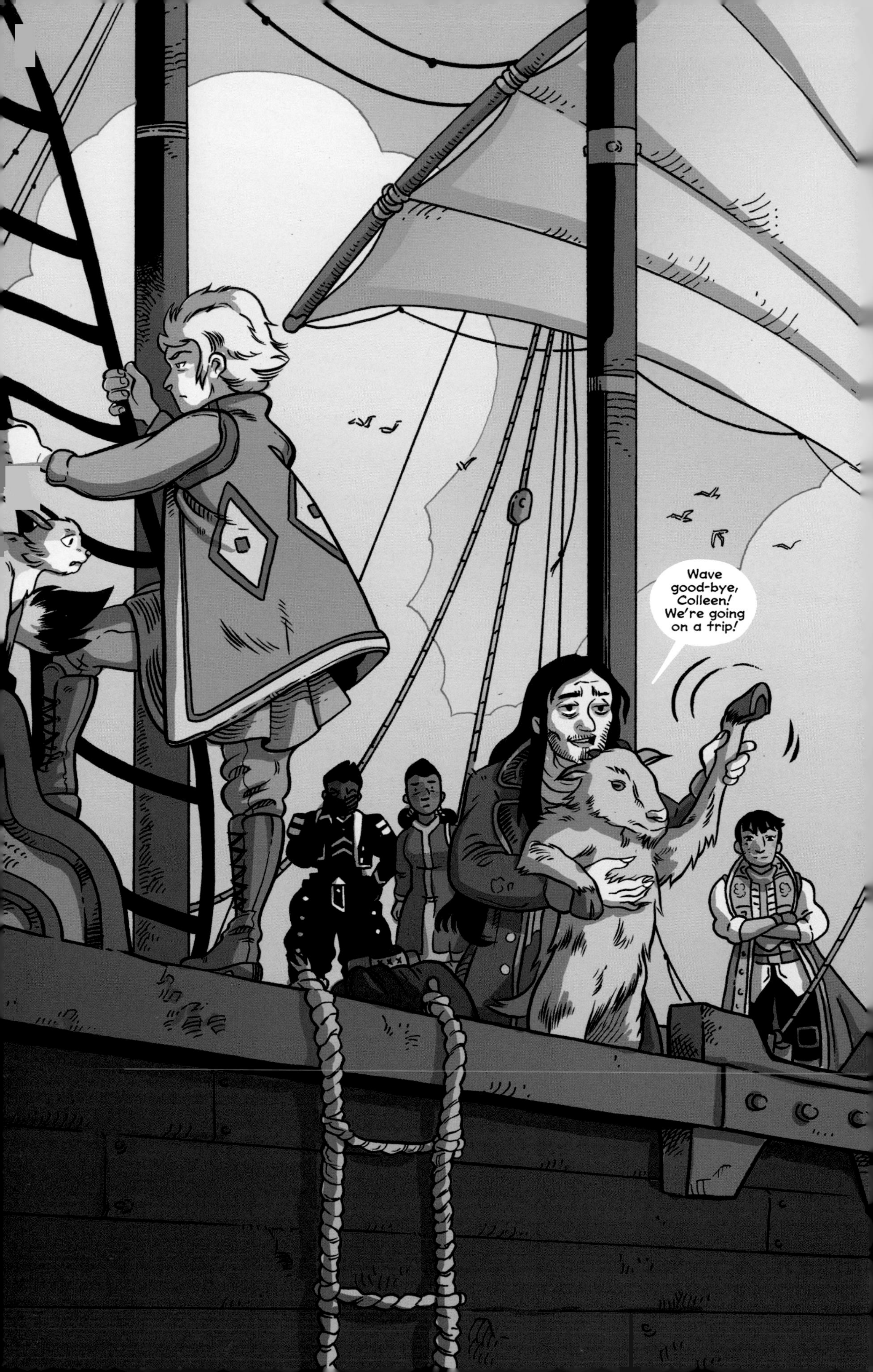
Wave good-bye, Colleen! We're going on a trip!

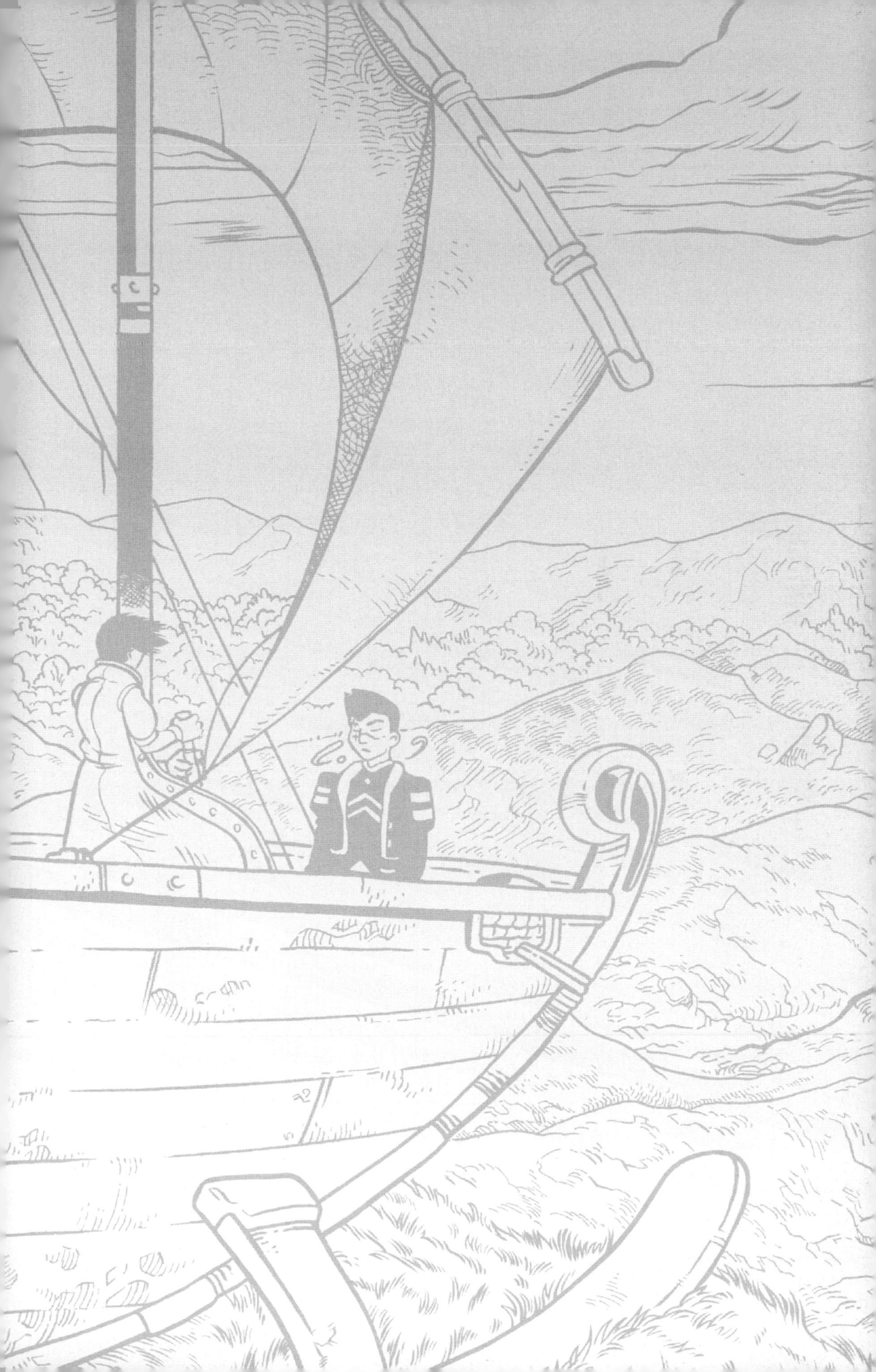

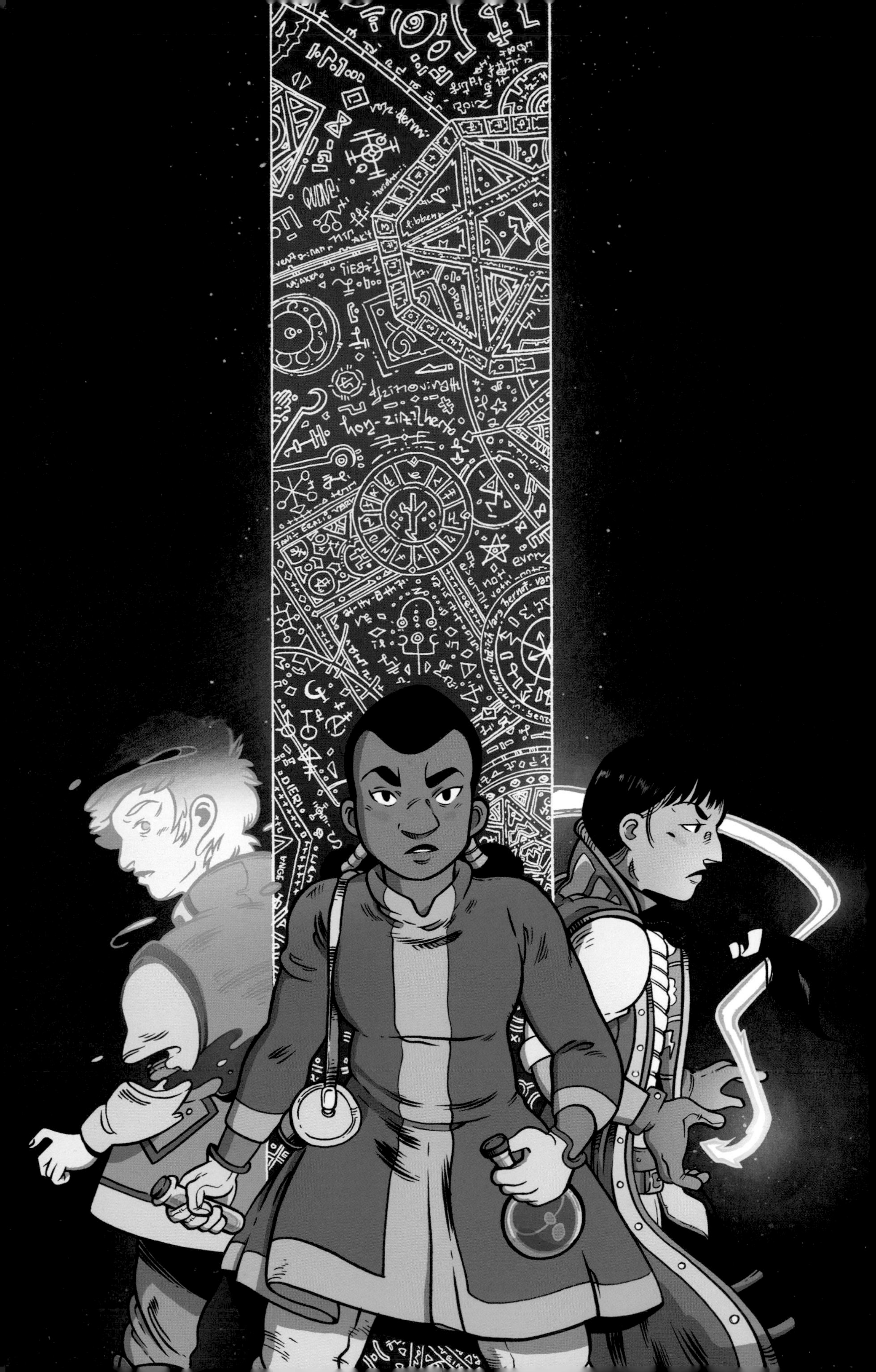

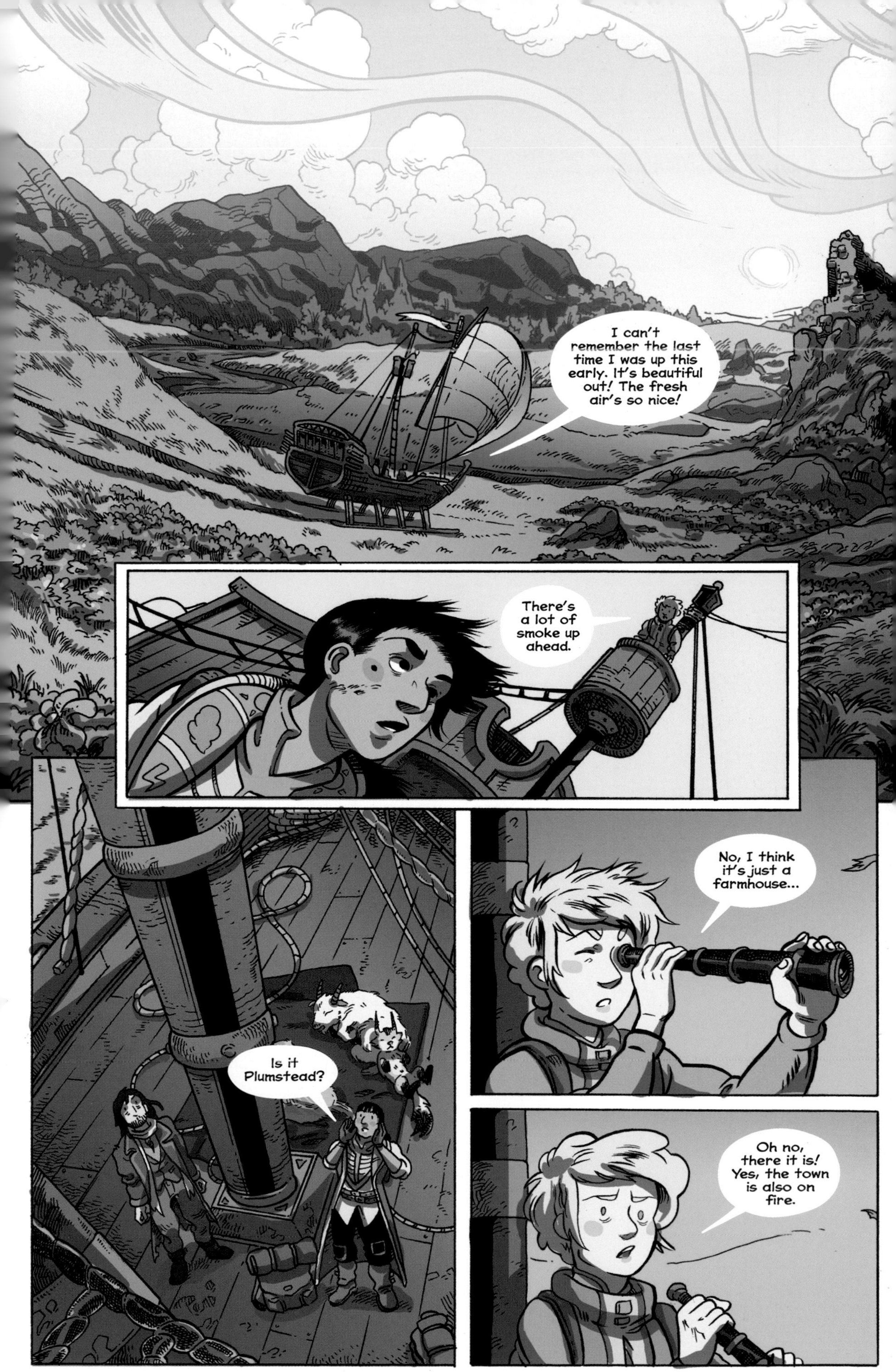
I can't remember the last time I was up this early. It's beautiful out! The fresh air's so nice!
There's a lot of smoke up ahead.
Is it Plumstead?
No, I think it's just a farmhouse...
Oh no, there it is! Yes, the town is also on fire.

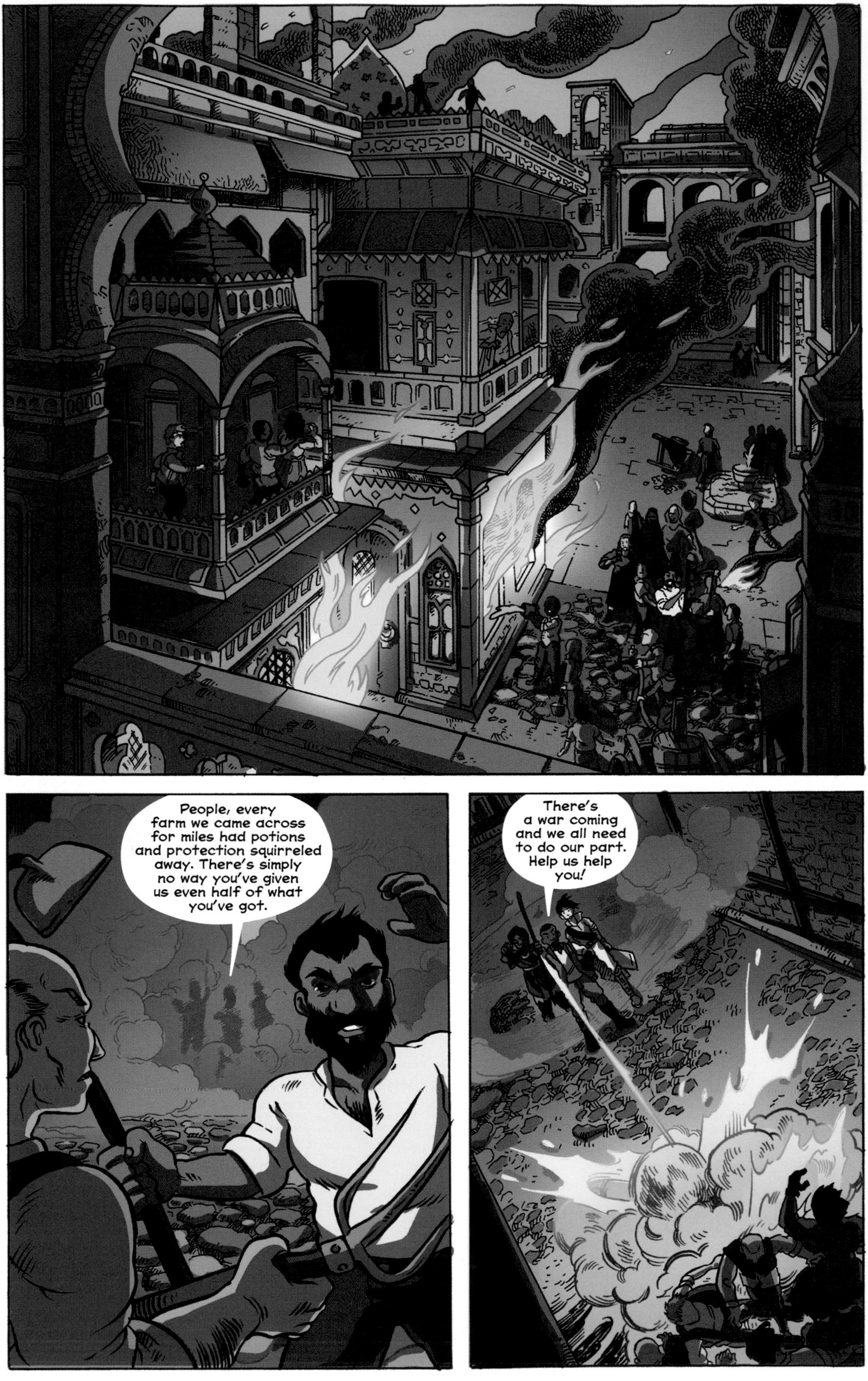
People, every farm we came across for miles had potions and protection squirreled away. There's simply no way you've given us even half of what you've got.
There's a war coming and we all need to do our part. Help us help you!

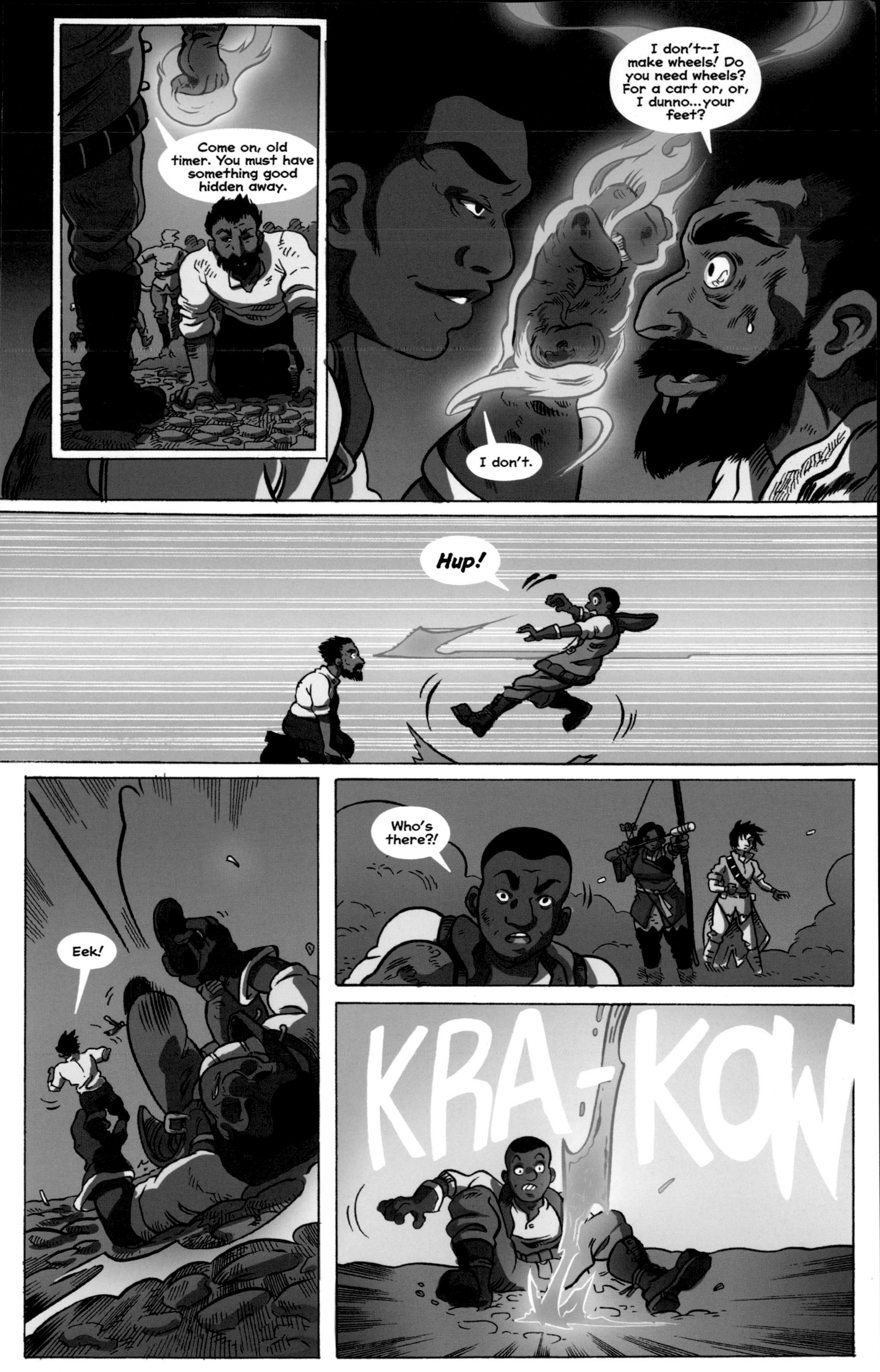
Come on, old timer. You must have something good hidden away.
I don't--I make wheels! Do you need wheels? For a cart or, or, I dunno...your feet?
I don't.
Hup!
Eek!
Who's there?!
KRA-KOW

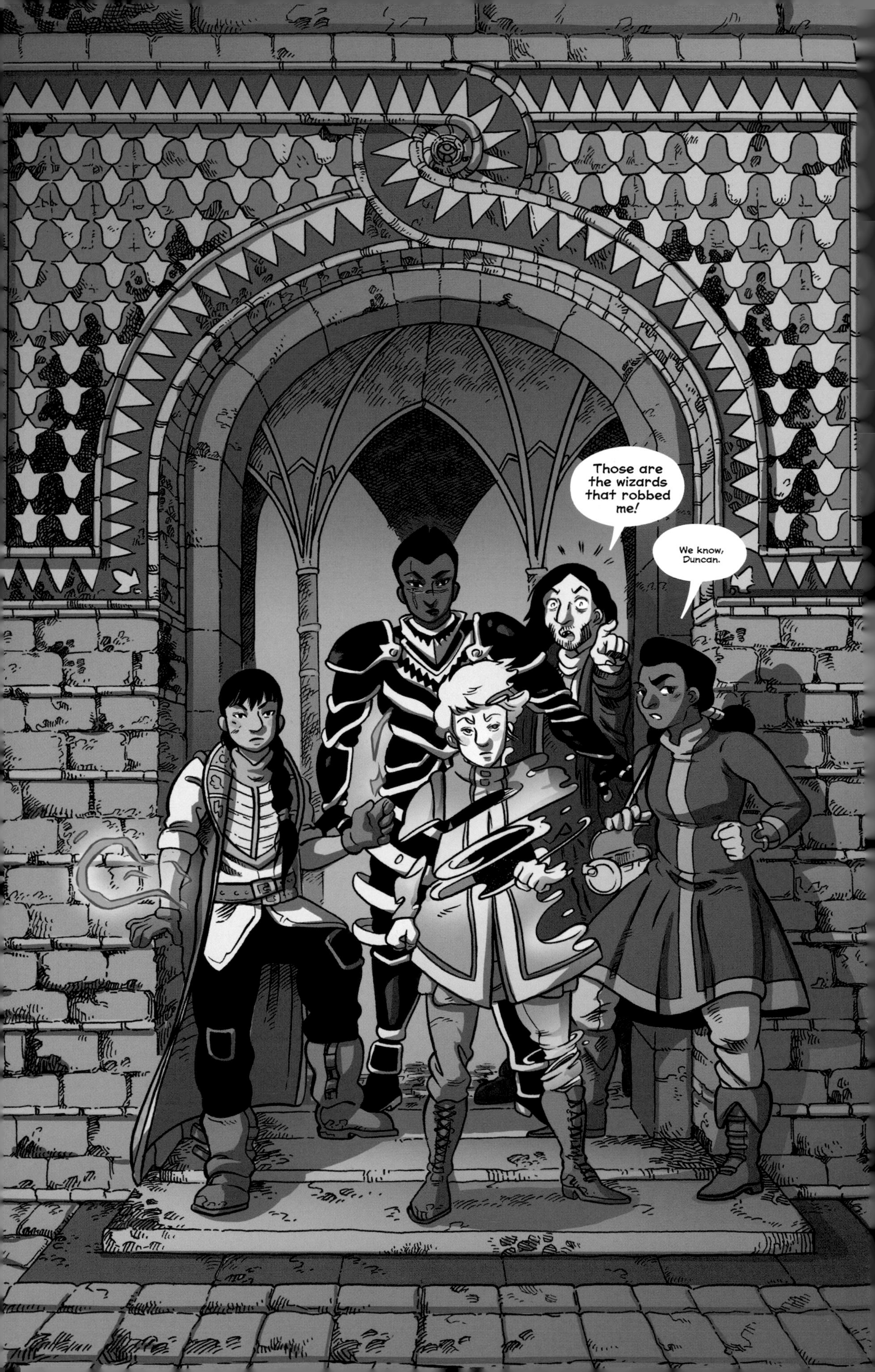
Those are the wizards that robbed me!
We know, Duncan.

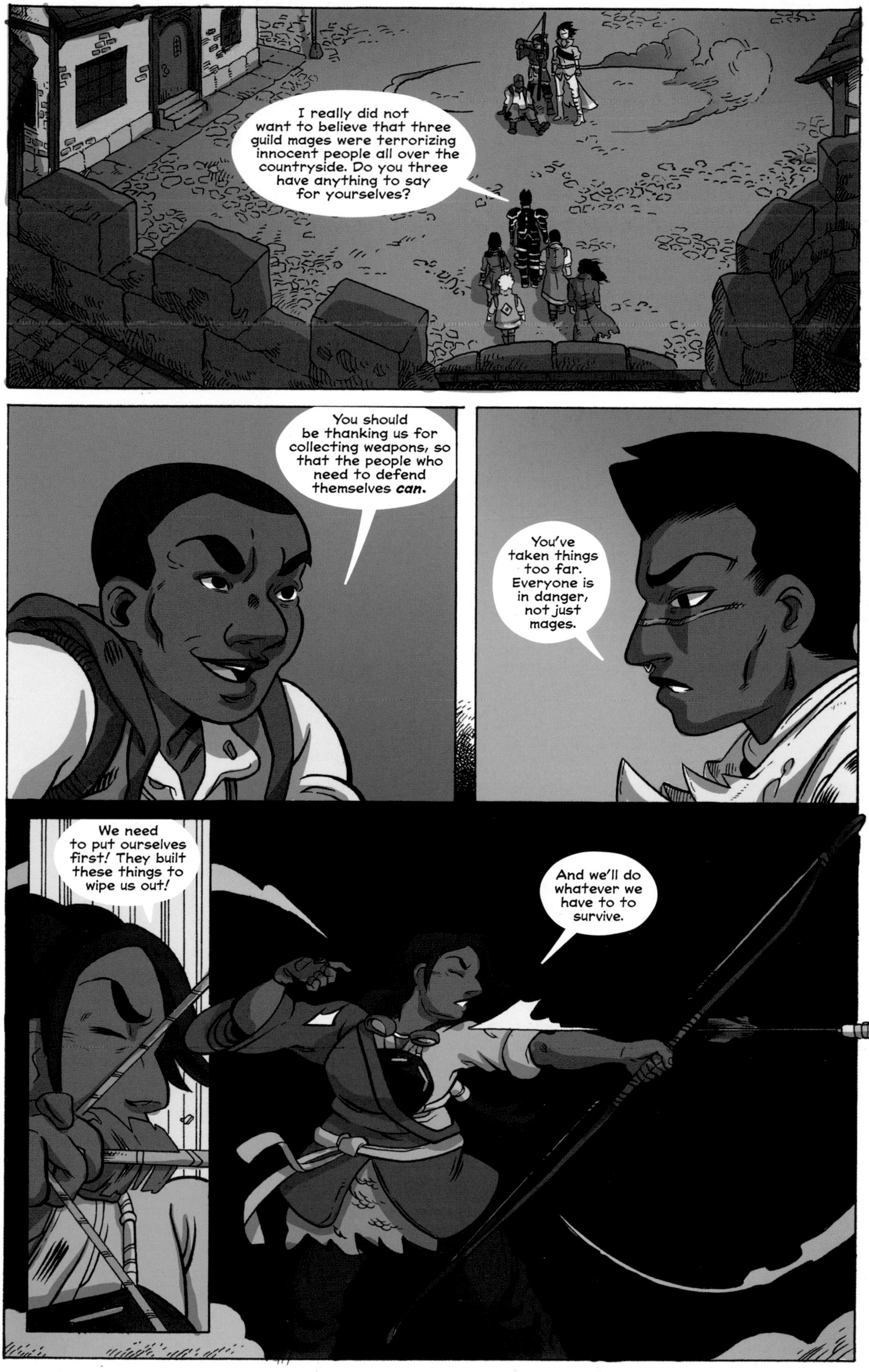
I really did not want to believe that three guild mages were terrorizing innocent people all over the countryside. Do you three have anything to say for yourselves?
You should be thanking us for collecting weapons, so that the people who need to defend themselves *can.*
You've taken things too far. Everyone is in danger, not just mages.
We need to put ourselves first! They built these things to wipe us out!
And we'll do whatever we have to to survive.

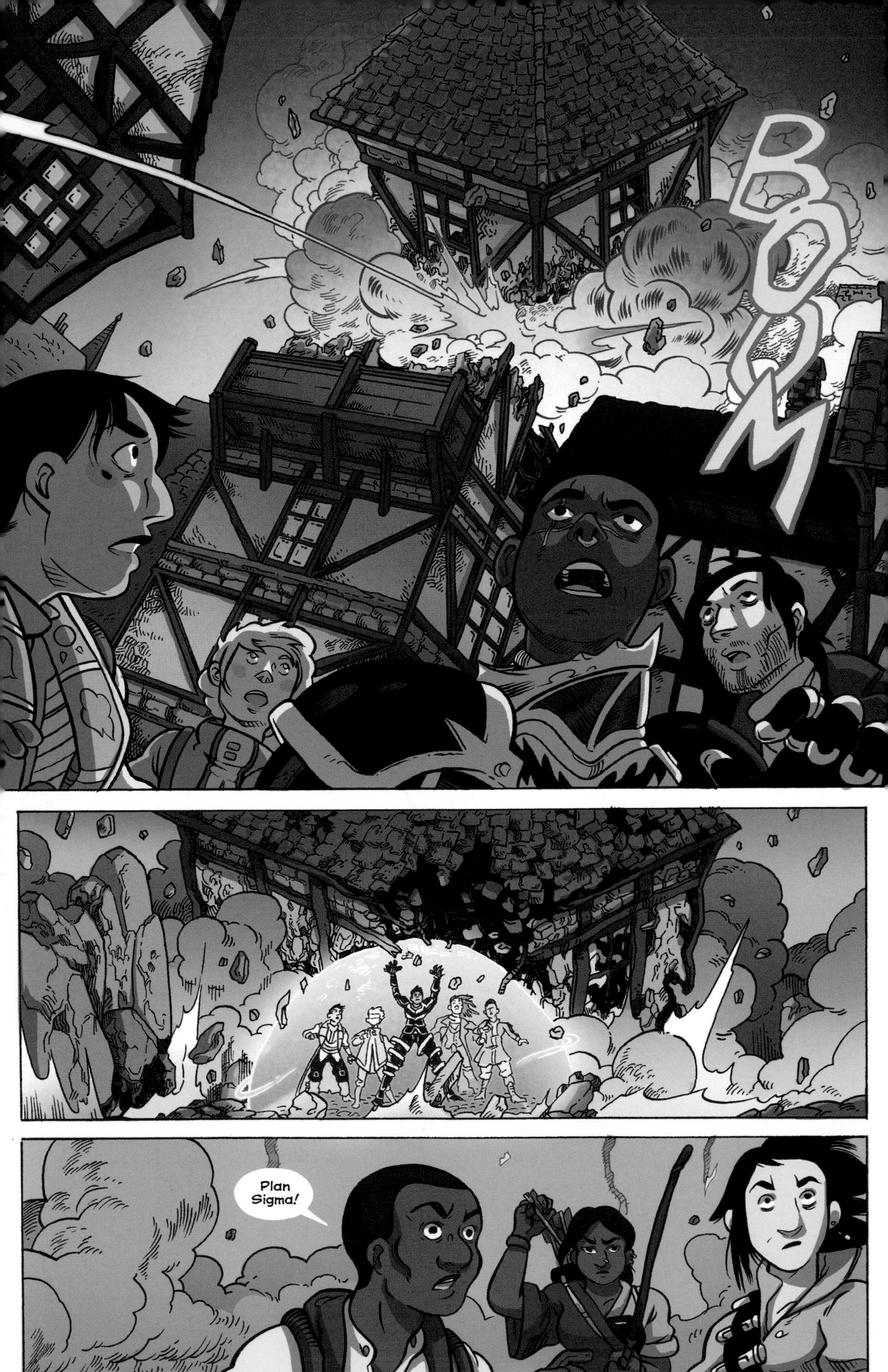
BOOM
Plan Sigma!

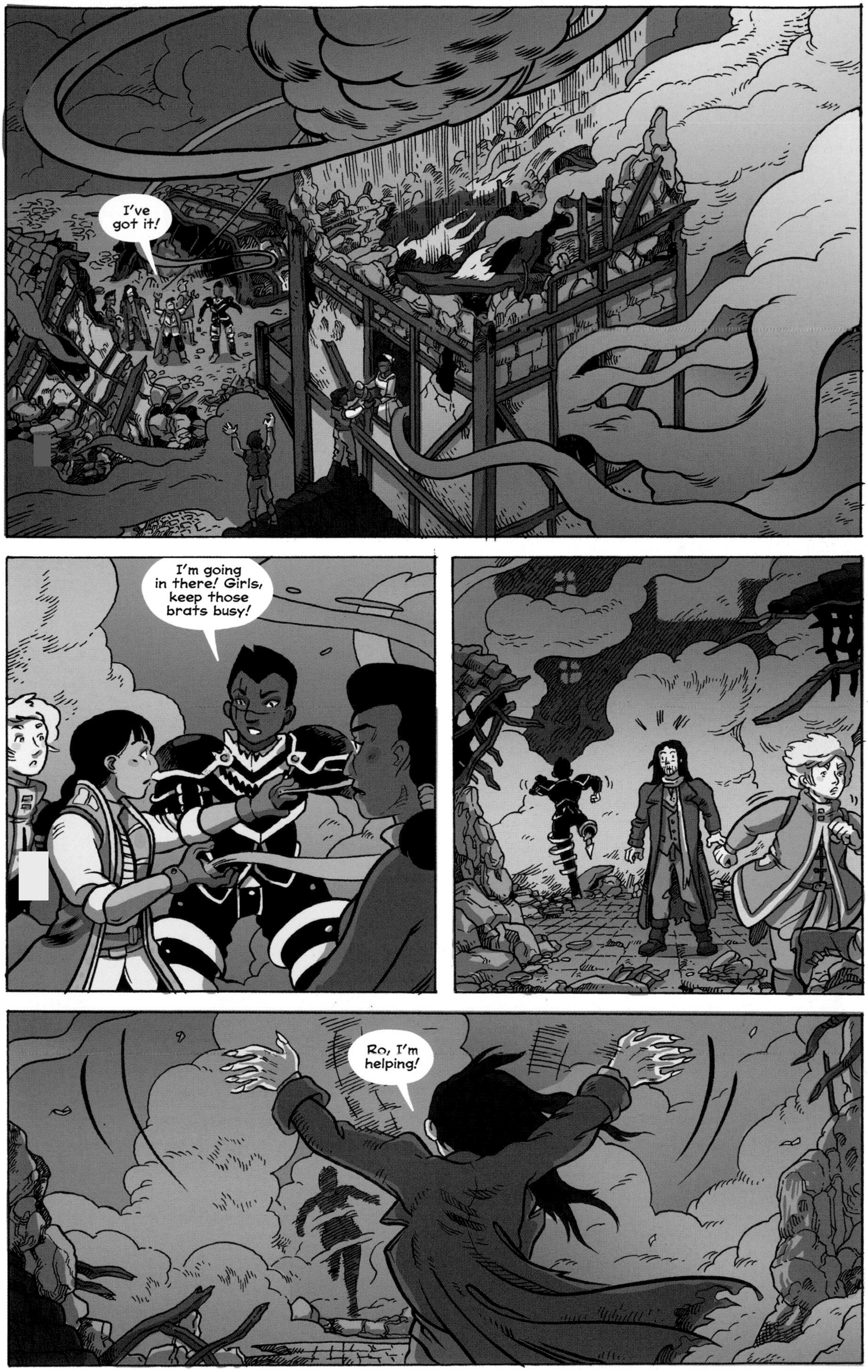
I've got it!
I'm going in there! Girls, keep those brats busy!
Ro, I'm helping!

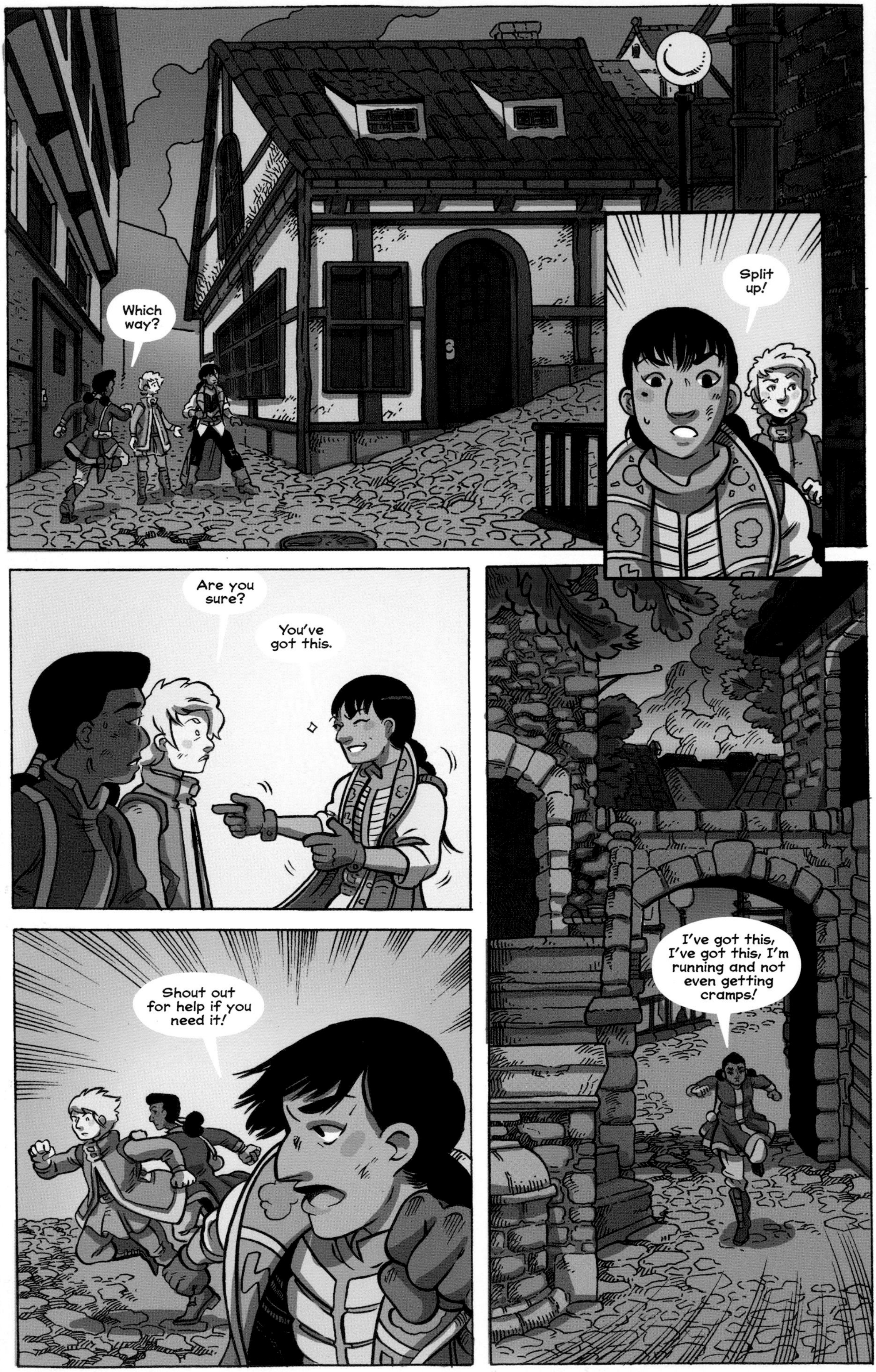
Which way?
Split up!
Are you sure?
You've got this.
Shout out for help if you need it!
I've got this, I've got this, I'm running and not even getting cramps!

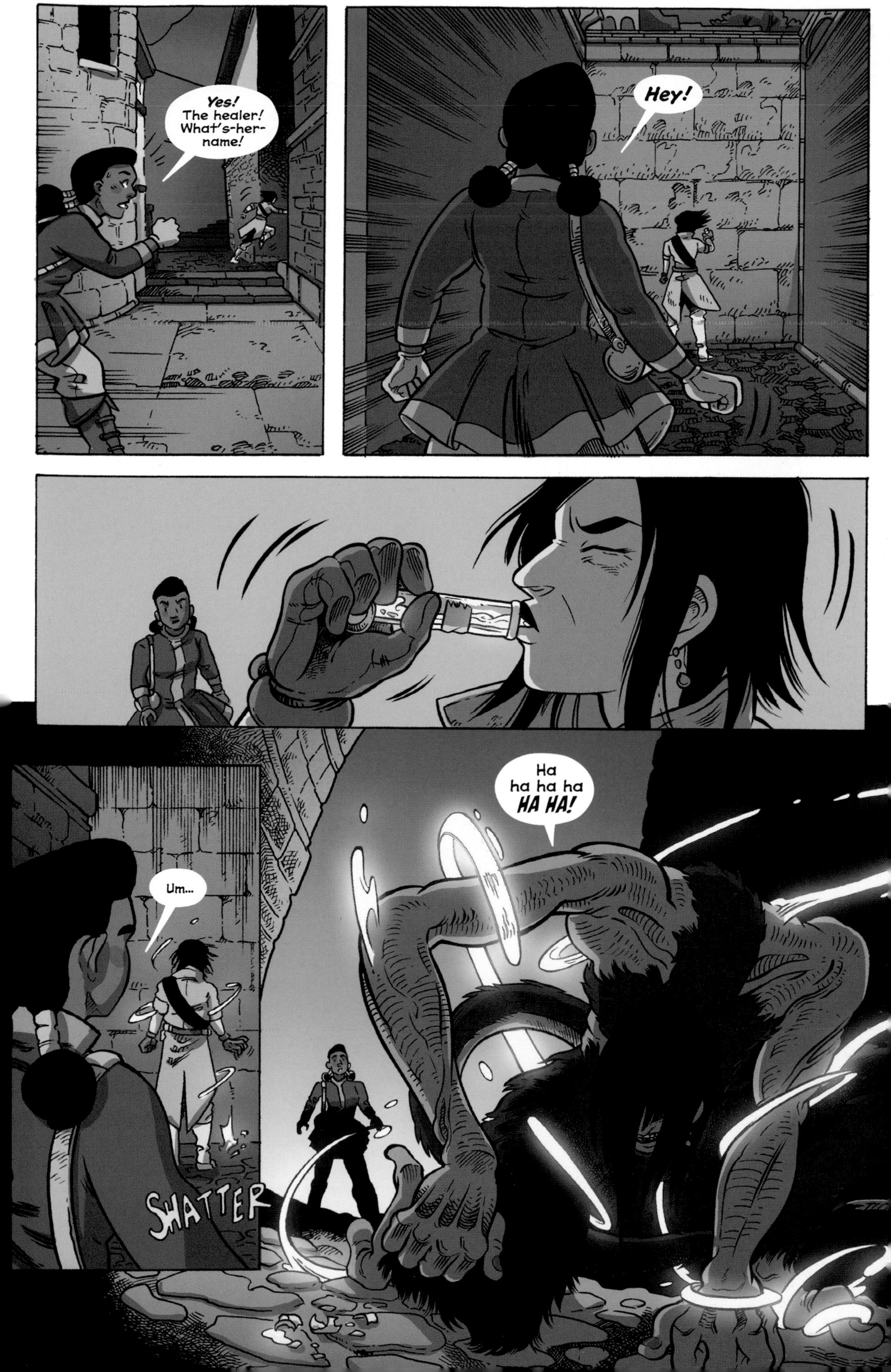
Yes! The healer! What's-her-name!
Hey!
Um...
SHATTER
Ha ha ha ha HA HA!

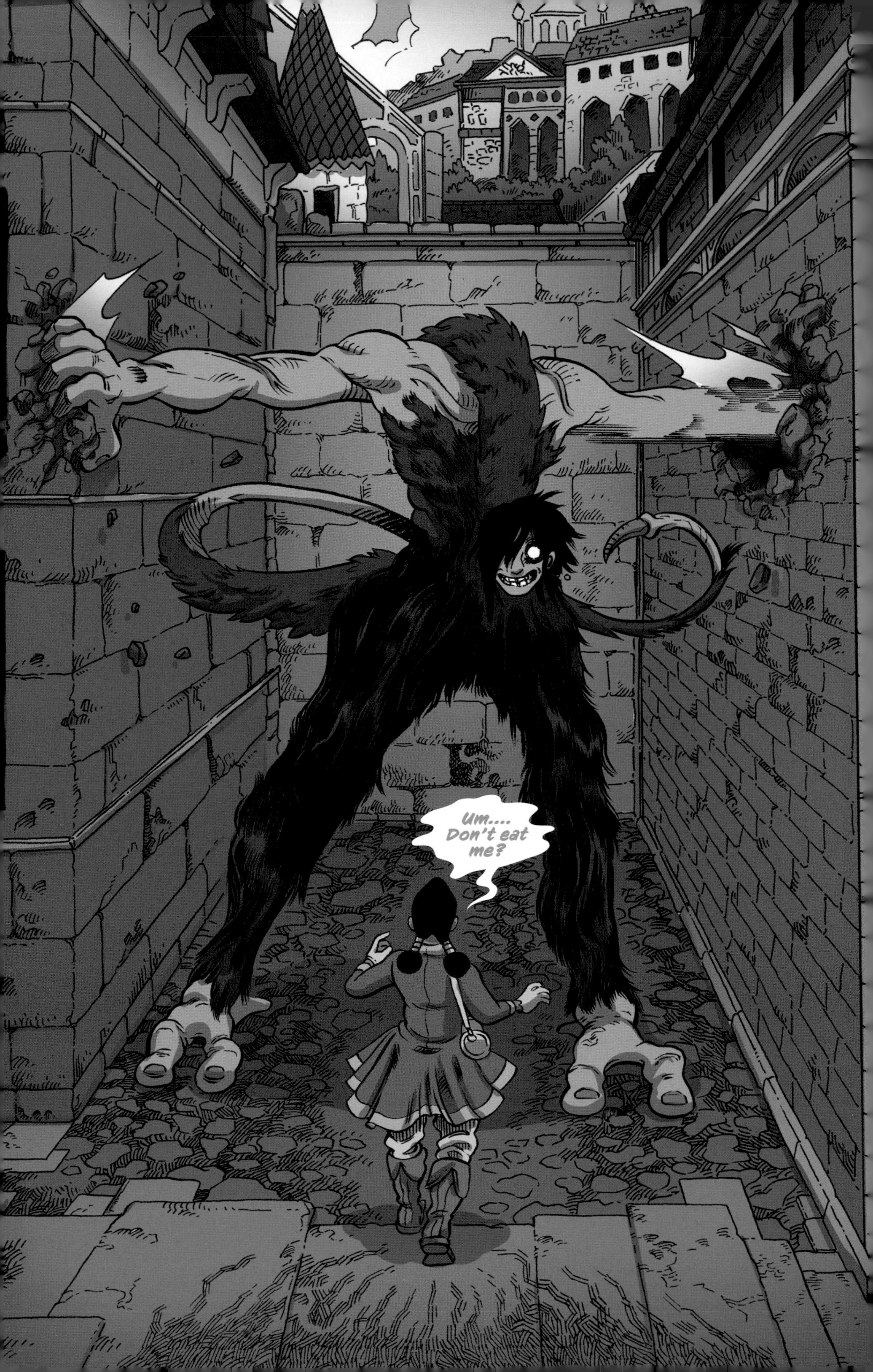
Um.... Don't eat me?

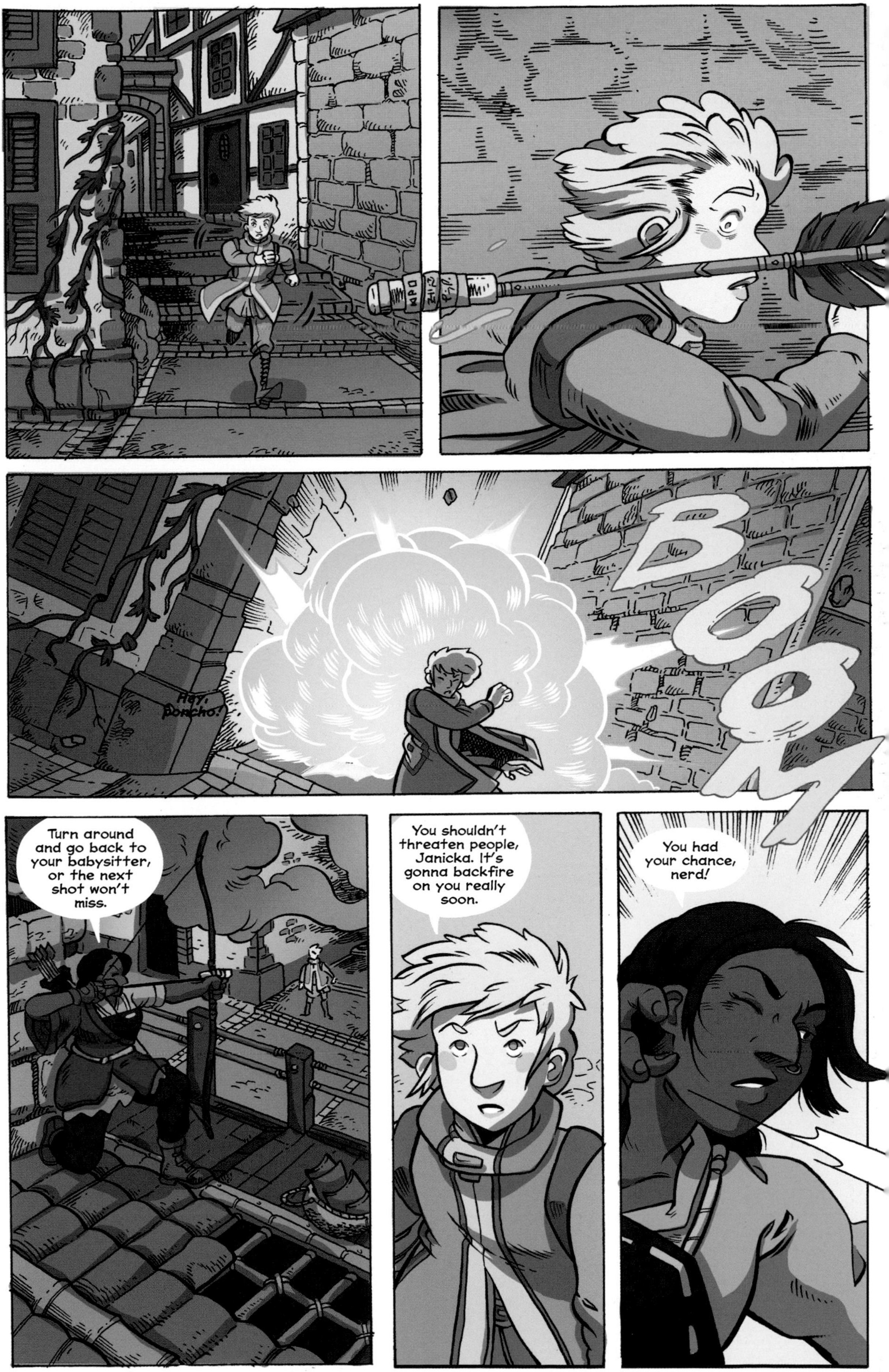
BOOM
Hey, Poncho!
Turn around and go back to your babysitter, or the next shot won't miss.
You shouldn't threaten people, Janicka. It's gonna backfire on you really soon.
You had your chance, nerd!

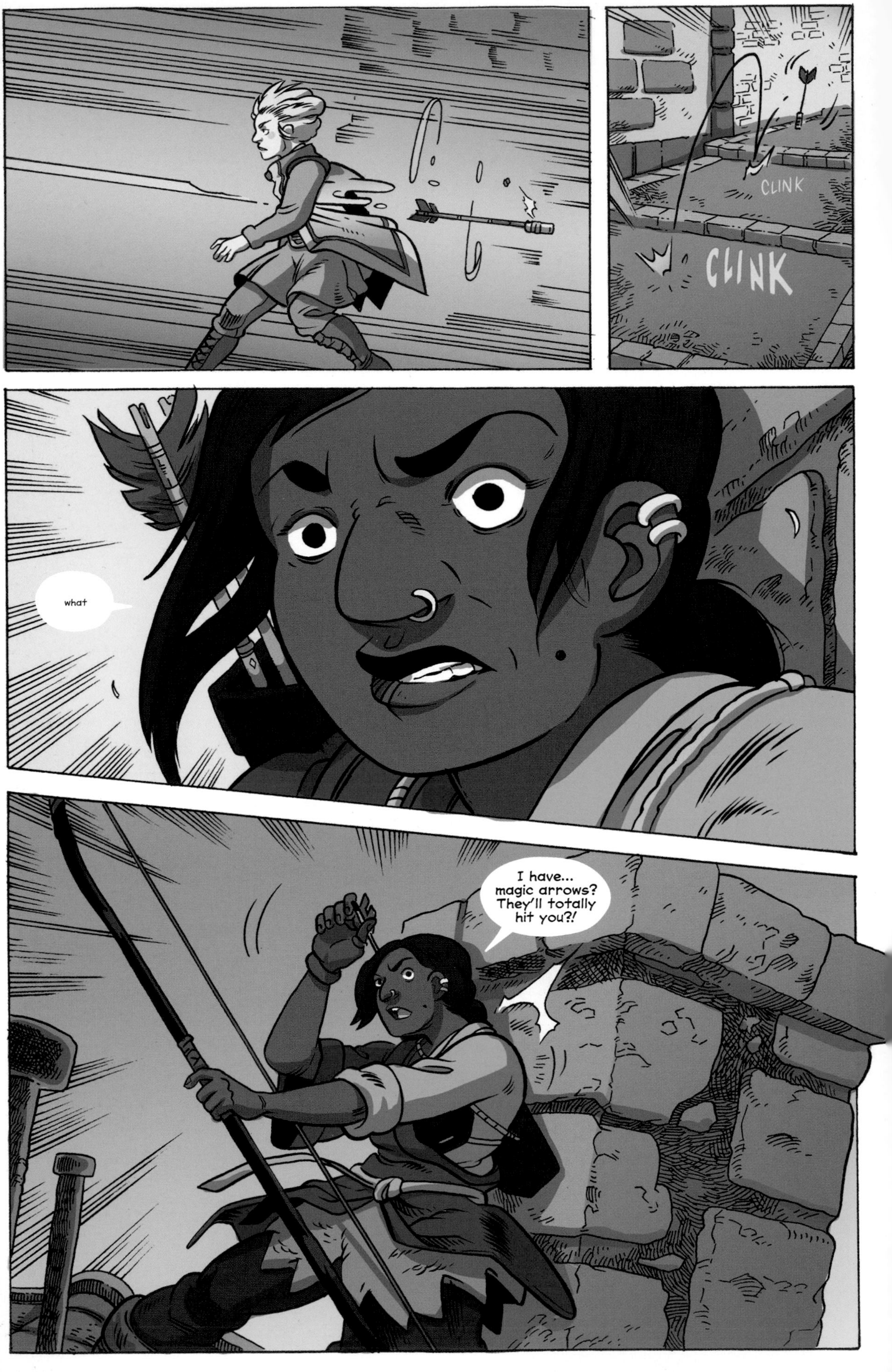

CLINK
CLINK
what
I have... magic arrows? They'll totally hit you?!

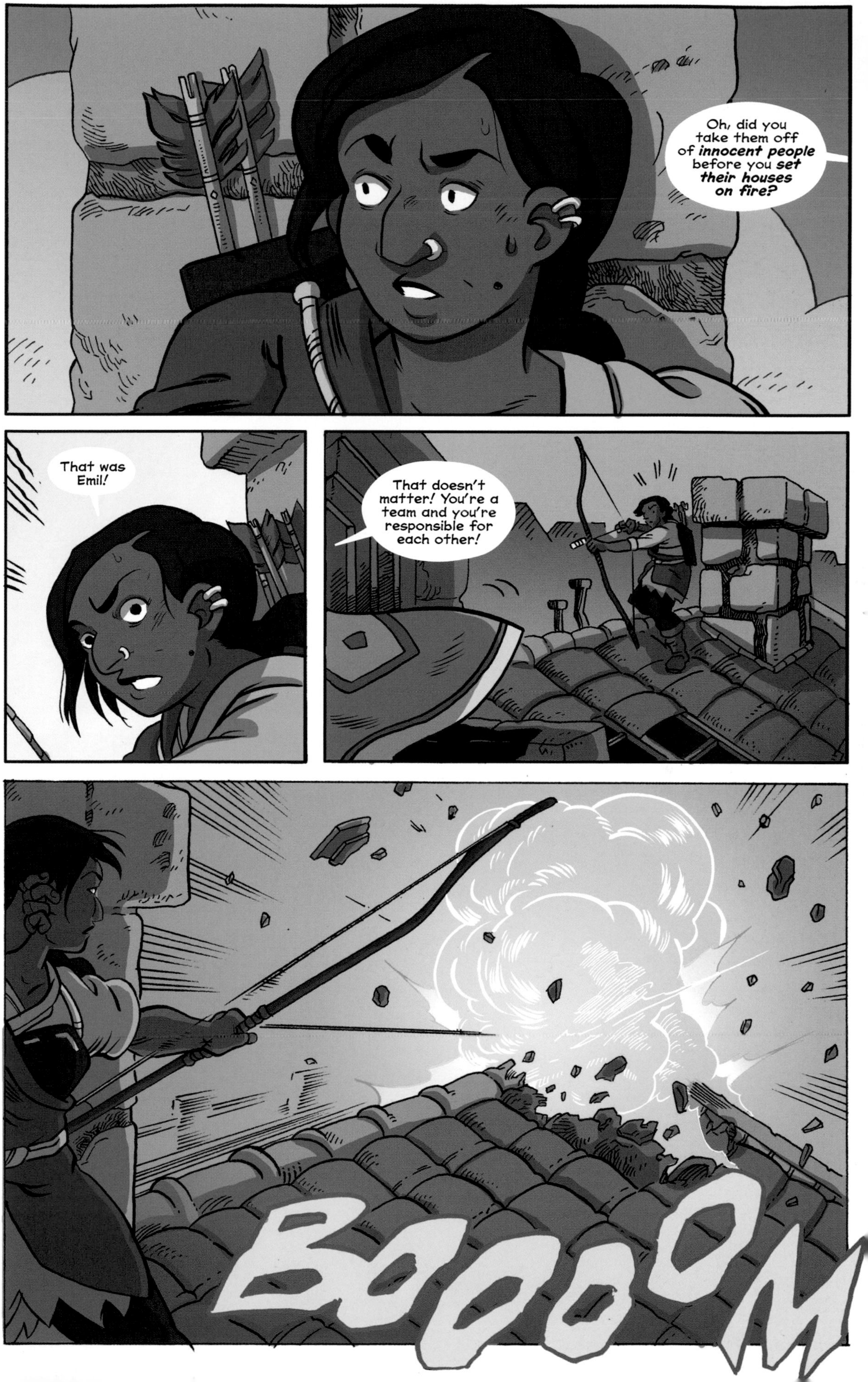
Oh, did you take them off of ***innocent people*** before you ***set their houses on fire?***
That was Emil!
That doesn't matter! You're a team and you're responsible for each other!
BOOOOOM

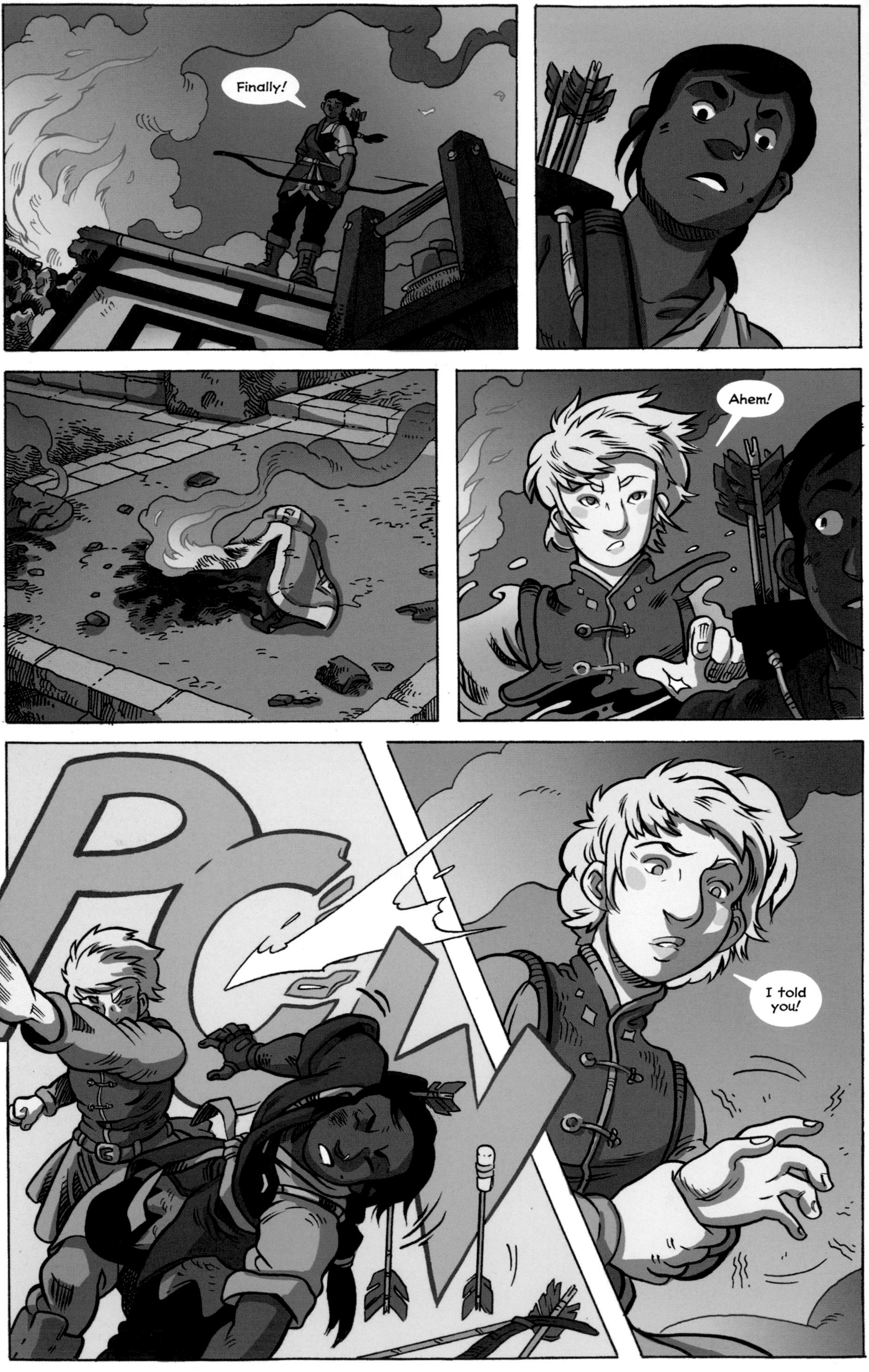
Finally!
Ahem!
I told you!

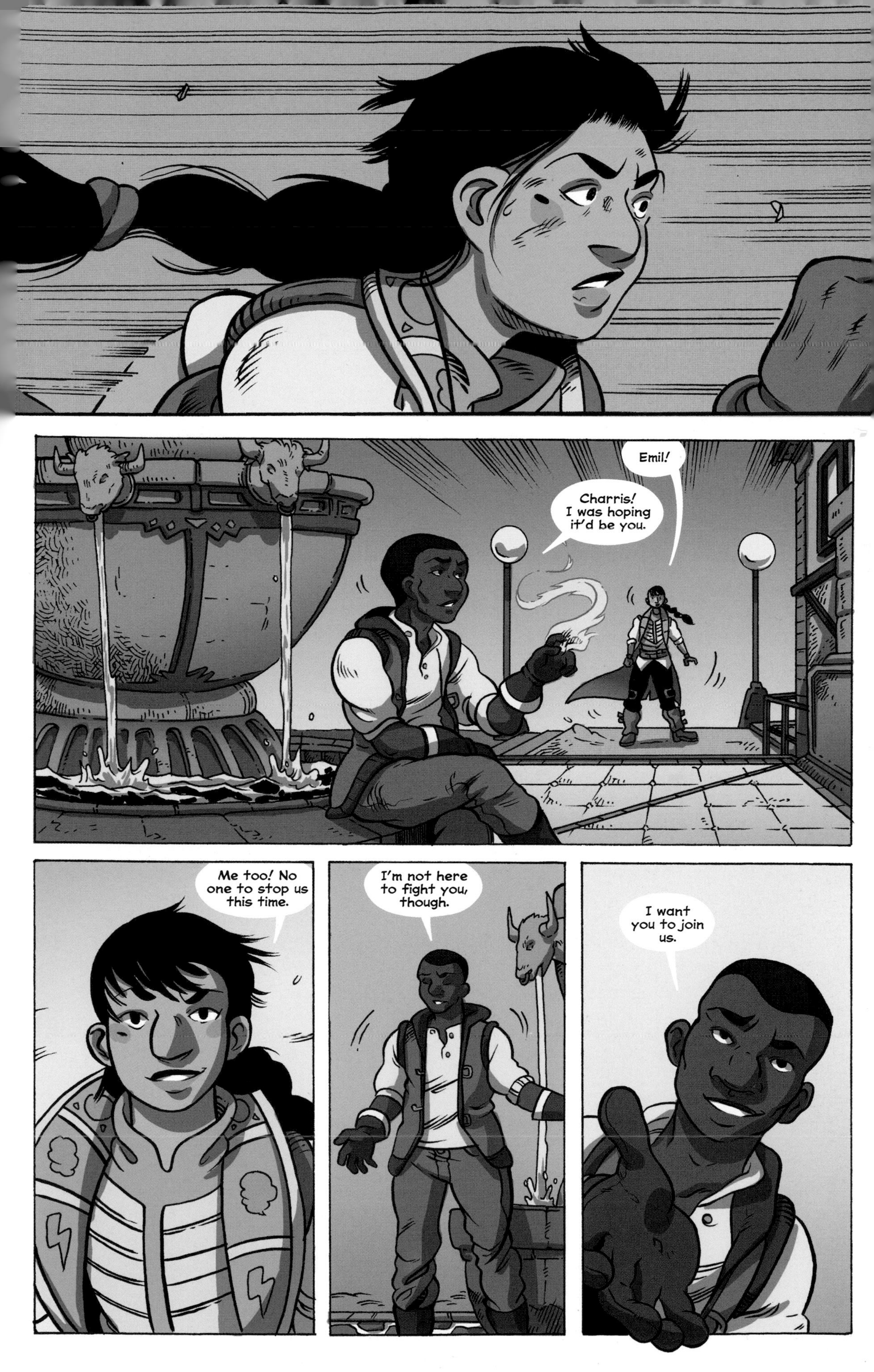
Emil!
Charris! I was hoping it'd be you.
Me too! No one to stop us this time.
I'm not here to fight you, though.
I want you to join us.

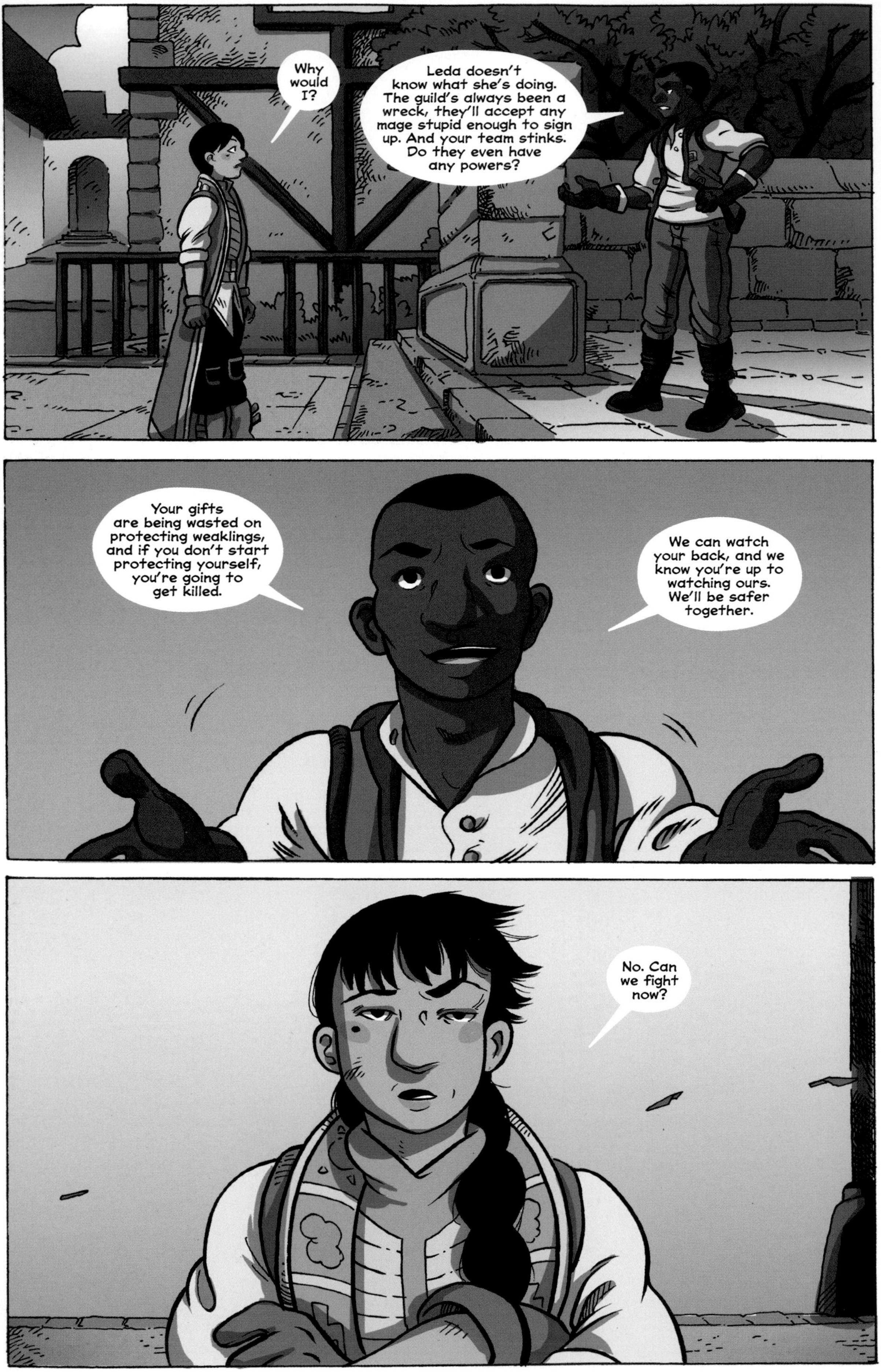
Why would I?
Leda doesn't know what she's doing. The guild's always been a wreck, they'll accept any mage stupid enough to sign up. And your team stinks. Do they even have any powers?
Your gifts are being wasted on protecting weaklings, and if you don't start protecting yourself, you're going to get killed.
We can watch your back, and we know you're up to watching ours. We'll be safer together.
No. Can we fight now?

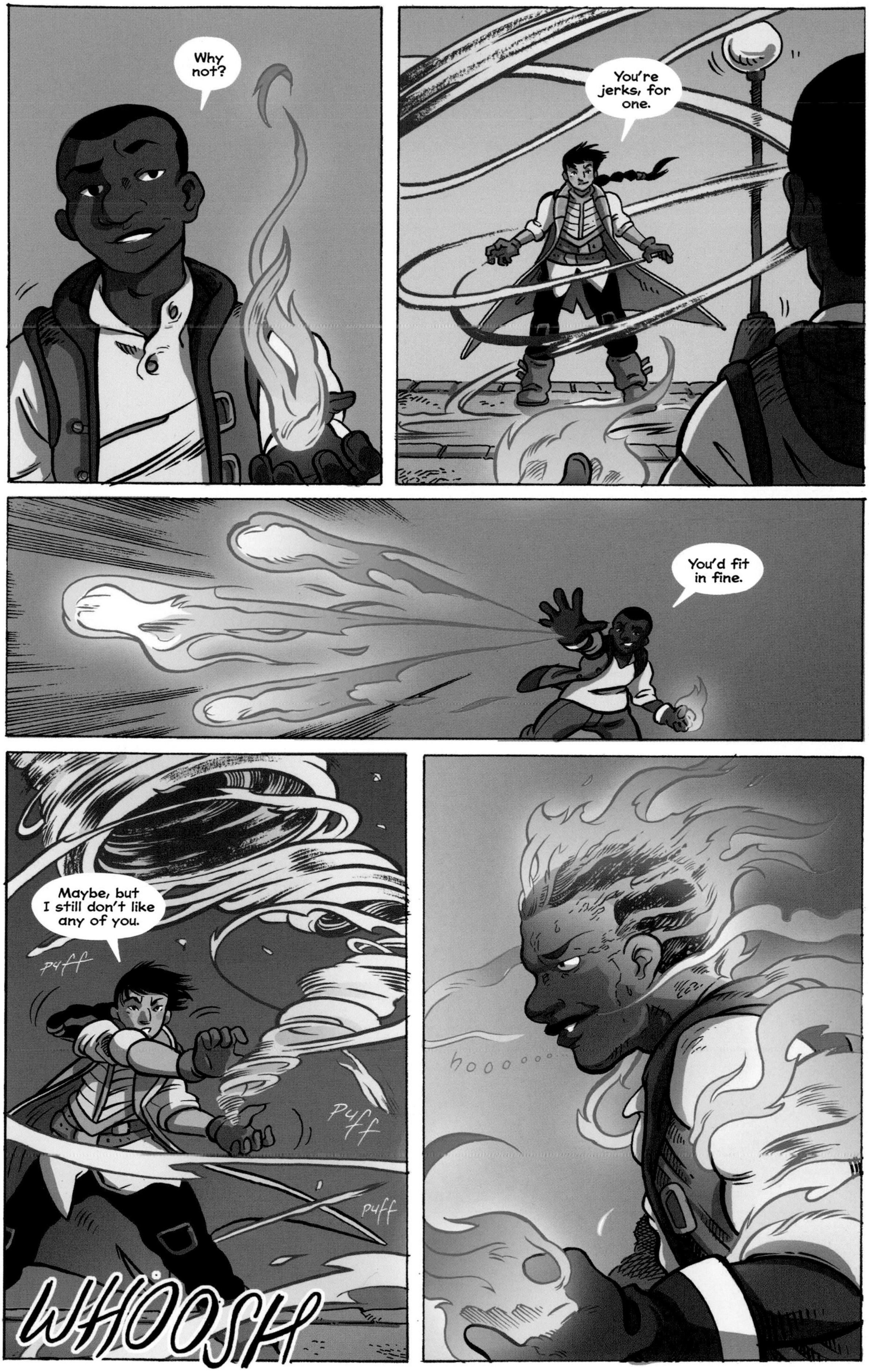
Why not?
You're jerks, for one.
You'd fit in fine.
Maybe, but I still don't like any of you.
puff
puff
puff
WHOOSH
hoooooo...

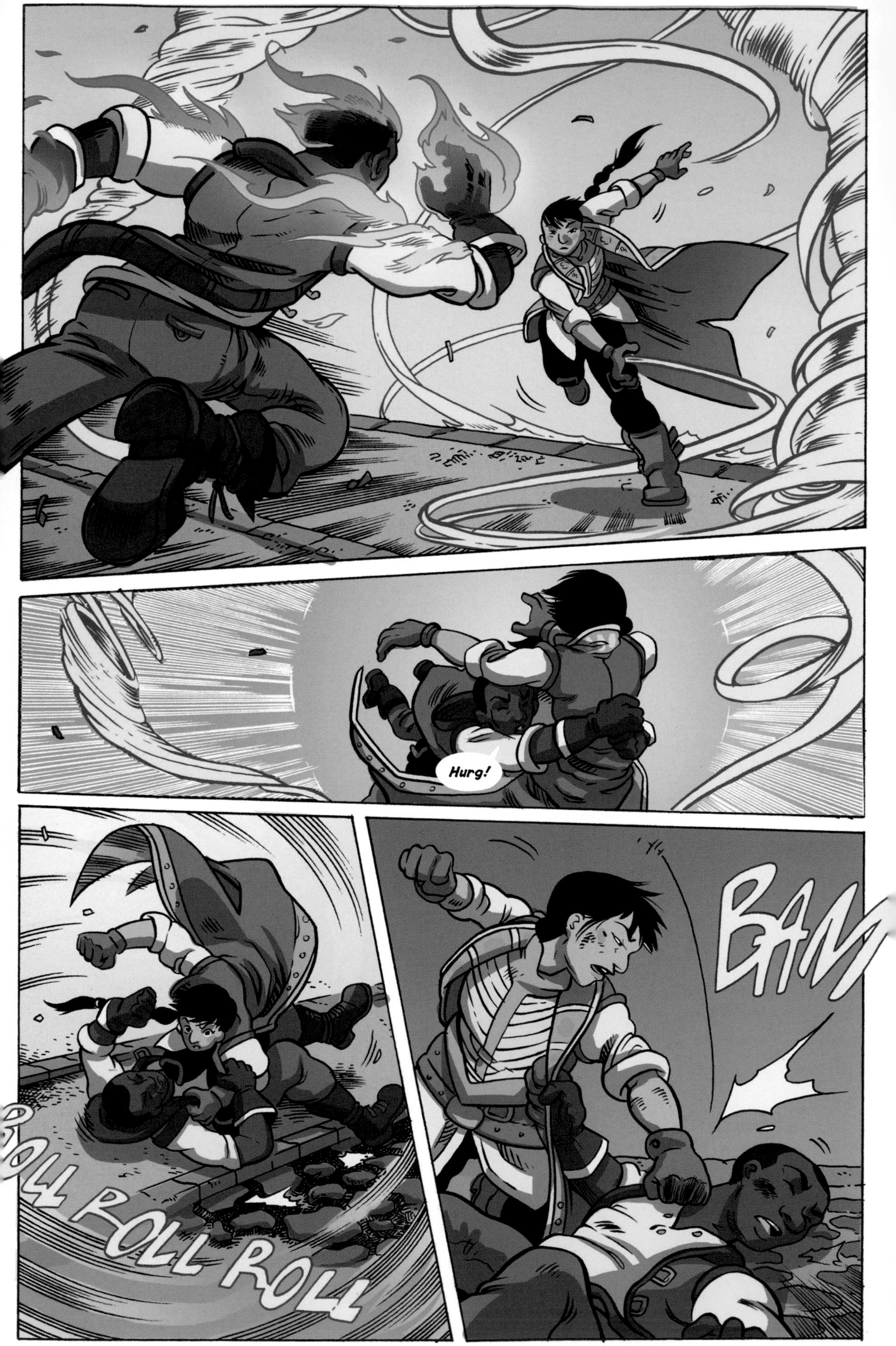
Hurg!
ROLL ROLL ROLL
BAM

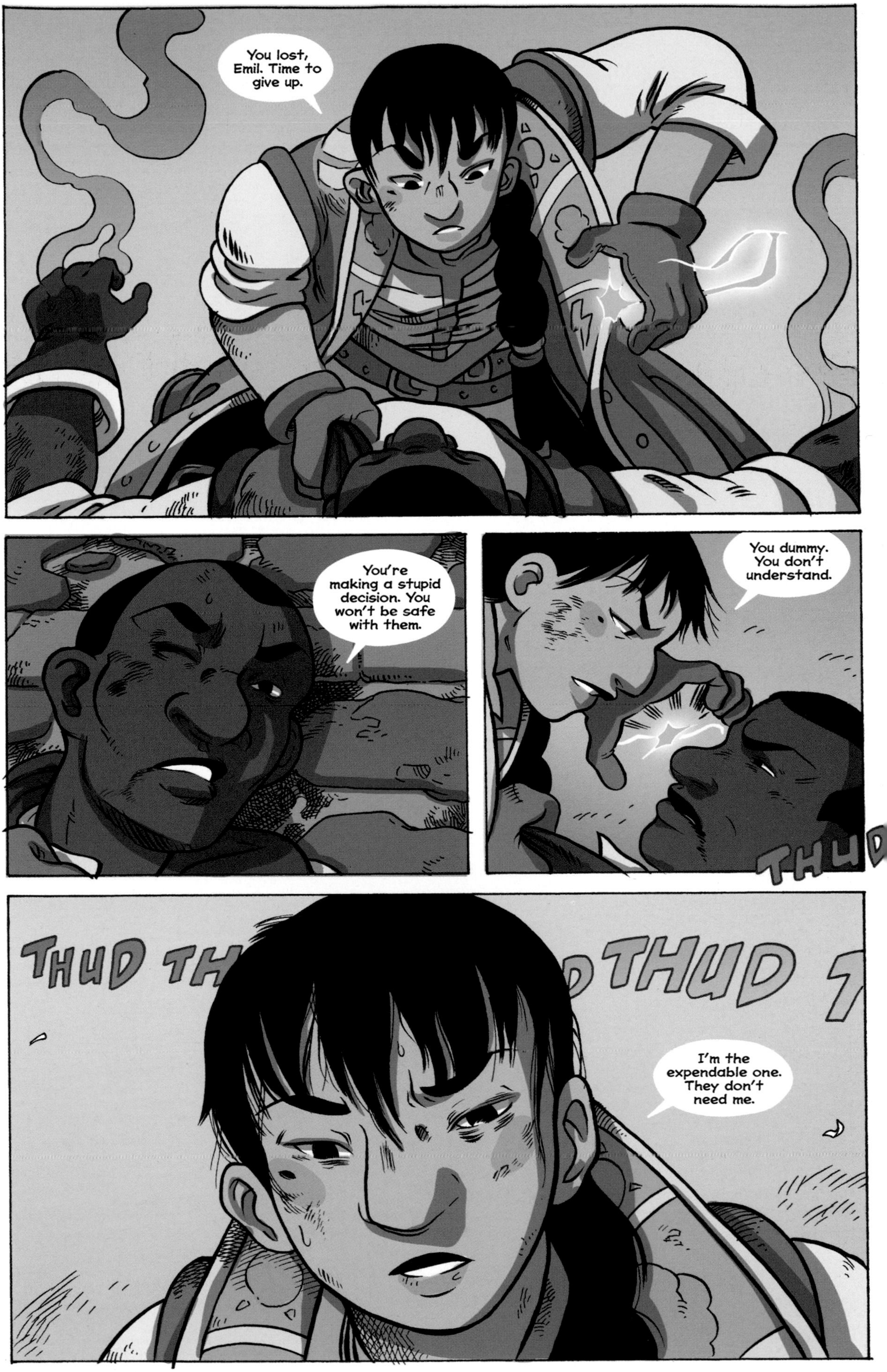
You lost, Emil. Time to give up.
You're making a stupid decision. You won't be safe with them.
You dummy. You don't understand.
THUD
THUD
THUD
I'm the expendable one. They don't need me.

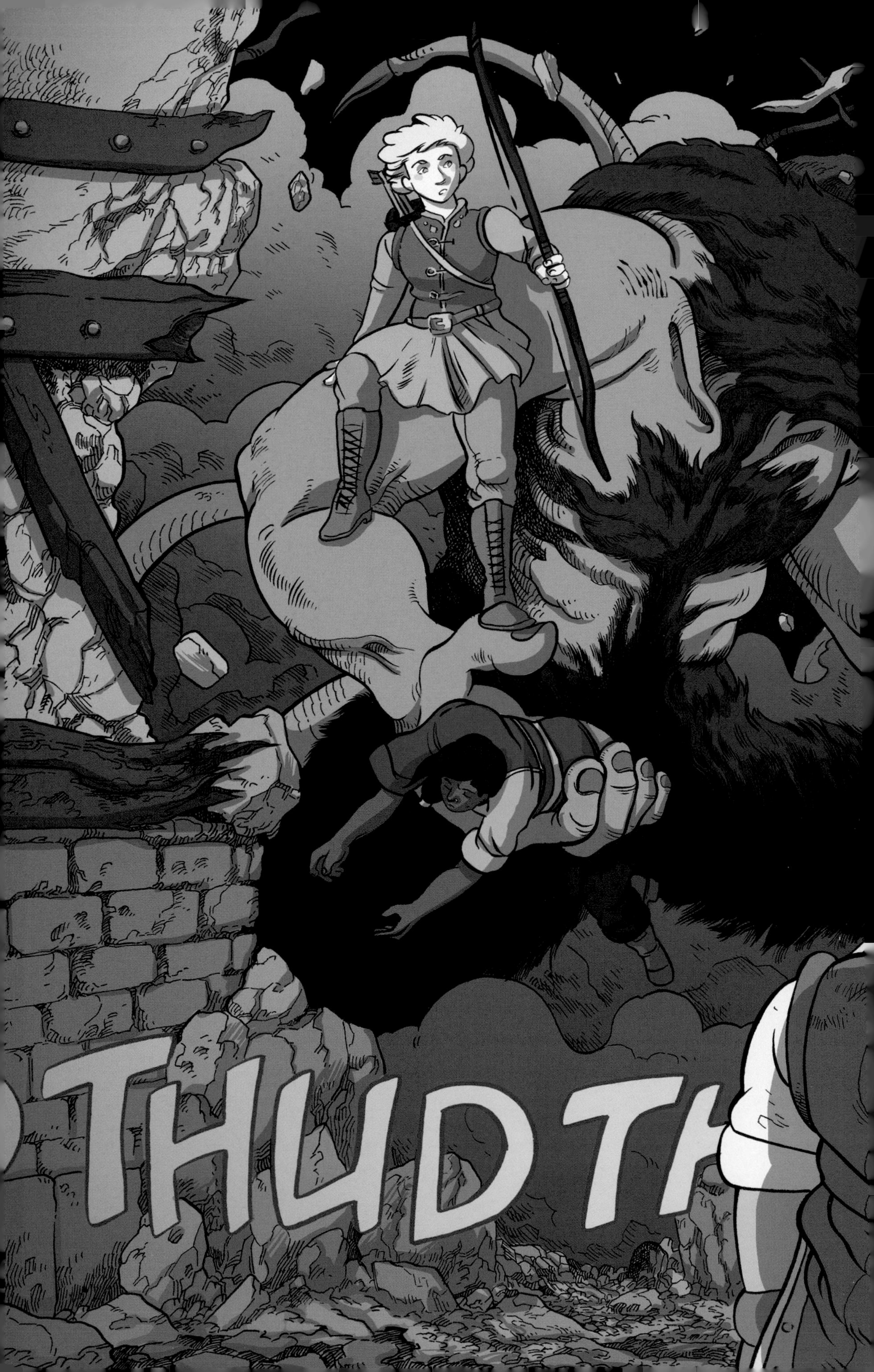
THUD

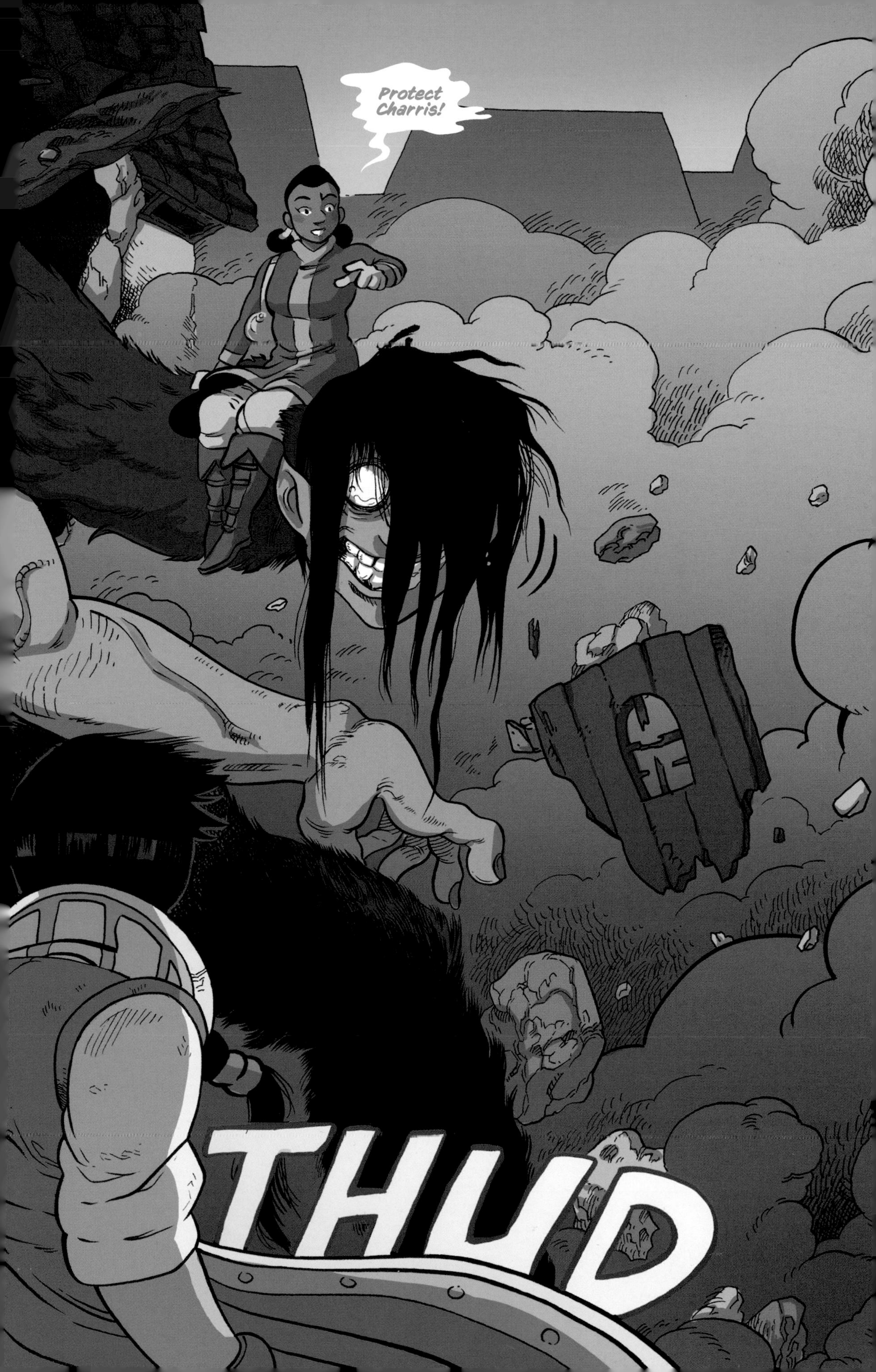
Protect Charris!
THUD

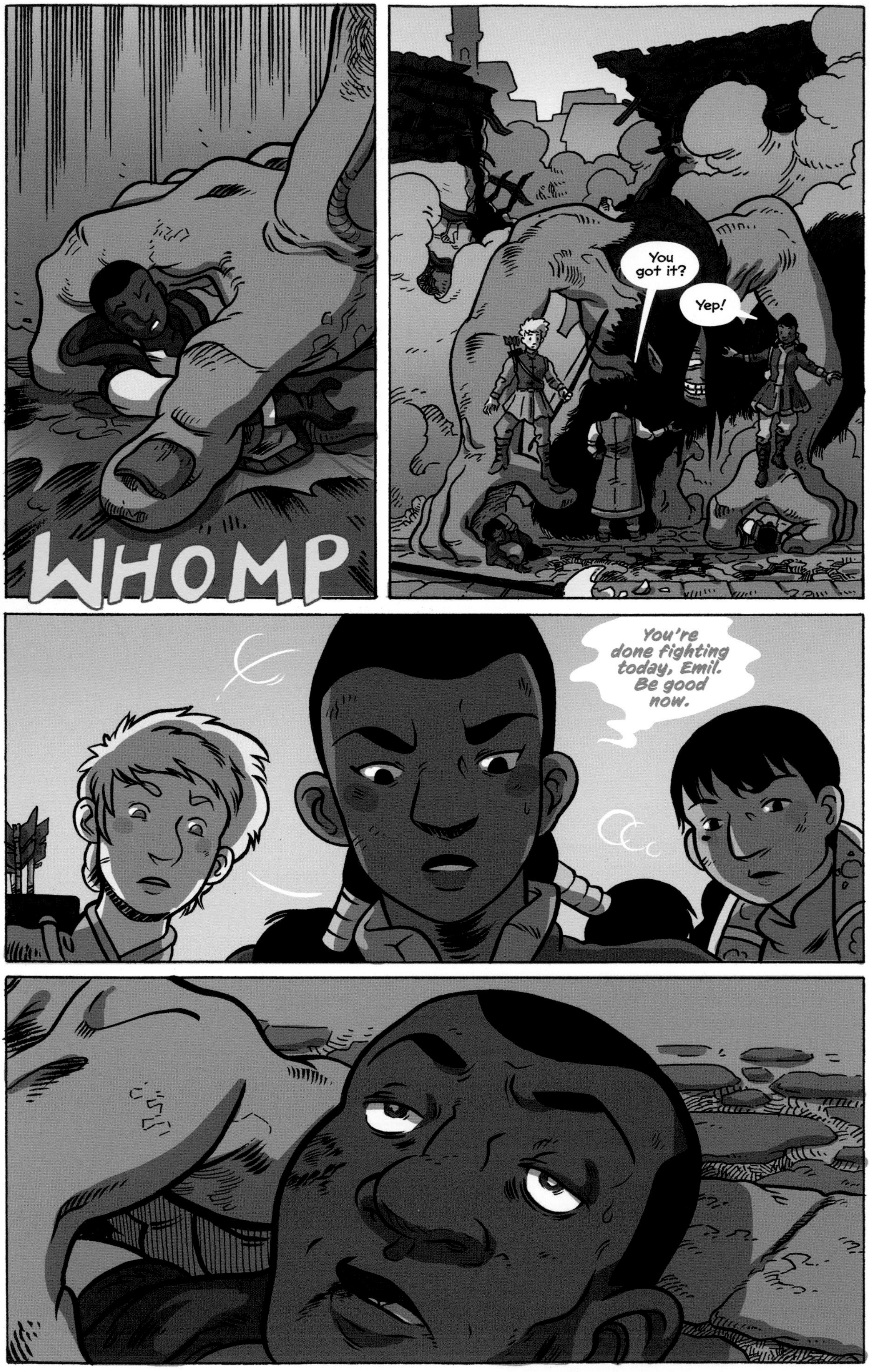
WHOMP
You got it?
Yep!
You're done fighting today, Emil. Be good now.

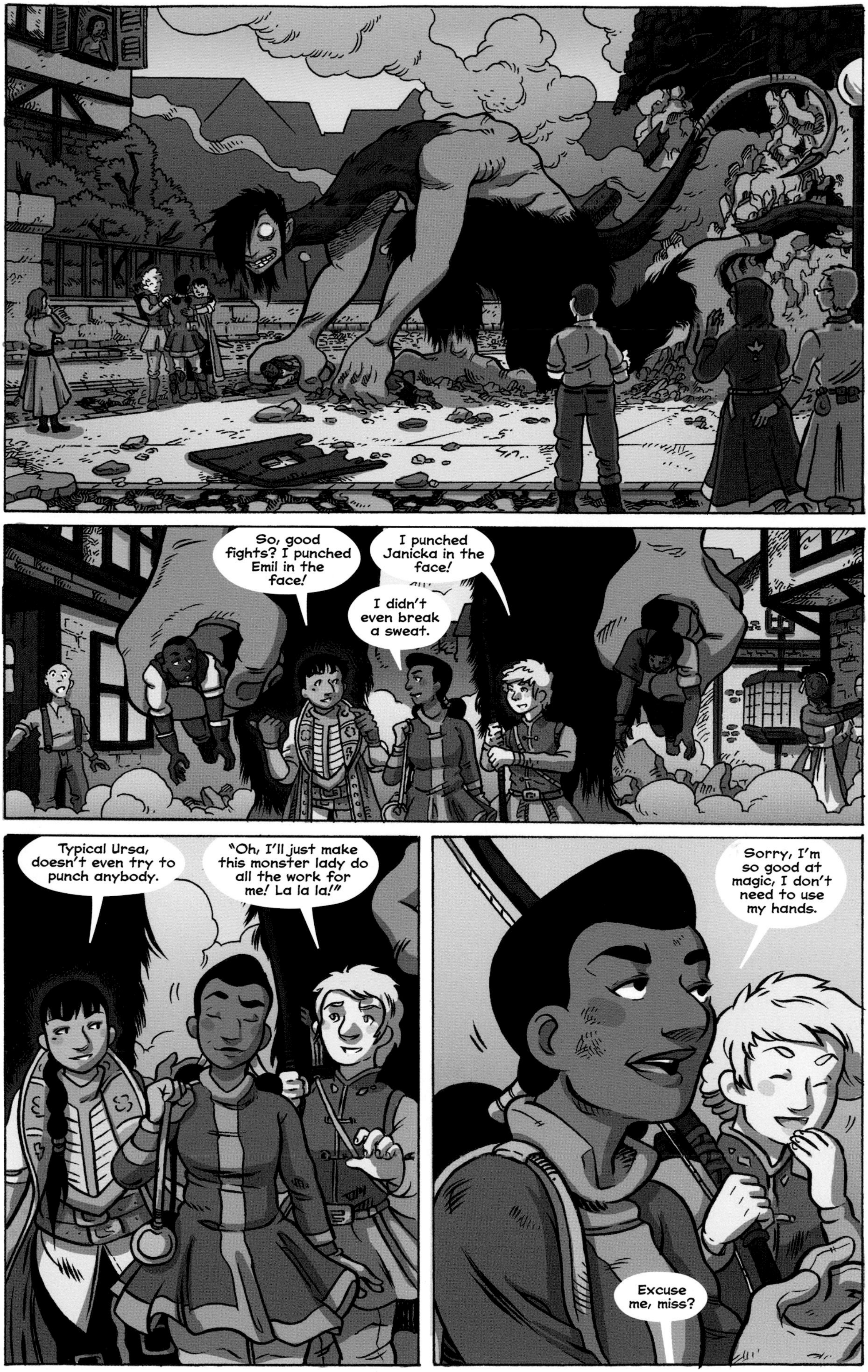

So, good fights? I punched Emil in the face!
I punched Janicka in the face!
I didn't even break a sweat.
Typical Ursa, doesn't even try to punch anybody.
"Oh, I'll just make this monster lady do all the work for me! La la la!"
Sorry, I'm so good at magic, I don't need to use my hands.
Excuse me, miss?

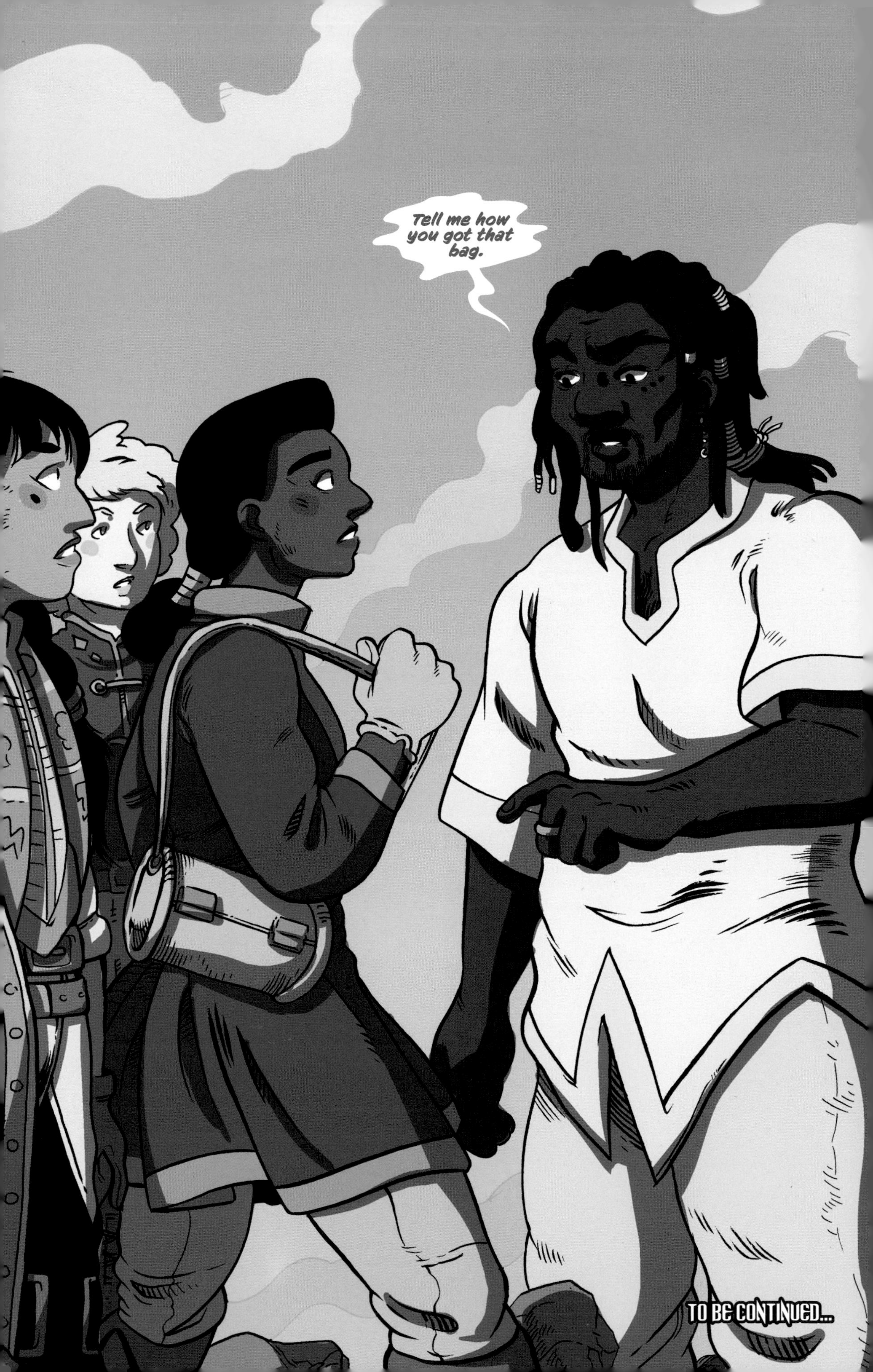
Tell me how you got that bag.
TO BE CONTINUED...

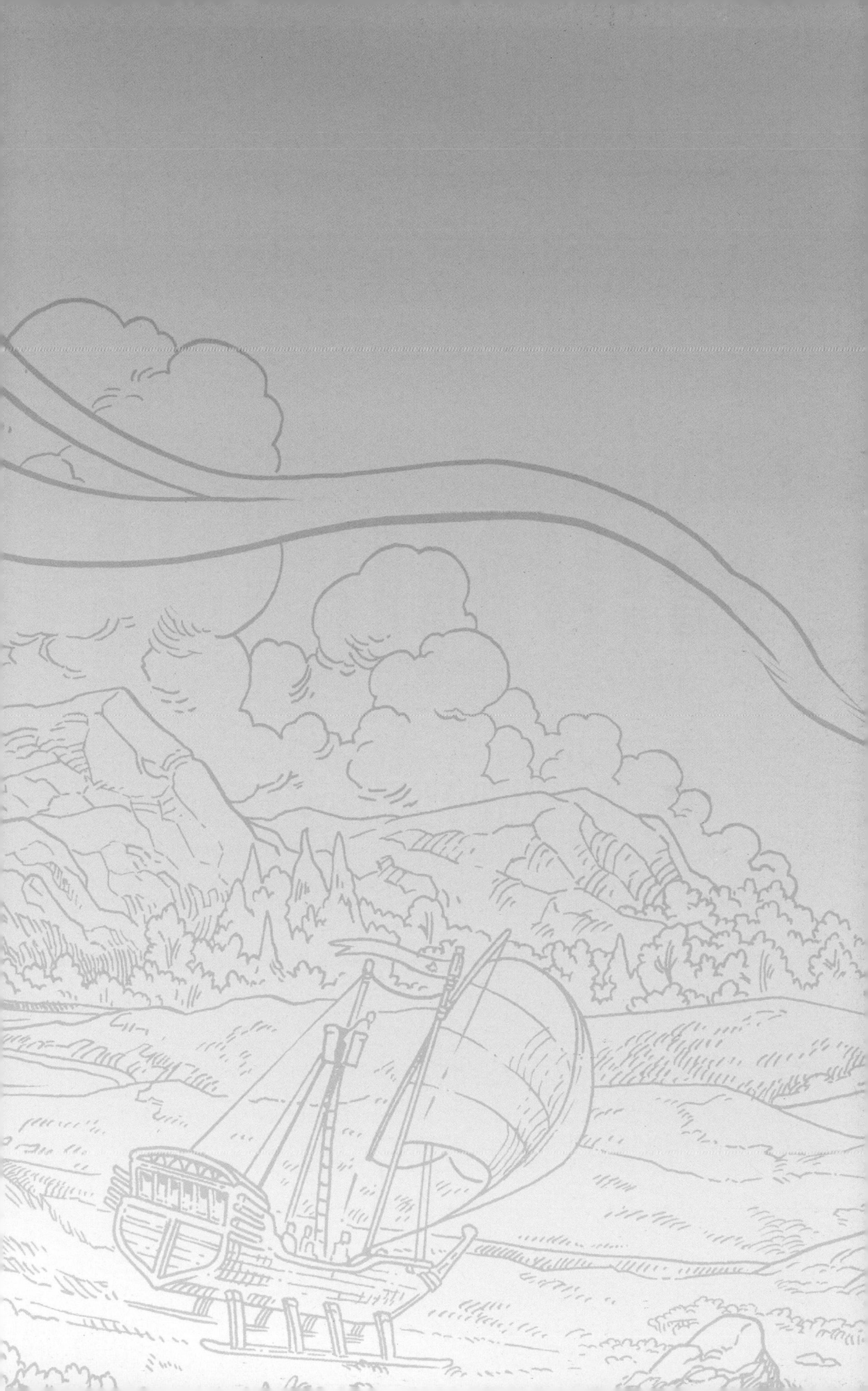

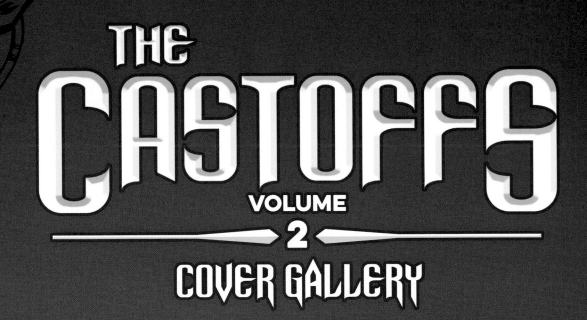

THE CASTOFFS

VOLUME
2
COVER GALLERY

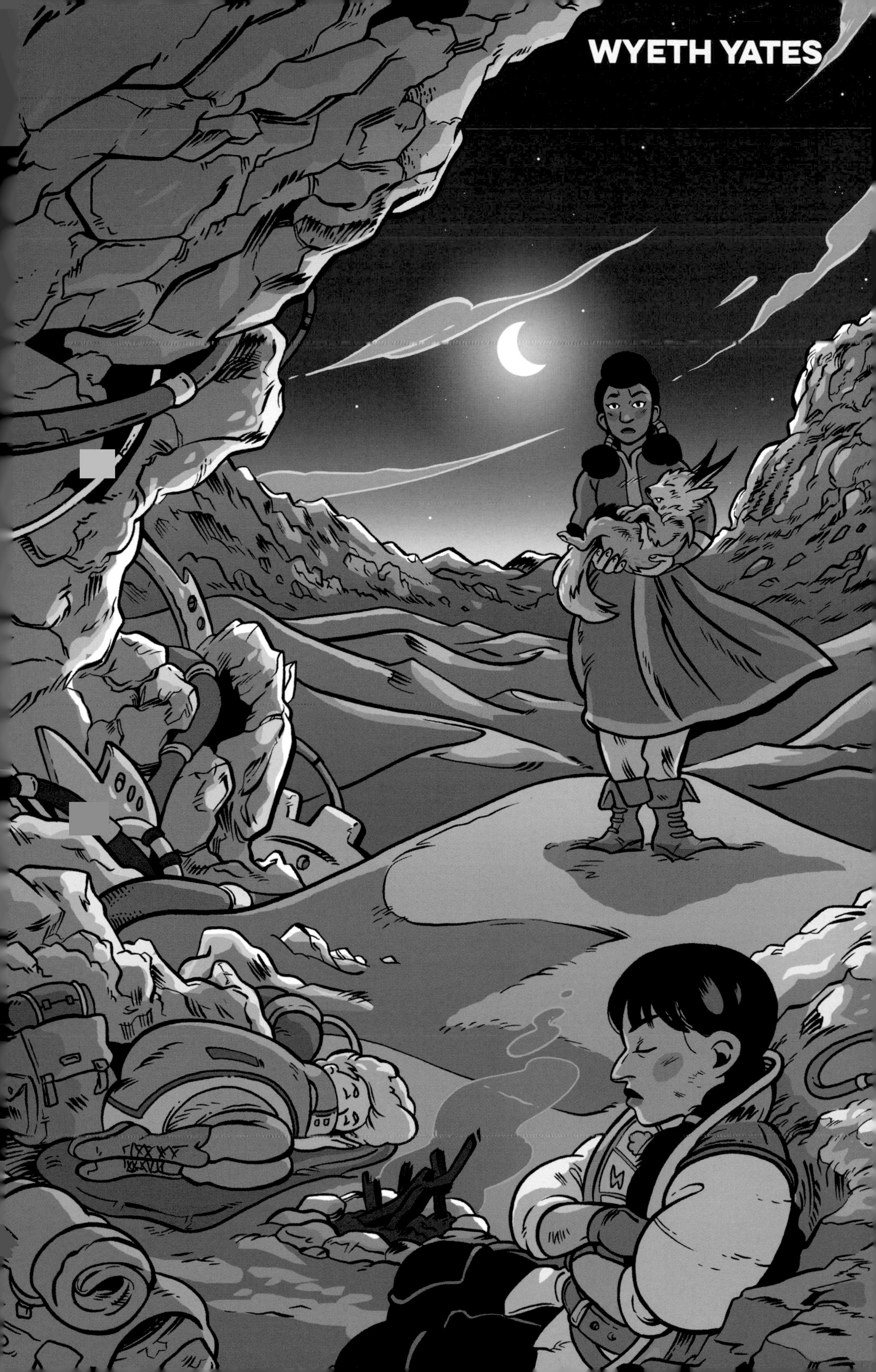
WYETH YATES

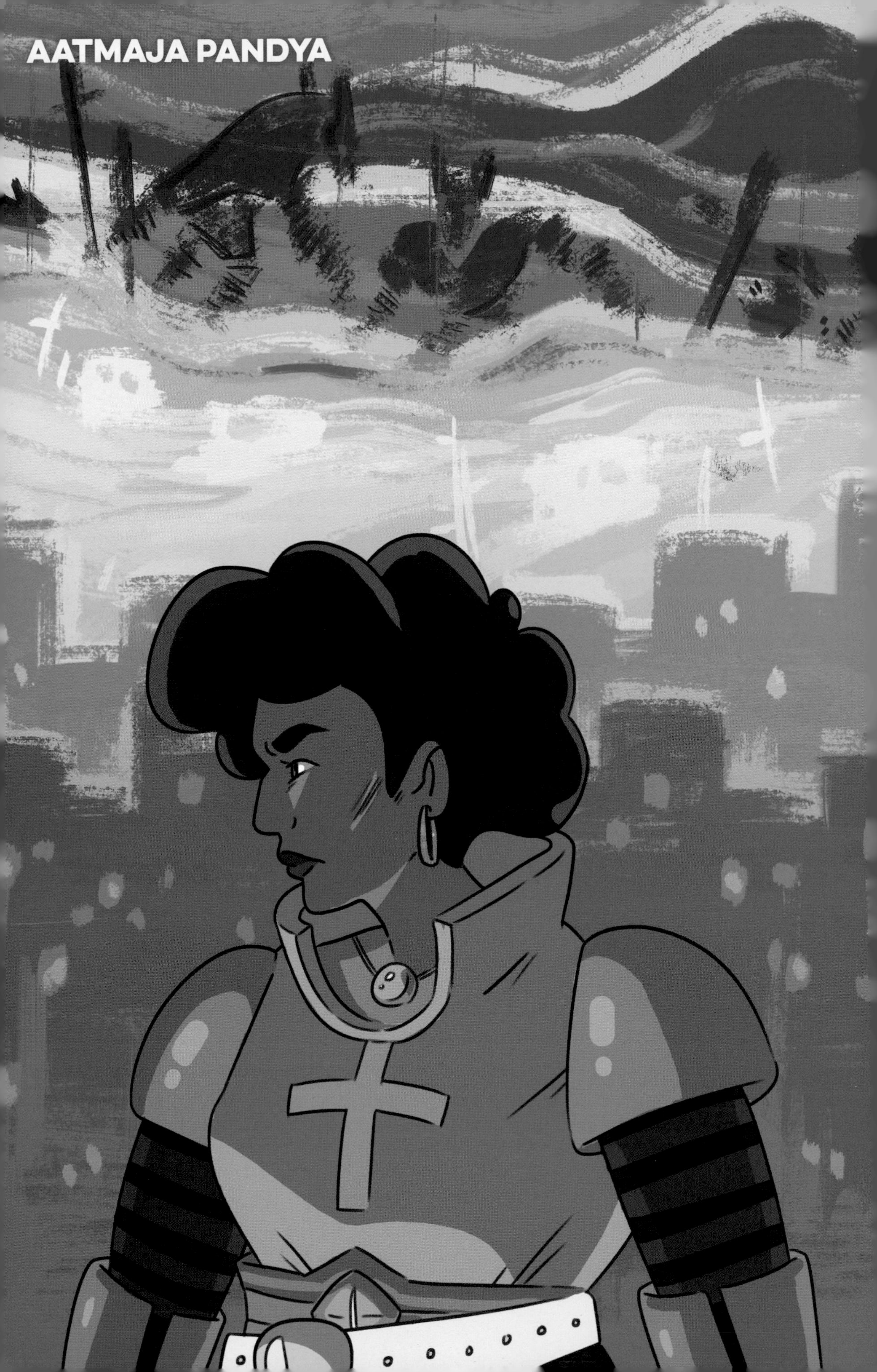
AATMAJA PANDYA

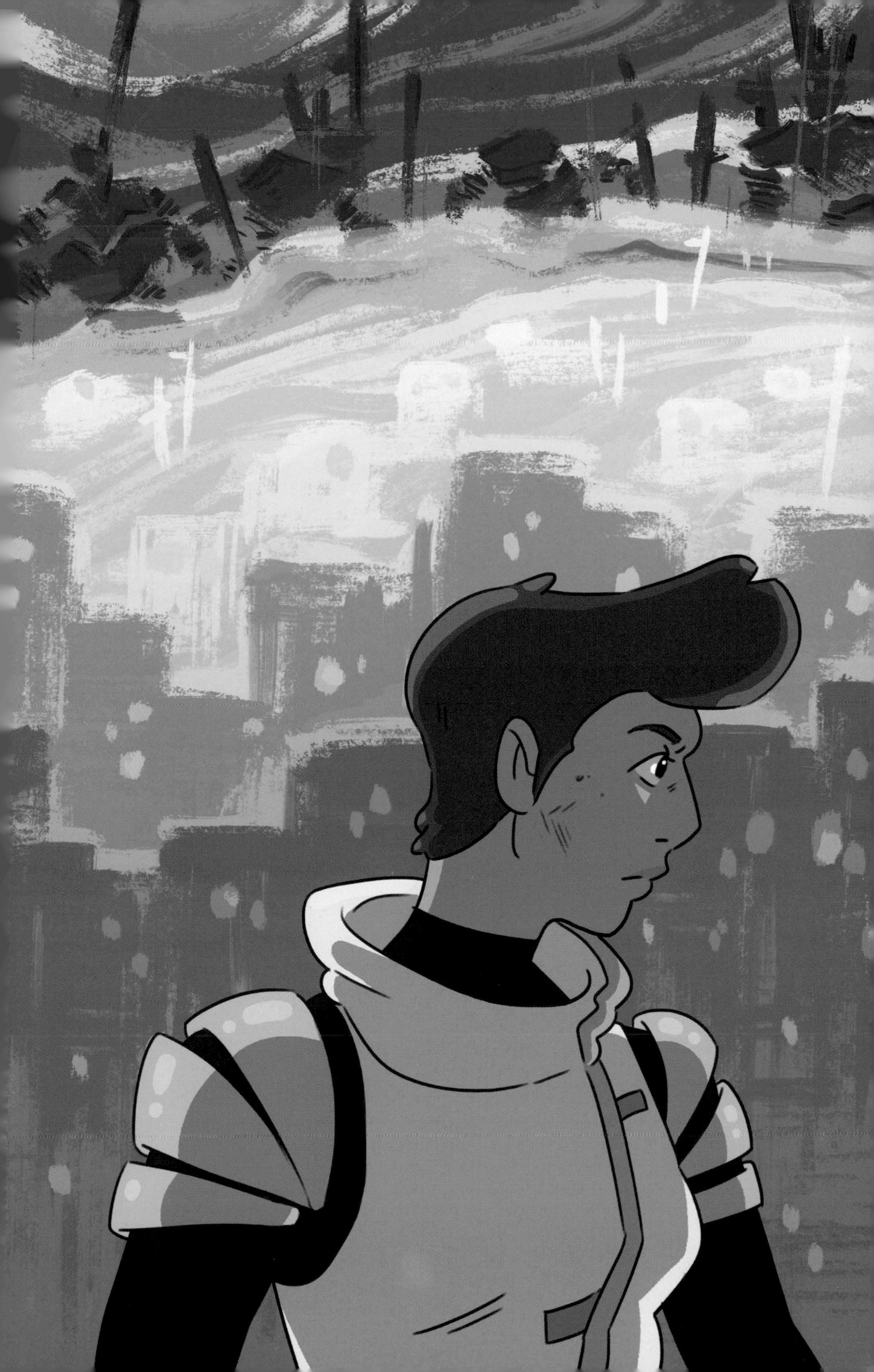

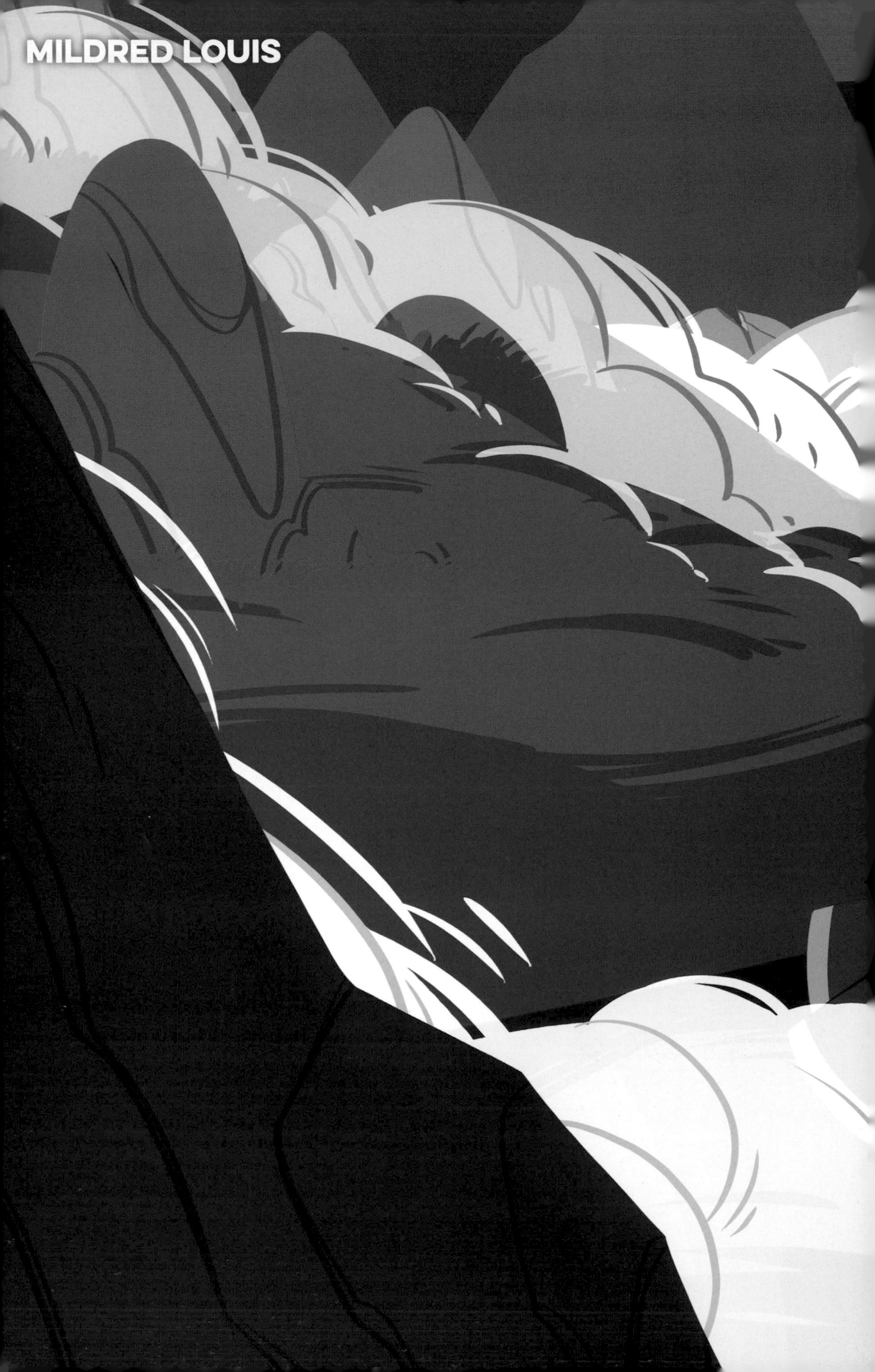
MILDRED LOUIS

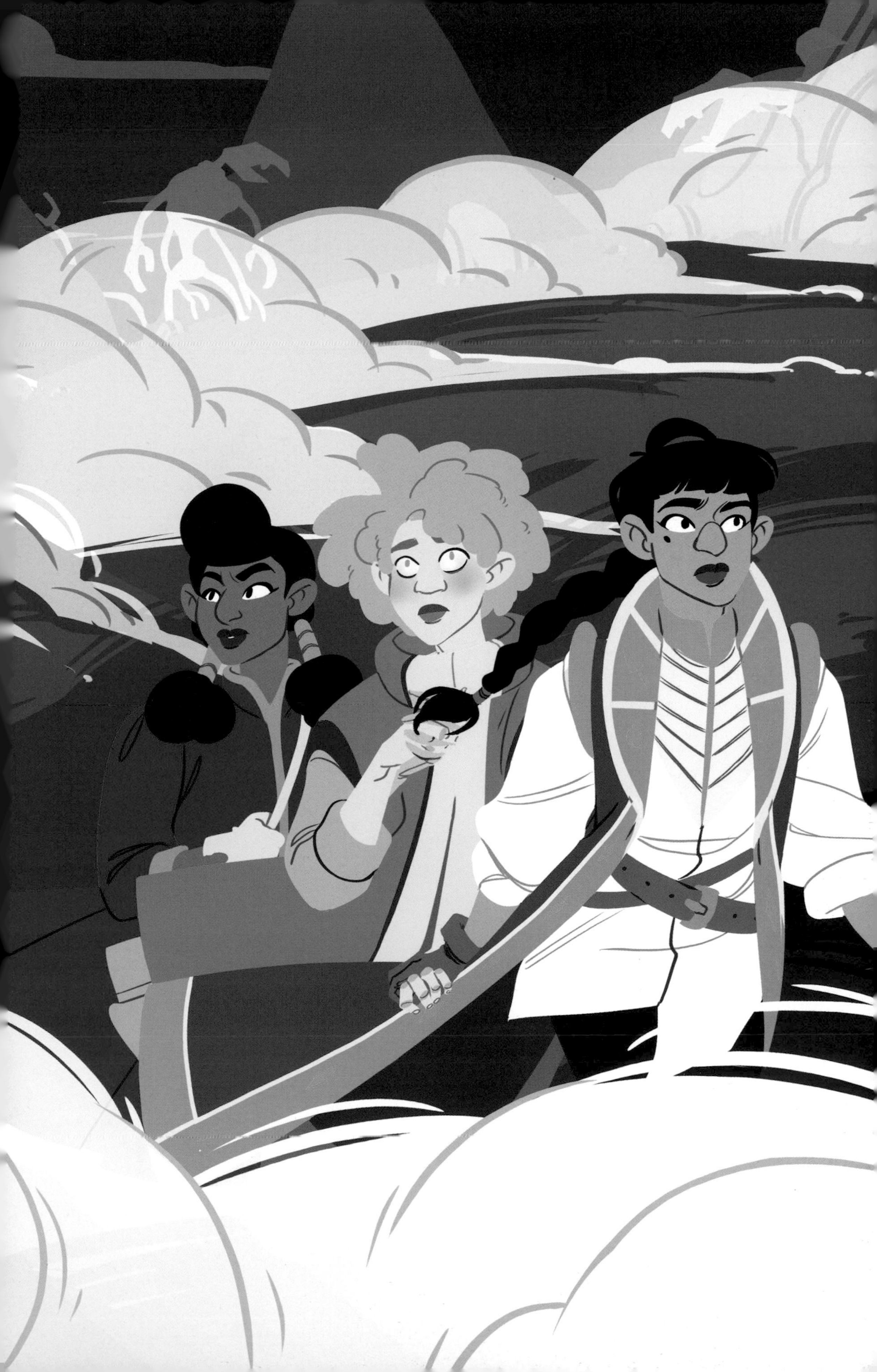

MYISHA HAYNES

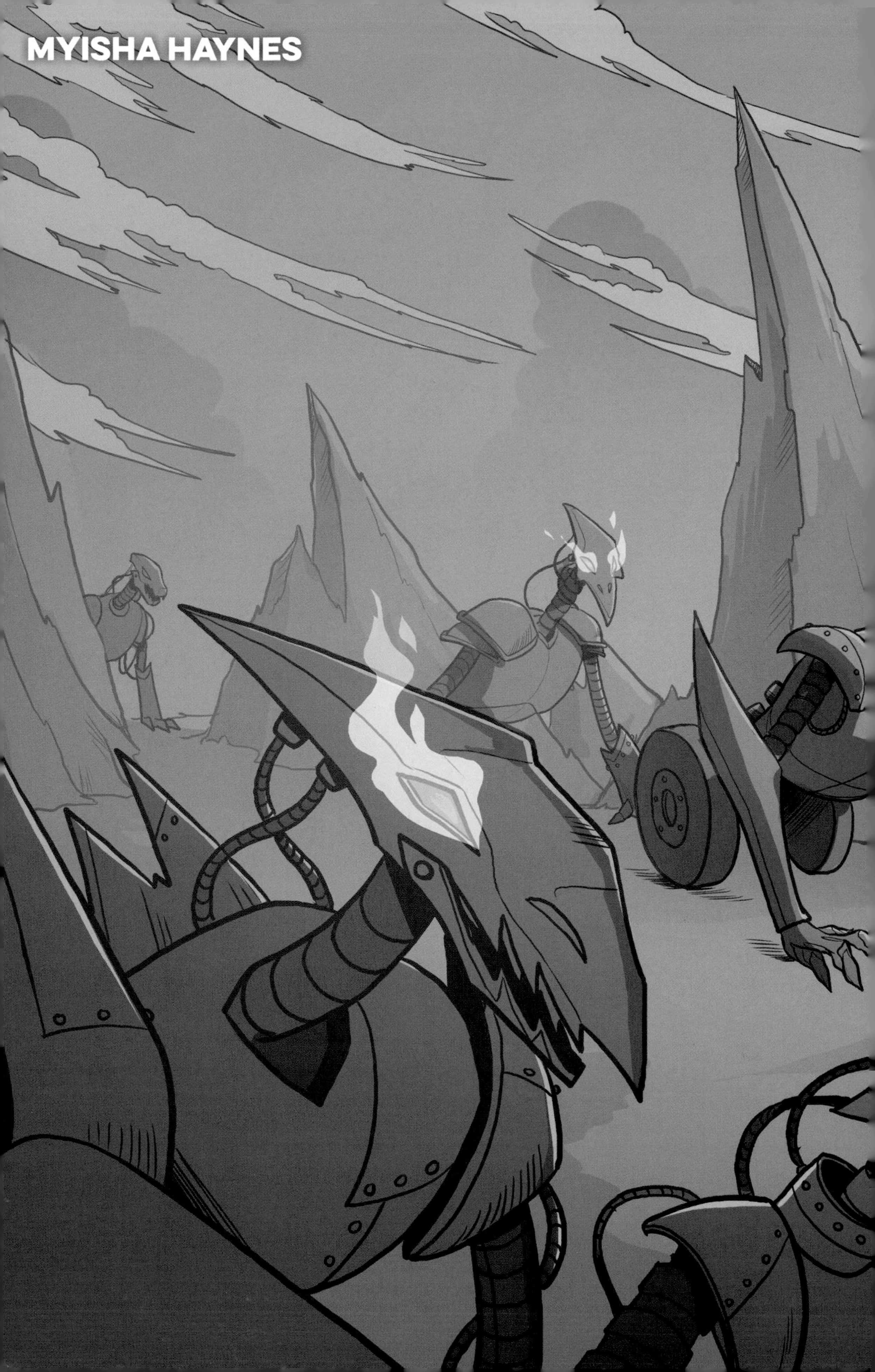

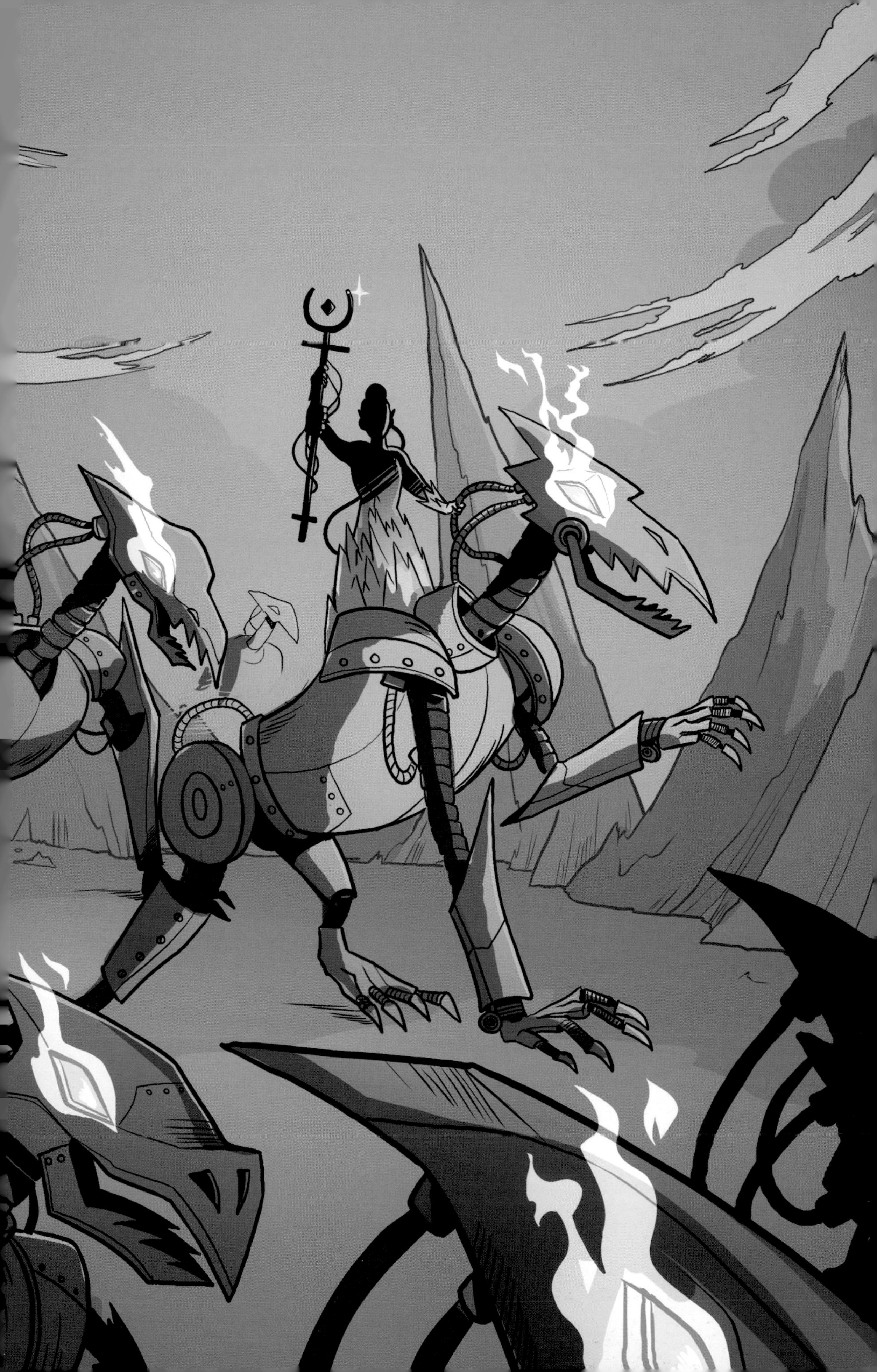

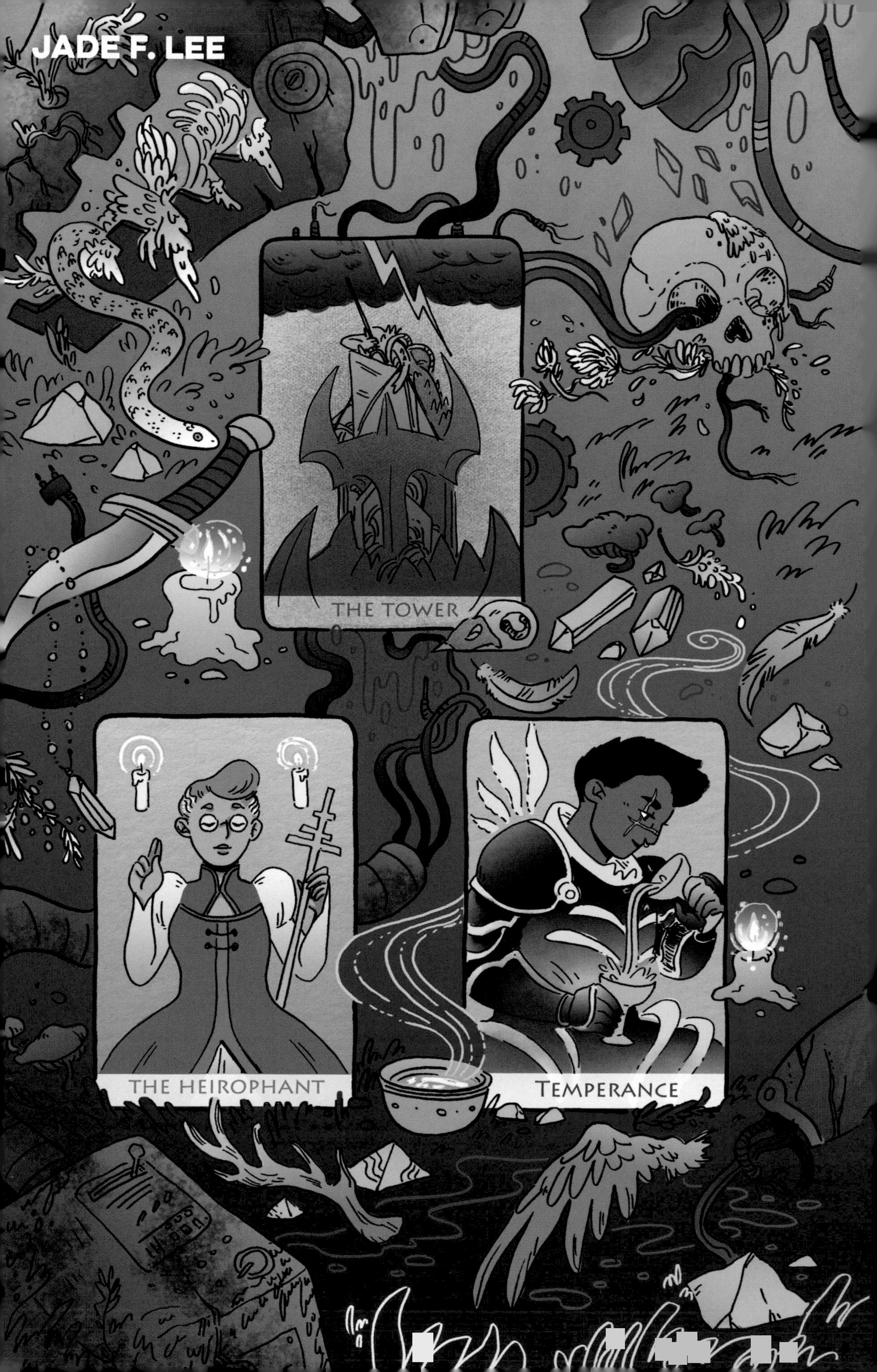
JADE F. LEE
THE TOWER
THE HEIROPHANT
TEMPERANCE

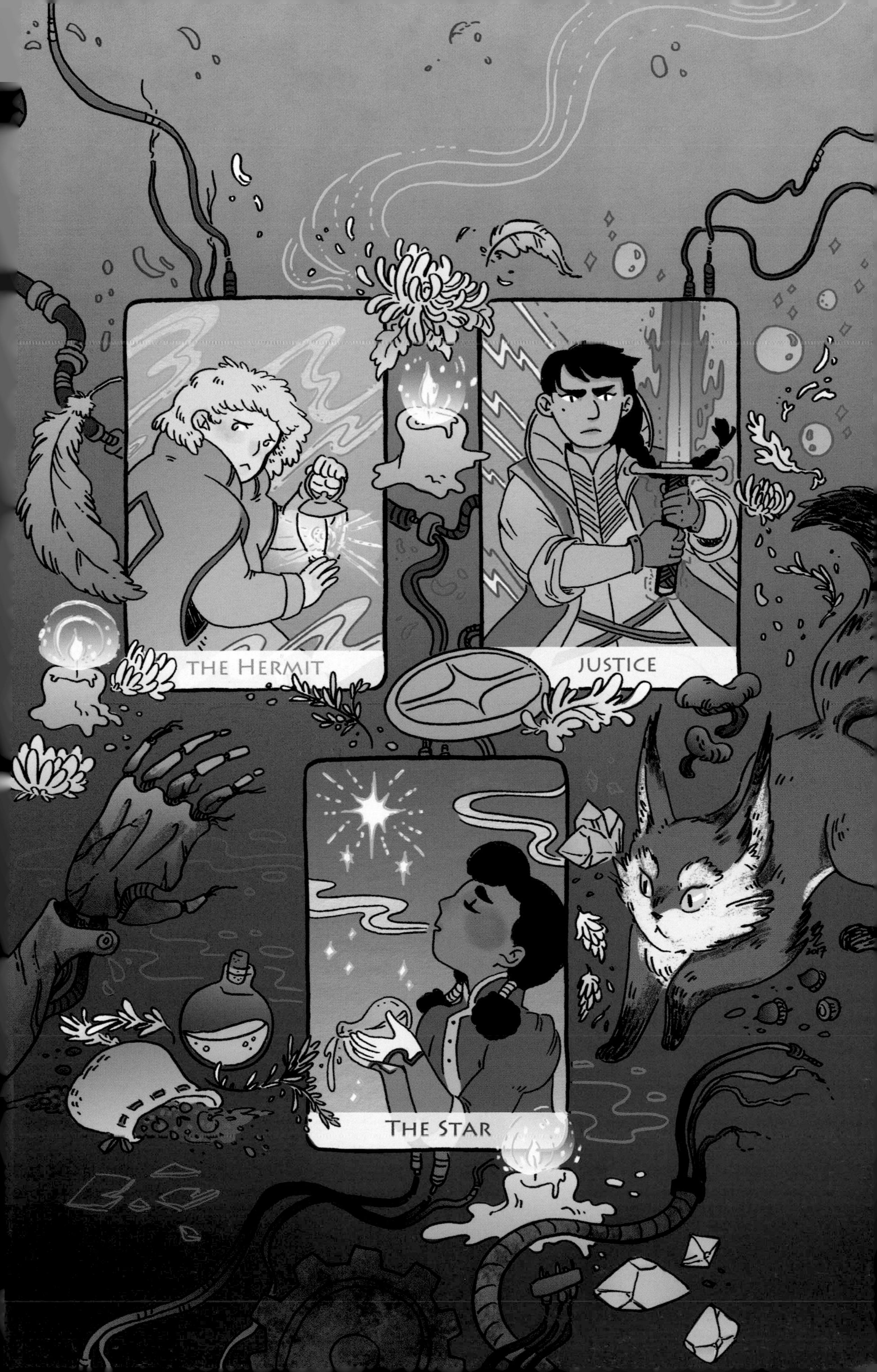
THE HERMIT
JUSTICE
THE STAR

MK REED

is the author of the graphic novels *Americus*, *The Cute Girl Network*, *Palefire*, and *Science Comics: Dinosaurs*. She also writes and draws the web comic *About A Bull*. Her work has appeared in anthologies like *Papercutter*, *Chainmail Bikini*, *The Big Feminist But*, and the Swedish magazine *Galago*. *Americus* was the winner of NAIBA's 2012 Carla Cohen Free Speech Award, and was a 2011 American Booksellers for Children's New Voices title. MK lives in Portland, Oregon, with her very tall husband.

BRIAN "SMITTY" SMITH

is a former Marvel Comics editor, and the co-creator of the *New York Times* bestselling graphic novel *The Stuff of Legend*. He is the writer and artist of the all-ages comic The *Intrepid EscapeGoat*, and the illustrator of *The Adventures of Daniel Boom AKA Loud Boy* series of younger reader graphic novels. He is also the artist of *Madballs* from Roar Comics.

WYETH YATES

is a cartoonist living in Brooklyn, NY. He is the writer and artist of *Hard Luck*, *The Other Gang*, and more. He lives with his wonderful partner and their two cats. If he gets lucky, he'll be drawing comics for the rest of his life. You can find more of Wyeth's work at www.wyethyates.com.

KENDRA WELLS

lives in Brooklyn and is an illustrator, colorist, podcaster, and level 4 half-orc fighter.

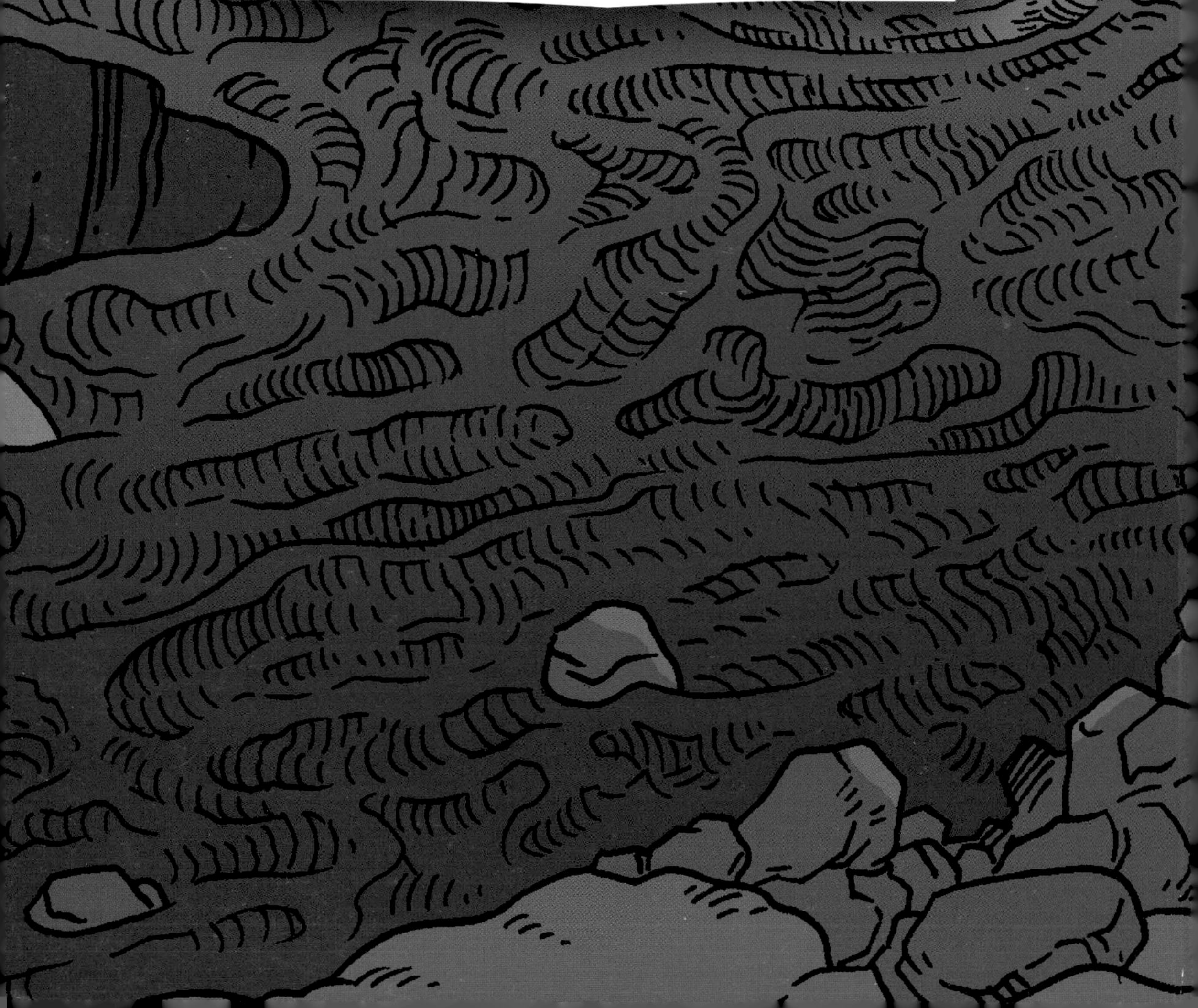